The Ernst & Young Tax Saver's Guide 2001

By Margaret Milner Richardson and the Tax Partners and Professionals of Ernst & Young LLP

Peter W. Bernstein, Editor

John Wiley & Sons, Inc.

New York • Chichester • Weinheim • Brisbane • Singapore • Toronto

In the preparation of this book, every effort has been made to offer current, correct, and clearly expressed information. The information included in this book is based on the Internal Revenue Code amended as of August 2000.

The information in the text is intended to afford general guidelines on matters of interest to taxpayers. The application and impact of tax laws can vary widely from case to case, however, based upon the specific or unique facts involved. Accordingly, this book is not intended to serve as legal, accounting, or tax advice. Moreover, tax rules and regulations often change. Readers are encouraged to consult with professional advisors for advice concerning specific matters before making any decision. The author and publisher disclaim any responsibility for positions taken by taxpayers in their individual cases.

ISSN: 1091-8027
ISBN: 0-471-39120-4 regular edition
ISBN: 0-471-41081-0 special edition

Printed in the United States of America

10 9 8 7 6 5 4 3 2 1

The Ernst & Young Tax Saver's Guide 2001

Contributing Authors

Larry J. Abowitz
Elizabeth N. Buchbinder
Diane C. Carruthers
Robert C. Coplan
Lauren A. Darling
Mark C.J. Fisher
David S. Hudson
David J. Kautter
Albert J. Kiss
Kyle H. Klein
James S. Kolan

Jeffrey A. Lear
Peter D. Lucido
Laura M. MacDonough
David J. Mangefrida, Jr.
Melinda S. Merk
Christopher N. Nelson
Martin Nissenbaum
Jane A. Rohrs
Charlene A. Schmidt
Darrin S. Stovall
Richard D. Wehrheim

Special thanks to Philip A. Laskawy, Chairman of Ernst & Young LLP; James S. Turley, Deputy Chair; Richard S. Bobrow, CEO of the Americas; Dennis Purdum, Chief Operating Officer for the Americas; William J. Lipton, Vice Chairman—Tax Services; Mark A. Weinberger, Director of National Tax; Sylvia J. Pozarnsky, National Director—Personal Financial Counseling; Martin Nissenbaum, National Director—Personal Income Tax Planning.

With more than 4,000 tax practitioners, Ernst & Young LLP has one of the largest professional tax practices in the United States. This book draws upon the experience of many of those professionals for its content.

ABOUT THE AUTHORS

Margaret Milner Richardson, now a partner at Ernst & Young LLP, served as the IRS Commissioner from 1993 through 1997. She is known for having begun the restructuring of the IRS, an effort that began the improvement of the agency's taxpayer service and efficiency, and reduced businesses' compliance burdens.

Ernst & Young, a global leader in professional services, helps clients to quickly and confidently make financial decisions designed to enhance value. Its 77,000 people in more than 130 countries have the industry and financial experience to provide fresh perspectives on operating in the new economy. Ernst & Young offers traditional audit and tax services, as well as customized services in corporate finance, online security, risk management, the valuation of intangibles and e-business acceleration. In addition, legal services are available in various parts of the world where permitted. A collection of Ernst & Young's latest ideas on the new economy can be found at www.ey.com/thoughtcenter.

Ernst & Young refers to the U.S. firm of Ernst & Young LLP and other members of the global Ernst & Young organization.

ABOUT THE EDITOR

Peter W. Bernstein is the editor of *The Ernst & Young Tax Guide*.

Contents

How to Use This Book

The Ernst & Young Tax Saver's Guide 2001 is a year-round tax planner with easy-to-follow, money-saving tax strategies. This book, with its concise explanations of key provisions of federal tax law, can also be used for quick reference to provide guidance on important personal and business transactions. It is not intended to give you line-by-line instructions on how to prepare your federal tax returns. A separate Ernst & Young publication—*The Ernst & Young Tax Guide*—is available for that purpose.

This book is organized into three sections:

Part I, Tax Strategies for Individuals, contains chapters that tell you what to include as income, what you can deduct, and how you calculate your tax. It also has chapters that relate specifically to your business travel and entertainment expenses; your home; retirement plans, such as IRAs and 401(k)s; charitable contributions; capital gains and losses; and mutual funds. In addition, sprinkled throughout all the chapters are money-saving tips about options and strategies you might consider to cut your tax bill. Part I concludes with a chapter on year-end planning for individuals.

Part II, How to Improve Your Financial Future, should help you with some of the tax considerations guiding your current investments. In addition, options you might consider to ensure yourself a comfortable and secure retirement are presented here. The chapter on estate planning offers tax-saving ideas on gifts, estate, and generation-skipping taxes.

Part III, Tax Strategies for Businesses, discusses many of the fundamental tax questions that confront the owner of any business. There is a special chapter on S corporations. The last chapter contains year-end planning suggestions that can save businesses money.

Among its many benefits, this book offers the following special features:

E&Y FOCUS:

This feature considers topics of current interest, such as leasing a car or deferred compensation plans, and suggests smart money moves that you may want to consider.

TAX*SAVER*

Highlighted throughout every chapter in the book are numerous *TAXSAVERS*—specific strategies and recommendations that can help you cut your tax bill.

TAX*ORGANIZER*

Do you need to save that receipt for tax purposes? *TAXORGANIZERS* point out things you need to do *now* to make it easier to file your taxes later.

TAXALERT

This feature highlights recent changes in the tax law that you should know about. Tax law changes that have been enacted recently are included. If you are aware of a new development in the law before the end of the year, you can often take timely and appropriate action and save yourself some money.

■ *Special chapters on year-end tax planning for individuals and businesses.* The prudent taxpayer must make decisions before December 31 about a number of important tax questions—for example, whether to report income now or defer it to next year and whether to pay a deductible expense this year or in the future.

■ *Important information on the tax aspects of "life-cycle events."* These are the occasions, transactions, and eventualities that most of us will almost certainly have to deal with at some time during our adult lives. A special index to the "life-cycle events" discussed in this book follows this introduction.

■ *Concisely presented rules of the tax law pertaining to individuals, estates, gifts, and business entities.* Included in each section are examples that show you how the rules work and "*TAXSAVERS*"—strategies to help you plan better.

The Ernst & Young Tax Saver's Guide contains two more features that will be of year-round use to individuals and businesses alike:

■ *Up-to-date tax tables*—the ones that you will use most often can be found at the end of this book; and

■ *Tax calendar*—month-by-month reminders of important tax action dates for individuals and businesses.

Index to Life-Cycle Events

This special index can be used to locate the sections of the text that contain important information on the tax aspects of "life-cycle events"—those milestones that most adults will be facing at one time or another during the course of their lives. By reading this information, you'll get off to a good start in understanding and planning for the tax consequences associated with various life-cycle events.

Changes in the Tax Law You Should Know About

As this book was being prepared in September 2000, Congress was still considering legislation that could affect individuals' tax planning for the coming year. We strongly encourage you to consult with your tax advisor for the most updated information.

To date, however, no new tax legislation has been enacted into law in 2000 that has had any direct effect on the tax planning of individual or small business taxpayers. Certain notable changes that will occur in 2000 and 2001 as a result of prior years' legislation are:

SELF-EMPLOYED HEALTH DEDUCTION

The deduction for health insurance expenses of self-employed individuals will be 60% for tax years 2000 and 2001. See Chapter 10.

ESTIMATED TAX PAYMENTS

If you have an adjusted gross income (AGI) of more than $150,000, you will need to pay in 108.6% of the prior year's tax liability for 2000 in order not to be subject to tax penalites. In the year 2001, you will need to pay in 110% of your prior year's tax liability. See Chapter 9.

DEDUCTIBLE IRAS

The adjusted gross income (AGI) phaseout limits for taxpayers who are active participants in employer-sponsored plans increase to $32,000–$42,000 for single taxpayers and $52,000–$62,000 for joint filers. See Chapter 5.

STUDENT LOAN INTEREST DEDUCTION

The maximum allowable deduction per taxpayer return is $2,000 in 2000. See Chapter 2.

ITEMIZED DEDUCTION FOR LONG-TERM CARE INSURANCE PREMIUMS

The amount of qualified long-term care insurance premiums that may be taken into account for 2000 is as follows: $220 in the case of an individual 40 years old or less; $410 in the case of an individual who is more than 40 but not more than 50; $820 in the case of an individual who is more than 50 but not more than 60; $2,200 in the case of an individual who is more than 60 but not more than 70; and $2,750 in the case of an individual who is more than 70. These limits are indexed annually.

UNIFIED ESTATE AND GIFT TAX CREDIT

A unified credit is available with respect to taxable transfers by gift and at death. The unified credit amount effectively exempts from tax a total of $675,000 in 2000 and 2001. See Chapter 13.

EXCLUSION FOR CONSERVATION EASEMENTS

An executor may elect to exclude from taxable estate 40% of the value of any land subject to a qualified conservation easement, up to a maximum exclusion of $300,000 in 2000. See Chapter 13.

10 Smart Tax Planning Tips

1. Start your planning early. This allows you time to take advantage of strategies that may take several months to implement.

2. Make your contributions to an IRA or Keogh plan early in the year. The combination of making contributions early in the year and compounding will make your money grow faster than if you wait until the last minute. See page 91.

3. Contribute the maximum to your 401(k) plan and start early in the year. If you wait too long, you may not be able to contribute the full amount because of limitations. See pages 95–96.

4. Do not take a lump sum distribution from your pension plan unless you roll it over to an IRA account in a timely manner. **Caution: there is a 20% withholding tax on lump sum distributions.** See page 100.

5. If you plan to work after your normal retirement date, consider how it will affect your Social Security benefits. Also, consider whether you would be better off applying for your benefits by age 62 or waiting until you are 65. See page 207.

6. If you have publicly traded stock that would generate a long-term capital gain if sold, consider using it to make your charitable contributions. (Your contribution deduction will be based on the fair market value of the stock and you won't have to pay tax on the gain.) See page 109.

7. Charitable contributions are subject to certain tax limitations. Some of your contributions to charities may not be deductible until a later year if you exceed the prescribed limits. Furthermore, if you do not meet the substantiation requirements the contribution won't be deductible at all. Also consider making your charitable contributions toward the end of your tax year. See page 111.

8. Replace personal debt with mortgage debt to the extent possible. Interest expense on mortgage loans is—subject to some limitations—deductible; personal or consumer interest is not. See page 44.

9. Consider the after-tax yield of an investment when comparing returns on different investments. See page 189.

10. Consider giving gifts to your children. You may want to shift income to them since children are usually in lower tax brackets and so pay less in taxes. However, if your children are under age 14, their income above certain levels will be subject to the special "kiddie tax" rates. See page 153.

I

Tax Strategies for Individuals

There are many tax-saving strategies you can use to lower your tax bill. This book has been organized to assist you in developing and implementing the tax-saving strategies most effective for you. The first step, as anyone who has collected information for an annual tax return knows, is to determine what portion of your income is subject to tax and what may not be. Income, of course, is not just the money you get in your paycheck. It includes interest and dividends, rent and royalties, pensions and annuities, alimony and separate maintenance payments, among many other things—all of which are explained in Chapter 1. We've also pointed out permissible ways you can reduce the amount of income you have to report.

The second step (described in Chapter 2) is to figure out which of the expenses you incurred during the year can be deducted to lower your taxable income. We've included suggestions about how you can maximize your deductions and therefore lower the amount of tax you owe. The chapters on Travel and Entertainment Expenses, Tax Planning and Your Home, IRAs and 401(k) Plans, Charitable Contributions, Capital Gains and Losses, and Mutual Funds explain in greater detail strategies that can help you deal with these important topics.

The third step, the calculation of your tax, is explained in Chapter 9. It involves several calculations—you need to figure out, for example, whether to claim the standard deduction or to itemize, and for some taxpayers, whether you are subject to the alternative minimum tax. We've tried to describe the process in as simple and straightforward a way as possible. The results can be richly rewarding.

The last step represents both an end and a new beginning. The sophisticated taxpayer can take steps at the end of the year that can defer taxes until next year. This is the primary focus of Chapter 10. If you can shift the tax from this taxable year to the next taxable year, you have saved the use of those deferred funds for a year. More important, Chapter 10 illustrates how a taxpayer can start planning so that less tax will have to be paid in future years.

1

What You Have to Include as Income

INTRODUCTION

The first step in determining how much in taxes you'll have to pay is to figure out your *taxable income*. That is the amount, figured by subtracting from your gross income certain adjustments and allowable deductions, upon which your tax is based. Your gross income includes income from all sources, such as:

- Alimony and separate maintenance payments
- Compensation for services, including salary, wages, tips, fees, commissions, and certain employee benefits
- Gains from dealings in property
- Gross income from a business
- Income from an interest in an estate or trust
- Income from paying off a debt for less than you owe
- Certain income from life insurance and endowment contracts
- Interest and dividends
- Pensions and annuities
- Rents and royalties
- Court awards in noninjury or nonsickness cases (e.g., job discrimination)
- Your share of income from a partnership or S corporation, whether it is distributed or not.

This chapter discusses what you have to include in calculating your taxable income. Along the way, you'll find many tax-saving suggestions that should help you lower your taxable income—and your tax bill.

WAGES, SALARIES, AND OTHER EARNED INCOME

As a general rule, you must include in your gross income everything you receive as payment for personal services including wages, salaries, commissions, and tips. If you receive property or services as compensation, you generally should include the fair market value of the property or services as wages in the year you receive it.

Unless you anticipate a tax rate increase next year, you will generally find it to your advantage to defer recognizing income, where permissible, to a later year. Usually the date of receipt determines the year income is taxable. So, failure to cash a check or refusal to accept a payment will not defer income.

E&Y FOCUS: Deferred Compensation Plans

Deferred compensation plans are designed by employers for executives who can afford to defer a portion of their earnings. Under such plans, you make an election to defer some portion of your income until a stated time; you are taxed on the deferred income only when it is received.

Deferrals can be made from your regular salary or from bonuses. You generally should make an election to defer income before that income is earned. Furthermore, you and your employer must enter into a written deferral agreement.

Deferred compensation plans serve one of two functions, depending on whether they are short-term or long-term plans:

- Short-term arrangements are generally most effective when used to take advantage of tax-rate changes. For example, suppose that in the current year the top rate on your taxable income is roughly 40% (39.6%). The next year you expect your top rate to drop to 31%. You might use a deferred compensation plan to shift income from one year to the next so that it will be taxed at a lower rate.

- Long-term arrangements are aimed primarily at providing key employees with bonuses and retirement income in excess of the amounts allowed by law to be provided under the employer's qualified pension and profit-sharing plans. Some experts are dubious about the benefits of long-term deferrals, mainly because they believe tax rates will be higher in the future than they are currently. If they're right, the deferred income would be taxed at a higher rate—defeating one of the primary purposes of deferring the income. It's worth noting that most deferred compensation plans include a provision for increasing the amounts deferred to reflect what you would have earned by receiving the payments up front and then investing them. Also, given the restrictions on qualified plans (plans entitled to tax-favored status), nonqualified plans continue to be popular with executives.

Make Sure You Collect Your Deferred Compensation. Many traditional "nonqualified" (i.e., unfunded) deferred compensation plans are based on an unsecured promise from your employer to pay compensation in the future. But how can you be sure your company will pay up?

Various arrangements have been developed to provide the employee with an additional sense of security that the promise will be honored without causing the income to be immediately taxable. One such device is known as a "rabbi trust," so named because the first arrangement approved by the IRS was developed by a synagogue for its rabbi.

Under a rabbi trust arrangement, amounts sufficient to pay the deferred compensation are placed into an irrevocable trust by your employer. Once in the trust, these amounts can be accessed by the employer's creditors only upon the employer's bankruptcy or insolvency; the amounts are not otherwise available for use by the original employer or a successor employer. This means that, unless the employer becomes bankrupt or insolvent, amounts in the rabbi trust will be available to pay the deferred compensation in future years.

"Noncash" Compensation. The following are some of the more common forms of noncash compensation that are subject to tax:

1. *Employer-provided automobile for personal use.* If your employer provided you with a car, your personal use of the car is considered taxable noncash compensation.
2. *Educational assistance.* You generally must include in income any educational expenses your employer paid for you, unless the courses are required by your employer, are job-related, or the expenses are paid for under a special plan meeting IRS requirements.
3. *Bargain purchase of employer's assets.* If you are allowed to purchase property from your employer at a price *below* its fair market value as compensation for your services, you must report as income the difference between the property's fair market value and the amount you paid for it (see the exception following under "Qualified employee discount").
4. *Stock options.* The difference between the stock's fair market value and the option price should generally be reported as additional income when you exercise an option to buy stock from your employer. A special rule, however, applies to certain stock options. This rule usually delays the tax until you sell or exchange your stock. (See pages 27–30 in this chapter.)
5. *Group term life insurance premiums for over $50,000 of coverage.* An employer's payments for group term life insurance premiums for coverage over $50,000 are considered to be additional income to you unless the beneficiary of the "over $50,000 life insurance" is an organization to which a contribution would be a charitable contribution.
6. *Club memberships.* If your employer provides you with a membership in a country club or similar social organization, you are subject to tax on the value of the membership.

Tax-Free Fringe Benefits. Certain fringe benefits you receive from your employer are specifically excluded from taxation. These include:

1. *No-additional-cost service.* If you receive services from your employer that are regularly offered for sale to customers and your employer incurs no substantial additional cost in providing them to you, you do not have to include the value of these services as income. *Example:* Stand-by space on flights for airline employees.

2. *Qualified employee discount.* You do not have to report additional income if the discount your employer extended to you is less than the discount your employer would regularly offer to customers. For the purchase of services, the discount must be less than 20% of the price regularly charged to customers. *Example:* Appliance retailers' discounted sales of their merchandise to their employees at the lowest discounted price offered to customers.

3. *Working condition fringe benefits.* You do not have to include in income the value of property or services provided to you by your employer if you would be entitled to a business deduction for such items on your personal return had you paid for these items. *Example:* Business periodical subscriptions.

4. *De minimis fringe benefits.* Fringe benefits items so small in value that it would be unreasonable or administratively impractical for your employer to account for them. *Examples:* Personal use of copying machine, occasional parties for employees.

5. *Tax-free employee parking and transit benefits.* An exclusion from gross income is allowed for an employee whose employer offers the choice between cash and parking or a transit benefit, and the employee chooses parking or a transit benefit. If the employee chooses cash, the amount offered is includible in income.

We've mentioned just a few examples. You should consult with your employer and your tax advisor to find out how to treat a particular item.

401(k) Plans. If your employer has a 401(k) plan or another plan that allows you to postpone income, you can elect to defer a certain amount of your salary on a pre-tax basis. Such amounts are withheld from your salary and are not reported as income until withdrawn from the plan. For further information about 401(k)s and other retirement plans, see Chapter 5.

TaxSaver

A key element of tax planning is reducing your income. One way to do that is to take advantage of your employer's 401(k) plan, particularly if the deductible amount you are permitted to contribute to an IRA is limited (see pages 88–91). With a 401(k), you can elect to defer up to a maximum of $10,500 in 2000.

Although the funds in your 401(k) plan are meant to be set aside for your retirement, you may still have access to them if you need money. Your plan may permit you to borrow from the plan, subject to strict rules. Despite the restrictions, you may be better off borrowing from your retirement fund than getting a loan from your bank. If the loan from the bank is for personal purposes, it could result in nondeductible interest. While a loan from your 401(k) plan does not generate deductible interest, the interest you pay is allocated to your account (although, of course, your rate of return may be lower than what your assets were earning prior to the loan). Your best bet might be to borrow from the equity in your home. The interest on such a loan would generally be tax deductible.

INTEREST AND DIVIDENDS

Interest that you receive on bank accounts, on loans that you have made to others, or from other sources is taxable. However, interest received on obligations of a state or one of its political subdivisions, the District of Columbia, or a possession of the United States or one of its political divisions is usually tax exempt for federal purposes. Interest paid by the IRS on a tax refund arising from any type of original tax return, if the refund is not issued by the 45th day after the later of the due date for the return (determined without regard to any extensions) or the date the return was filed, is taxable. (The interest rates on such payments are set periodically by the IRS.)

Qualified State Tuition Programs

Qualified state tuition programs (QSTPs) are tax exempt. Gifts made to a QSTP are eligible for the gift tax exclusion and the student/participants are not taxed until they receive distributions.

"Qualified higher education expenses" are tuition, fees, books, supplies, equipment required for the enrollment or attendance at a college or university (or certain vocational schools), and room and board.

U.S. Saving Bonds

U.S. saving bonds are direct obligations of the United States government. Two series of bonds are available: Series EE bonds and Series HH bonds. Both are subject to federal income tax, though in some circumstances (explained below) interest on Series EE bonds may be deferred for many years, and if used for certain educational purposes may even be exempt from tax. Both series of bonds, however, are exempt from state and local income taxes.

Series EE Bonds. These are bonds that are issued at a discount—that is, they're purchased at a fixed amount, and are redeemed at a higher amount depending upon how long the bonds are held. Cash method taxpayers have the option of reporting income on the bonds when the bonds are redeemed or reporting it annually as it accrues. Accrual method taxpayers must report the income as it accrues.

TaxSaver

Series EE bonds can be an interesting tax-sheltered investment in two ways. First, because most individuals are cash-method taxpayers paying taxes on income as it is received, interest income from Series EE bonds is not recognized until it is received (i.e., when the bonds are redeemed). But, there is a second way you can shelter your interest income from Series EE bonds for an even longer time. If, instead of redeeming the bonds when they come due, you exchange them for Series HH bonds (that pay interest semiannually), you can avoid recognition of the accumulated Series EE bond interest until the Series HH bonds are redeemed.

Example: *Clay purchases $7,500 worth of Series EE bonds, which pay interest of 4% per year. In slightly more than seven years, the bonds will have grown in value to $10,000. Instead of redeeming them at that point, he exchanges them for $10,000 worth of Series HH bonds, which pay interest at the rate of 4% per year. The $2,500 of interest income earned over the years on the Series EE bonds would not be taxable at the date of exchange but would be deferred. Clay will receive $400 of taxable interest income per year on the Series HH bonds. The $2,500 of deferred interest income on the Series EE bonds would not be taxable until the Series HH bonds reach final maturity or are redeemed.*

There is, however, a limitation on the purchase of EE bonds. An individual may purchase only up to $30,000 per year.

The interest received on EE bonds depends on when the bonds are purchased. Different rules apply to bonds purchased before May 1995, from May 1995 through April 1997, and in May 1997 and beyond. The Treasury site at http://www.publicdebt.treas.gov/sav/savtypes has more details.

TAXSAVER

Under current law, interest on EE bonds purchased from January 1, 1990, may be exempt from federal tax, if their redemption proceeds are used for certain educational purposes. To be eligible for the tax exemption, the purchaser of the bonds must be at least 24 years of age, and the proceeds from the sale of the bonds must be used to pay for the qualified higher educational expenses of either the purchaser, his/her spouse, or dependents. The tax break begins to phase out for married taxpayers filing jointly who have adjusted gross income of $81,100 in 2000. For single taxpayers and heads of household filers, the phaseout begins at $54,100. The break is not available if you are married filing separately. Caution: a young couple whose income increases significantly may find that, by the time their child is ready for college, they are no longer eligible to claim the tax exemption.

Series HH Bonds. These are current income securities: interest is paid at a fixed rate semiannually. Interest must be reported in the year in which it is received. Since March 1, 1993, new issues have paid a 4% rate of interest. (See discussion above for a tax deferral opportunity using Series EE and Series HH bonds.) You can only get Series HH bonds in exchange for Series E or EE bonds.

TAXSAVER

Both Series EE and HH bonds are subject to estate, inheritance, gift, or other excise taxes—whether federal or state—but they are exempt from all other taxes imposed on the principal or interest by any state, U.S. possession, or local taxing authority.

TaxSaver

Millions of dollars worth of Series (single) E and (single) H saving bonds continue to be held by the public. Most are earning interest. Some, however, have reached final maturity and no longer earn interest; others are nearing their final maturity dates. The chart below shows the extended maturities that have been announced by the U.S. Treasury. Series E bonds that have reached final maturity should be redeemed or exchanged for Series HH bonds.

Extended maturities

Series	Date of Issues	Interest-bearing Life
E	May 1941–Nov. 1965	40 years
	Dec. 1965 and later	30 years
H	June 1952–Jan. 1957	29 yrs., 8 mos.
	Feb. 1957 and later	30 years
EE	All issues	30 years
HH	All issues	20 years

Dividends. Dividends are distributions of money, stock, or other property paid to you by a corporation. You may also indirectly receive dividends through a partnership, an estate, or a trust. In most cases, dividends are taxable as ordinary income. Some dividends, however, are treated as capital gain distributions. The distributions are nontaxable if the distribution is considered to be a return of capital or if the distribution is in the form of stock or stock rights. You should be informed by the corporation making the distribution about the nature and amount of the dividends at the time of distribution. Dividend distributions from a mutual fund, such as interest on dividends earned from the fund's investment securities, are generally considered ordinary income for tax purposes. See Chapter 8, Mutual Funds.

Stock Dividends and Stock Rights. Generally, the receipt of stock dividends or stock rights in a company is not taxable, unless the shareholder is permitted to choose between stock (or stock rights) and cash or other property (e.g., a dividend reinvestment plan). If you receive a nontaxable distribution from a company, the adjusted basis of your old stock must be apportioned between the old and the new stock (or stock rights) based on their relative market values.

Example: If you owned 100 shares of XYZ Company that you purchased at $10 a share and you then received another 100 shares as a stock dividend, your adjusted basis for your 200 shares would be $5 a share. You are not required to allocate basis to nontaxable stock rights received if the value of the rights is less than 15% of the fair market value of the stock on the date of distribution.

Mutual fund dividends declared in October, November, and December to shareholders of record in those months are considered paid on December 31 of that year even if the distribution isn't actually paid until January of the next year. For a further discussion, see Chapter 8, Mutual Funds.

RENTAL INCOME AND EXPENSES

Rental income includes any payment you receive for the use or occupation of property. If you receive property or services as rent, the fair market value of the property or services you receive is income. (See Chapter 4 for a discussion of vacation home rentals and depreciation issues.)

CAPITAL GAINS AND LOSSES

For the most part, everything you own and hold for personal and investment purposes is a capital asset. (See Chapter 7, Capital Gains and Losses, for a discussion of how sales of capital assets are taxed.)

SELLING YOUR HOME

A gain on the sale or exchange (including condemnation) of your principal residence is taxable, although the law provides for a large exclusion. If you have a loss on the sale, under current law you cannot deduct it. (See Chapter 4 for more information about the tax consequences of home ownership as well as for tax-saving strategies that involve your home.)

INCOME FROM BUSINESS AND OTHER INVESTMENTS

Sole Proprietorship, Partnership, and S Corporation Income

In a sole proprietorship, you and your business are the same taxpayer. You report gross profit or loss for the year from the sole proprietorship on Form 1040, and it becomes part of your adjusted gross income. In contrast with a sole proprietorship, a partnership is an entity that is separate from the individual taxpayers that are its owners. While a partnership is not an entity subject to federal income tax, if you are a member of a partnership, you are liable individually for tax on your share of partnership income, even if such income is not distributed to you. S corporations generally do not pay federal income tax. Instead, S corporation income typically is taxed directly to the shareholders based on their respective ownership percentage, regardless of whether such income is distributed to them. Like partnerships, S corporations separately report items of income, gain, deduction, and loss that may be subject to special treatment by their shareholders. For a more complete discussion about the taxation of business income, see Part III, Tax Strategies for Businesses, especially Chapter 15, Determining Income, Deductions, and Taxes for Your Business.

"At-Risk" Limitation Provisions

The deduction for business and other investment losses held directly or through partnerships or S corporations is generally limited to the amount by which you are considered to be "at risk" in the activity. You are considered at risk for the amount of cash you have invested in the venture and the basis of property invested plus certain amounts borrowed for use in the activity.

Borrowed amounts that are considered at risk are (1) loans for which you are personally liable for repayment or (2) loans secured by property, other than that used in the activity. Generally, liabilities that are secured by property within the activity for which you are not otherwise personally liable are not considered to be at risk. An exception: if nonrecourse financing—financing for which you are not personally liable—is secured against real property used in the activity, you may be considered at risk for the amount of the financing.

If you are a partner in a partnership or a shareholder in an S corporation, you are also considered to be at risk for your undistributed share of partnership or S corporation income. The at-risk provisions apply to individuals and closely held corporations (corporations in which five or fewer individuals own more than 50% of the stock). For S corporations or partnerships, the at-risk rules apply to the shareholder or the partner. An exception: closely held corporations engaged in certain equipment leasing and active qualifying businesses are not subject to the at-risk rules.

The law provides a broad list of activities (including the holding of real estate acquired after 1986) that are subject to the at-risk provisions. Each investment activity is considered separately. However, S corporations and partnerships can aggregate investments in similar activity categories. If the "at-risk" provisions apply to you, you should consult with your tax advisor.

Passive Activity Losses and Credits

Under current law, individuals, estates, trusts, closely held corporations, and personal service corporations are generally prohibited from deducting net losses generated by passive activities. (Passive activities are discussed below.) In addition, tax credits from passive activities are generally limited to the tax liability attributable to such activities. Disallowed passive activity losses are suspended and carried forward to offset passive activity income generated in future years. Similar carryforward treatment applies to excess credits.

Defining Passive Activities. A passive activity involves the conduct of any trade or business in which you do not materially participate. You are treated as a material participant only if you are involved in the operations of the activity on a regular, continuous, and substantial basis. If you are not a material participant in an activity, but your spouse is, you are treated as being a material participant and the activity is not considered passive.

Seven Tests. The IRS has seven alternative tests you can meet to be considered a material participant. If you satisfy any one of these tests, you will be considered a material participant in an activity. These tests are:
1. You participate in the activity for more than 500 hours during the taxable year;
2. Your participation during the taxable year constitutes substantially all of the participation of all individuals;
3. You participate for more than 100 hours during the taxable year and no one else participates more;
4. The activity is a significant participation activity (SPA) for the taxable year, and your participation in all SPAs during the taxable year exceeds 500 hours. An SPA is an activity in which an individual participates for more than 100 hours, but does not otherwise meet a material participation test;
5. You materially participated in any 5 of the 10 preceding taxable years;
6. The activity is a personal service activity, and you materially participated for any three preceding taxable years. A personal service activity involves performance of personal services in the fields of health, law, engineering, architecture, accounting, actuarial sciences, performing arts, consulting, or any other business in which capital is not a material income-producing factor; or
7. Based on all the facts and circumstances, your participation is regular, continuous, and substantial during the taxable year.

Defining an Activity. The proper grouping of business operations into one or more activities is important in determining the allocation of suspended losses, measuring your material participation, separating rental and nonrental activities, and determining when a disposition of an activity has occurred. IRS regulations define an activity as any "appropriate economic unit for measuring gain or loss." What constitutes an "appropriate economic unit" is determined by looking at all facts and circumstances. The regulations list five factors that are to be given the greatest weight. They are:
1. Similarities and differences in types of business;
2. The extent of common control;
3. The extent of common ownership;
4. Geographical location; and
5. Interdependence between the activities.

Generally, taxpayers must be consistent from year to year in determining the business operations that constitute an activity. Furthermore, rental and nonrental activities may only be grouped together in a limited number of circumstances. Consult your tax advisor for more information.

Rental Activities. Rental activities are generally considered passive activities. However, the personal use of a dwelling unit for the greater of 14 days or 10% of the time that it is rented out to others is considered use of a personal residence and is not considered a passive activity.

IRS rules provide other exceptions for which activities involving the use of tangible property are not deemed a rental activity.

Real estate professionals who meet certain eligibility thresholds and materially participate in rental real estate activities may offset rental real estate losses against all sources of taxable income.

Only individuals and closely held C corporations can qualify for this special rule. An individual taxpayer will satisfy the eligibility requirements for any tax year if more than one-half of the personal services (with more than 750 hours) performed in trades or businesses by the taxpayer during such a tax year are performed in real property trades or businesses in which the taxpayer materially participates. Personal services performed as an employee are not considered in determining material participation unless the employee has more than a 5% ownership in the employer. However, independent contractor realtor services would qualify for this purpose. For closely held C corporations, the eligibility requirements are met if more than 50% of the corporation's gross receipts for the tax year are derived from real property trades or businesses in which the corporation materially participates.

Example: During 2000, a self-employed real estate developer earned $100,000 in fees from projects the developer spent 1,200 hours developing. In addition, the developer incurred rental real estate losses of $200,000 from properties which the developer spent over 800 hours managing during 2000. The developer performs no other personal services during the year and has no other items of income or deduction. Because the developer (1) materially participated in the rental real estate activity, (2) performed more than 750 hours in real property trades or businesses, and (3) performed more than 50% of the developer's total personal service hours in real estate trades or businesses in which the developer materially participated, the developer will have a net operating loss of $100,000 to carry back (and the excess to carry forward) to offset any source of income.

Limited Partnerships. Limited partnership interests are considered passive because a limited partner is generally not a material participant. If you have an interest in a limited partnership, you should check with your tax advisor to see if exceptions apply.

In general, working interests in any oil and gas property that you hold directly or through an entity that does not limit your liability is not considered passive, whether or not you are a material participant.

TaxSaver

One way to increase the deductibility of your passive activity losses is to convert the interest expense from nondeductible passive activity interest to deductible residential interest. You can accomplish this shift by borrowing against your personal residence and using the proceeds to repay passive activity loans. Interest on borrowings of up to $100,000 secured by your personal residence is usually fully deductible regardless of how the proceeds are used.

Exception for Active Real Estate Participation. An exception to the passive loss rules applies to real estate rental activities in which you are an active participant. For this purpose, "active" participation requires a significant but lesser amount of involvement than does "material" participation. Active involvement would include making management decisions such as approving "new tenants" or making capital expenditures. You are considered to have not actively participated in the rental activity if, at any time during the tax year, you own less than a 10% interest in the activity. Each tax year, you can deduct up to $25,000 of passive losses (or claim the equivalent amount of credits) arising from real estate rental activities against income from nonpassive sources, such as salary, interest, and dividends. The $25,000 maximum deduction is reduced (but not below zero) by 50% of the amount by which your adjusted gross income exceeds $100,000. Thus, this deduction is completely phased out if your adjusted gross income is $150,000 or more. Adjusted gross income, for this purpose, is figured without counting taxable Social Security benefits, IRA contribution deductions, and any passive activity loss.

Example: Ron's adjusted gross income, figured without taxable Social Security benefits, IRA contribution deductions, and any passive activity loss, is $120,000. He has rental losses of $25,000. If Ron's income had been less than $100,000, he would have been able to deduct the full $25,000 rental real estate loss. Because his income is over $100,000, Ron's $25,000 loss is reduced by $10,000 [50% × ($120,000 − $100,000)]. The disallowed loss of $10,000 can be carried over to future years and deducted (based on these same limitations).

Dispositions of Passive Activities. If you completely dispose of a passive activity in a fully taxable transaction, you can then claim previously disallowed (i.e., suspended) losses. In addition, for dispositions made prior to January 1, 1995, if you dispose of a "substantial part" of a passive activity in a fully taxable transaction, you also may be able to deduct the portion of your suspended losses attributable to that part of your investment assuming that you can determine with reasonable certainty the amount of the losses attributable to that part of your investment. For dispositions made after January 1, 1995, you must dispose of "substantially all" of a passive activity in order to deduct that same portion. If you dispose of a passive activity by selling your interest to a related party, you will not be able to deduct any suspended losses until the related purchaser disposes of the interest in a taxable transaction to an unrelated person. You may also be able to deduct suspended losses in a passive activity if your interest is disposed of in various other ways, including abandonment, death of the taxpayer, gifts, and installment sales of entire interests. Special rules may apply. You should consult your tax advisor for further clarification and requirements.

Social Security and Other Benefits

Social Security and Equivalent Railroad Retirement Benefits

A portion of your Social Security benefits may be subject to tax. Whether and how much depends upon the extent to which your provisional income (a technical term we will explain below) exceeds certain thresholds:

- $32,000 in the case of a married taxpayer filing a joint return—$0 if married filing separately, unless the spouses lived apart for the entire taxable year.
- $25,000 for all other taxpayers.

Provisional income is your adjusted gross income **plus** tax-exempt interest; income earned in a foreign country, Puerto Rico, or a U.S. possession that is not included in your gross income; plus tax-free foreign housing and one-half of the Social Security benefits you received.

For taxpayers with provisional income in excess of the thresholds, there is a two-tier system for determining the amount of the Social Security benefits included in income. How much is included will depend on whether your provisional income is in excess of:

- $44,000 in the case of a married taxpayer filing a joint return—$0 if married filing separately, unless the spouses lived apart for the entire taxable year.
- $34,000 for all other taxpayers.

For married joint filers with provisional income between $32,000 and $44,000, and for unmarried taxpayers with provisional income between $25,000 and $34,000, the amount of the Social Security benefit that is included in income is the lesser of one-half of the benefits received or one-half of the amount by which the provisional income exceeds the applicable threshold.

Example: For 2000, George and Harriet file a joint return. They have an adjusted gross income of $27,000. They received $7,500 in tax-exempt interest and $8,000 in Social Security benefits. The amount of Social Security benefits that they included in income is computed as follows:

Adjusted gross income	$27,000
Plus: Tax-exempt interest	7,500
Plus: One-half of the Social Security benefits received	4,000
Provisional income	$38,500
Less: Threshold base	32,000

Excess of *provisional income* above threshold base	$ 6,500
One-half of the excess	$ 3,250
One-half of the Social Security benefits	$ 4,000
The amount included in income	$ 3,250

(The lesser of one-half of the excess of the provisional income over the base amount or one-half of the Social Security benefits)

For those whose provisional income is in excess of the $44,000 and $34,000 applicable thresholds, not only does the amount of Social Security benefits included in income increase but the computation of the includible amount becomes more complicated.

For joint filers with provisional income in excess of $44,000 and unmarried filers with provisional income in excess of $34,000, the portion of Social Security benefits received that is included in income is the *lesser* of:

- 85% of Social Security benefits received, or
- the sum of the following amounts:

  a) the smaller of (1) the amount that would have been included in income if the threshold did not apply or (2) $6,000 for joint return filers or $4,500 for unmarried taxpayers; plus

  b) 85% of the excess of the provisional income over the higher threshold amount.

Example: Instead of $38,500 provisional income, as in the prior example, George and Harriet have $61,000 provisional income comprised of $45,000 adjusted gross income, $9,000 in tax-exempt interest, and $7,000 in Social Security benefits (one-half of the $14,000 Social Security benefits they received).

Provisional income	$61,000
Threshold amount	44,000
Excess of provisional income over threshold	$17,000
1) 85% of excess	$14,450
2) The amount that would have been included (50% of their Social Security benefits)	$ 7,000
3) Statutory amount for joint filers	6,000
4) The lesser of 2) or 3)	$ 6,000
5) The sum of 1) and 4)	$20,450
6) 85% of Social Security benefits ($14,000 × .85)	$11,900
Amount includible in income	$11,900

For married individuals filing separately, taxable Social Security benefits are calculated as the lesser of 85% of the taxpayer's provisional income.

The table below shows the portion of $10,000 in Social Security benefits received that would be included in taxable income of unmarried and joint filers at various income levels.

Amount of $10,000 in Social Security Benefits Included in
Taxable Income

Provisional Income	Single	Joint
$25,000	None	None
34,000	$4,500	$1,000
38,000	7,900	3,000
44,000	8,500	5,000
50,000	8,500	8,500

TAXALERT

Tax-exempt income is added to your adjusted gross income for purposes of calculating how much, if any, of your Social Security benefits will be subject to tax. Keep this in mind when evaluating the after-tax rate of return of tax-exempt investments versus taxable investments.

Disability

Generally, you must report as income amounts you receive for your disability through an employer-paid accident or health insurance plan.

TAXSAVER

If you pay part of the cost of a disability plan, then any amounts you receive that are attributable to your payments will not be taxed to you. For example, if you pay $25 into a disability plan for every $75 your employer puts into the plan, one-quarter of the amounts you receive will not be taxed to you.

Pensions or Annuities

As a general rule, if you did not pay any part of the cost of your pension or annuity, and your employer did not withhold part of the cost of the contract from your pay while you worked, the amounts you receive each year are fully taxable. For more information about IRAs, Keoghs, and Simplified Employee Pensions (SEPs), see Chapter 5.

What to Exclude from Income. If you paid part of the cost of your annuity, the portion of an annuity payment representing the return of your "investment in the contract" can be excluded from your gross income. The excludable portion is the payment received times the "exclusion ratio," that is, the investment in the contract divided by the expected return under the contract. The "expected return under the contract" is the total amount that you or someone you designate can expect to receive under the contract based on actuarial considerations. The exclusion is determined as of the first day of the first period for which an annuity payment is received. Once computed, the ratio ordinarily will not change.

Where the annuity starting date is after November 18, 1996, the excludable portion must generally be determined by dividing the investment in the contract by the number of anticipated payments determined under a table provided in the Internal Revenue Code.

For annuities that began payments before 1987, tax-free recoveries will continue even if the annuity owner outlives his or her life expectancy. However, if your first annuity payment was after 1986, the portion of a payment excluded from your gross income cannot exceed the unrecovered investment in the contract immediately before the receipt of such payment.

If annuity payments (from annuities with starting dates after 1986) cease because the annuity owner dies before his or her total contributions have been recovered, the amount of the unrecovered investment is allowed as a miscellaneous itemized deduction to the annuity owner for his or her last taxable year. However, the deduction is not subject to the 2% floor on miscellaneous itemized deductions. Similar rules apply where the contract provides for payments to be made to a beneficiary.

TaxSaver

Annuities are popular investments to earn income and defer taxes. Earnings accumulate and are not taxed until you receive payments. For more on annuities, please see Chapter 11, Investment Planning.

Lump Sum Distributions.   Lump sum distributions you receive from a qualified retirement plan—an employer's pension, stock bonus, or profit-sharing plan—may qualify for special tax treatment. A lump sum distribution is the distribution within a single tax year of an employee's entire balance, excluding certain amounts forfeited or subject to forfeiture, from all of the employer's qualified pension plans, all of the employer's qualified stock bonus plans, or all of the employer's qualified profit-sharing plans. The distribution must have been made:
1. Because of the employee's death,
2. After the employee reaches age 59½,
3. Because of the employee's separation from service (does not apply to self-employed persons), or
4. After a self-employed individual becomes totally and permanently disabled.

As with an annuity, you may recover tax-free your cost basis in the lump sum distribution. In general, your cost basis is:
1. Your total nondeductible contributions to the plan;
2. The total of your taxable one-year term costs of life insurance;
3. Any employer contributions that were taxable to you; and
4. Repayments of loans that were taxable to you.

You must reduce your basis by amounts previously distributed to you tax-free.

You also may be able to receive special tax treatment on the remainder of the distribution:

Long-Term Capital Gain Treatment. If you were at least age 50 on January 1, 1986, you may choose to treat a portion of the taxable part of a lump sum distribution as a long-term capital gain taxable at a 20% rate. This treatment applies to the portion you receive relating to your participation in the plan before 1994.

Capital gains treatment is not available for lump sum distributions received after 1999 by individuals who were less than 50 years old on January 1, 1986, or for lump sum distributions from an IRA.

Special Averaging Method. You may elect to use a 10-year special averaging method to calculate the tax on the ordinary income portion of a lump sum distribution, including the capital gain portion for which you did not elect capital gain treatment. To use special averaging, you must have been at least age 50 on January 1, 1986, elect to use special averaging for all lump sum distributions received during the year, and have been a participant in the plan for five or more years. You can make this election only once in a lifetime.

The tax rates used in the 10-year averaging calculation are the rates in effect for 1986. (See Table 1.1.)

TABLE 1.1 Tax Rate Schedule for the 10-Year Averaging Calculation

If the amount is:		The tax is:		Of the amount over—
Over—	But not over—			
$–0–	$1,190	—	11%	$–0–
1,190	2,270	$130.90 +	12%	1,190
2,270	4,530	260.50 +	14%	2,270
4,530	6,690	576.90 +	15%	4,530
6,690	9,170	900.90 +	16%	6,690
9,170	11,440	1,277.70 +	18%	9,170
11,440	13,710	1,706.30 +	20%	11,440
13,710	17,160	2,160.30 +	23%	13,710
17,160	22,880	2,953.80 +	26%	17,160
22,880	28,600	4,441.00 +	30%	22,880
28,600	34,320	6,157.00 +	34%	28,600
34,320	42,300	8,101.80 +	38%	34,320
42,300	57,190	11,134.20 +	42%	42,300
57,190	85,790	17,388.00 +	48%	57,190
85,790	—	31,116.00 +	50%	85,790

To get an idea of how special averaging works, assume that your income was received equally by 10 different persons in the current year and that each of these people had no other income. As a result, most of the income is taxed at the lowest rates on the single taxpayer tax-rate schedule. The tax for these fictional individuals is then added up and becomes your tax on the distribution.

TaxSaver

The 10-year averaging method may be so beneficial to you that you elect to have the long-term capital gain portion of the lump sum distribution included in the 10-year averaging computation rather than have it taxed as long-term capital gain. The tax should be figured both ways to see which is the lowest.

Lump sum distributions from an IRA do not qualify for the special averaging method.

TaxAlert

For tax years beginning before 2000, a five-year special averaging method was available. This method has been eliminated after 1999.

Individual Retirement Arrangements (IRAs). In general, distributions from an IRA are taxed in much the same way as an annuity. The portion of each distribution that is attributable to nondeductible contributions, if any, is excluded from your taxable income. The portion of each distribution to be excluded is determined by dividing undistributed nondeductible contributions by your total IRA account balance. If no nondeductible contributions have been made, then the entire distribution is considered ordinary income. If you take a distribution from a Roth IRA, you are generally considered to have withdrawn your nontaxable contributions first unless you converted a traditional IRA into a Roth IRA and are taking a premature distribution. (See Chapter 5 for more details about IRAs.)

Other Income

Interest-Free and Below-Market-Rate Loans

Certain interest-free and below-market-rate loans must be treated as loans bearing interest at a statutory rate. This may cause the imputed interest to be treated as a gift, compensation, or other payment, as described below.

An interest-free or below-market loan is a loan on which no interest is charged or on which interest is charged at a rate below the applicable federal rate (AFR), set monthly by the IRS. Such a loan is generally treated as an arm's-length transaction in which you, as the borrower, are deemed (1) to have received a loan that requires the payment of interest at the applicable federal rate and (2) to have received an additional payment equal to the difference between the AFR and the no-interest or low-interest rate. The additional payment is treated as a gift, dividend, contribution to capital, payment of compensation, or other payment, depending on the nature of the transaction. In effect, two transactions are deemed to have occurred. One results in interest income to the lender and interest expense to the borrower to the extent that the interest at the statutory rate exceeds the actual interest paid. This is known as "foregone interest." In the second transaction, the lender is considered to have paid to the borrower the amount of "foregone interest" in the form of a gift, dividend, compensation, or other payment, depending on the nature of the relationship between the two parties.

Below-Market Demand Loans. If one party receives a below-market gift demand loan or other demand loan (one payable in full at any time upon the lender's demand), the lender will be treated as having made a transfer to the borrower on the last day of the calendar year of an amount equal to the "foregone interest." This amount will be treated as a gift, compensation, dividend, or other payment as appropriate. An identical amount will be treated as a payment of interest by the borrower at the same time. Therefore, the borrower may be entitled to deduct a part of that amount as interest expense. Loans with indefinite maturities are treated as demand loans.

Below-Market Term Loans. If one party receives a below-market "gift" term loan (one that is not a demand loan), the lender is treated as having made a gift on the loan date equal to the excess of the amount borrowed over the present value of all principal and interest payments required by the terms of the loan. The present value is determined using the applicable federal rate established monthly by the IRS. The borrower is treated as if he or she paid the lender interest on the last day of the calendar year.

If one party receives a term loan (other than a gift term loan), the lender is deemed to have transferred an amount equal to the excess of the loan over the present value of all principal and interest payments to the borrower. The transfer is treated as having occurred on the date the loan was made. The amount will be considered a dividend, compensation, or other payment as appropriate. An amount equal to this excess will be treated as original issue discount. Accordingly, the original discount rules apply. The borrower and the lender will be treated as paying or receiving interest on an economic accrual basis over the term of the loan. (Original issue discount is discussed on page 249.)

The applicable federal rate used in the calculations discussed above is based on the average yield on U.S. Treasury obligations. Different rates will be used for short-, intermediate-, and long-term loans. Semiannual compounding is required for both term and demand loans.

Exceptions: The rules for below-market loans do not apply to:
1. Gift loans between individuals that in the aggregate do not exceed $10,000, provided the loan proceeds are not directly used to purchase or carry income-producing assets;
2. Gift loans between individuals not exceeding $100,000, where the borrower's net investment income does not exceed $1,000 and there is no motive to avoid paying tax;
3. Gift loans between individuals not exceeding $100,000, where the borrower's net investment income exceeds $1,000 and there is no motive to avoid paying tax (the amount of interest income and expense imputed is limited to the net investment income);
4. Compensation or corporate/shareholder loans that in the aggregate do not exceed $10,000, provided the principal purpose of the loan is not avoiding taxes; and
5. A mortgage loan made to an employee who has moved where the beneficial rate is contingent on continued employment.

TaxSAVER

Imputed interest may result in one or both parties of the transaction recognizing taxable income without an offsetting deduction, even though no money changed hands. To avoid this, be sure that the loans carry an appropriate market interest rate and that interest payments are made when due. For term loans, the interest rate is the applicable federal rate in effect on the date the loan is made; for demand loans, the rate is the applicable federal short-term rate in effect on each day the loan is outstanding.

Restricted Property Received for Services

The excess of the fair market value of restricted property received for services performed over the amount (if any) paid for such property should be included in income as compensation in the year your interest in the property becomes transferable or is not subject to a substantial risk of forfeiture. Restricted property includes both real and personal property that is subject to some form of restriction, such as a limitation on transferring the property or a risk of forfeiture upon leaving employment before a specified date. However, restricted property does not include either money or an unsecured promise to pay money or property in the future. Generally, the fair market value is determined at the time the property becomes transferable or nonforfeitable.

Instead of deferring the recognition of income until your interest in the property becomes transferable or is no longer subject to a substantial risk of forfeiture, you may elect in the year of transfer to include in your income the fair market value of the property at the time of receipt (disregarding restrictions other than ones that by their terms will never lapse) minus the amount (if any) paid for such property. Generally, this election must be made within 30 days of the transfer of the property. However, if this election is made and the property is subsequently forfeited, you may only deduct the excess of the amount originally paid for the property (if any) over the amount realized (if any) from the forfeiture. This means that you can't deduct the amount you included in income as a result of the election.

TaxSaver

The election to include in your income the fair market value of the property at the time of receipt can produce tax savings if the property appreciates in value by the time the restrictions lapse. This election defers recognizing the gain on the appreciation until the property is sold and the appreciation would be taxed as capital gain rather than ordinary income. However, you need to consider the value of money over time for the taxes you will currently pay as well as the possibility of forfeiting the property.

The holding period for the restricted property begins on the first date on which your rights are either transferable or not subject to a substantial risk of forfeiture. If, however, you elect to include in your income the fair market value of the property, the holding period begins on the date of actual transfer.

If you perform services in return for restricted property, the person for whom you perform such services is allowed a deduction for the same amount and in the same year in which you report income. For transfers to employees, regulations generally require withholding by the employer (although withholding is not required for the deduction).

Unemployment Compensation

Generally, unemployment compensation benefits are fully taxable. However, if the unemployed worker contributed nondeductible amounts to the unemployment compensation fund during employment, unemployment compensation is not taxable until an amount equal to those nondeductible amounts has been received.

Health and Accident Benefits

Benefits received under a qualified employer-sponsored health or accident plan for the reimbursement of medical expenses and payments for permanent injury or loss of a bodily function can be excluded from your gross income. Reimbursements for medical expenses that you claimed as an itemized deduction in a previous year must be included in gross income.

Benefits received under an employer-funded, self-insured, medical reimbursement plan by employees who are officers, shareholders, or highly compensated individuals can be excluded from income only if the plan does not discriminate in favor of these employees.

Life Insurance Contracts

Generally, amounts you receive under a life insurance contract paid by reason of the death of the insured, whether in a single sum or otherwise, are not included in your gross income.

Any interest paid along with life insurance death proceeds is taxable.

Any proceeds received upon the surrender of a life insurance contract by the insured are taxable to the extent that the amount received (including amounts recovered tax-free prior to the exchange) is in excess of the amounts paid in. A loss is not deductible.

Accelerated Death Benefits (Viatical Settlements)

Amounts a terminally or chronically ill person receives on the sale or assignment of the death benefit of a life insurance contract to a viatical settlement provider generally are excluded from gross income. To be considered terminally ill, an insured person must obtain certification from a physician that the person has a condition that is expected to result in death within 24 months. A chronically ill person is defined as someone who has been certified by a licensed health care practitioner within the previous 12 months as (1) being unable to perform at least two activities of daily living for at least 90 days as a result of the loss of functional capacity; or (2) requiring supervision because of cognitive impairment. Activities of daily living include eating, toileting, transferring, bathing, dressing, and continence.

A qualified viatical settlement provider is any person who regularly engages in the trade or business of buying life insurance contracts on individuals who are terminally ill or chronically ill. The viatical settlement provider generally must be licensed in the state where the insured resides, meet certain disclosure requirements, and meet standards intended to ensure that the chronically or terminally ill person receives reasonable payments for the sale or assignment.

Modified Endowment Contracts

In general, a modified endowment contract is one in which the accumulated amount paid by the taxpayer under the contract at any time during the first seven contract years exceeds the sum of the average annual premiums for paid-up insurance that would have been paid within the first seven years. Modified endowment contracts entered after June 21, 1988, are taxable as follows:

1. Amounts received under the contract are treated first as income and then as a recovery of investment in the contract.
2. Loans under the contract, as well as loans secured by the contract, are treated as amounts received under the contract except for certain loans relating to funeral expenses.

3. An additional 10% tax is imposed on amounts received that can be included in income. This additional tax does not apply to any distribution (a) made on or after you turn age 59½; (b) due to your becoming disabled; or (c) that is part of a series of substantially equal periodic payments made over your life or life expectancy or for the joint lives or life expectancies of you and your beneficiary.

Certain Living Expense Contracts

You can exclude from your gross income amounts received under an insurance contract that pays you for living expenses in excess of your normal living expenses resulting from the loss of the use of your principal residence due to a casualty.

Dividends on Life Insurance and Endowment Policies

Dividends on most unmatured life insurance or endowment policies are treated as a partial return of the premiums paid and are not included in your gross income until they exceed the accumulated net premiums paid for the contract.

Alimony and Similar Payments

If you receive payments of alimony or separate maintenance, you must include them in figuring your gross income. Conversely, if you pay alimony or separate maintenance to a former spouse, you may deduct such payments from your gross income. Payments received from a property settlement or for child support are not considered alimony and therefore are not considered income to the recipient (or deductible to the payor).

TaxSaver

The tax consequences of alimony versus other payments need to be carefully considered in working out divorce or separation agreements. For example, if you receive property with a tax basis that is substantially less than its current value, you will be subject to tax on the difference between the tax basis of the property and the amount you receive when you sell the property. You should consult your tax advisor on such matters. (See page 37 for a further discussion of alimony.)

Tax-Exempt Interest

Interest on certain obligations of a state, territory, U.S. possession, or any political subdivision can be excluded from gross income. In addition, if you earn interest on tax-exempt bonds issued in your home state, the interest will generally not be subject to state or local tax. Special rules apply to interest on arbitrage and industrial development bonds. Tax-exempt interest on certain municipal bonds issued after August 7, 1986, is a tax preference item for AMT purposes. (See discussion on page 154.)

TAX*SAVER*

Higher income tax rates increase the appeal of tax-exempt bonds and mutual funds that invest in these bonds, especially for taxpayers in the 39.6% top marginal tax bracket. As tax rates rise, taxable securities must provide a higher yield in order to match the tax-effected yield offered by tax-exempt bonds of similar quality and time to maturity. For example, to a taxpayer in the 31% bracket, a taxable bond yielding 8.70% is comparable to a municipal bond with a 6.0% tax-exempt yield. However, a taxpayer in the 39.6% bracket would need almost a 10% yield on a taxable bond to match the municipal bond's 6.0% return. And considering the fact that some states have income tax rates over 10%, the combined federal and state marginal tax rate, taking phaseouts and other back-door tax increases into account, can exceed 50%. Thus, an investor living in such a high-tax state would need a 12% taxable bond to achieve the same after-tax return as a 6% municipal bond.

The following table demonstrates the yield you would have to earn on a taxable bond in order to generate the same after-tax earnings as a tax-exempt bond would provide at a correspondingly lower yield.

Equivalent Yield Needed from a Taxable Bond

Tax-Exempt Yield	*Your Combined Federal, State, & Local Marginal Tax Bracket*						
	28%	*31%*	*33%*	*36%*	*39.6%*	*42%*	*46%*
4.00	5.56	5.80	5.97	6.25	6.62	6.90	7.41
4.50	6.25	6.52	6.72	7.03	7.45	7.76	8.33
5.00	6.94	7.25	7.46	7.81	8.28	8.62	9.26
5.50	7.64	7.97	8.21	8.59	9.11	9.48	10.19
6.00	8.33	8.70	8.96	9.38	9.93	10.34	11.11
6.50	9.03	9.42	9.70	10.16	10.76	11.21	12.04
7.00	9.72	10.14	10.45	10.94	11.59	12.07	12.96

Group Term Life Insurance Paid by Employers

Generally, the cost for group term life insurance paid by an employer for the benefit of employees can be excluded from your gross income, as long as the premiums do not exceed the cost for $50,000 of life insurance.

If the group term life insurance plan discriminates in favor of highly compensated employees, then the cost of this insurance is fully taxable to such employees. For purposes of this rule, highly compensated employees include certain corporate officers and certain shareholder-employees.

E&Y FOCUS: Employee Stock Options

Many employers grant stock options to employees as a reward for services rendered or to be rendered. Stock options allow an employee to buy a specified amount of stock of his or her employer at some set price and for a stated period of time. For example, your employer might grant you an option to purchase stock in the company at $10 per share—its market price at the time of the grant. If the market price of the stock rises to, say, $15 per share, you would be able to buy the stock at a discount of $5 per share—that is, at the $10-per-share option price rather than the $15 market value. But if the value of the stock never goes above the $10 exercise price, you would let your option lapse.

Merely holding unexercised options may be viewed as providing the option holder with significant economic benefits. Options can be seen as an opportunity to ''ride the market'' without committing personal capital to a risk that the value of the stock may fall. If the market price of the employer's stock increases, the holder of unexercised options benefits from this appreciation just as a shareholder would. That's because the option holder can acquire the appreciated stock for a known bargain price simply by exercising the option.

Incentive Stock Options

Incentive stock options (ISOs) are options that meet certain rules set forth in the law and are afforded special tax treatment. An ISO can be received and exercised without recognition of income if certain requirements are met. An ISO has the following tax consequences:

1. No taxable income will be recognized by the employee when the ISO is granted or exercised.
2. The income will be taxed as a capital gain when the employee sells stock acquired on the exercise of an incentive stock option, provided the holding period requirements are met.
3. The employer will not be able to deduct the bargain element of the option as an expense, as long as the gain on the option is treated as a capital gain.
4. The difference between the option price and the fair market value at the time the option is exercised is an adjustment for the alternative minimum tax.

This favorable treatment is available provided that:

1. You do not dispose of the stock within two years after the option is granted and you hold the stock for at least one year from the date the option is exercised. If these requirements are not met, you will recognize ordinary income on the difference between the option price and the fair market value at the date the option is exercised or the gain on the date the shares are sold, if lower. Any amount realized in excess of the fair market value on the date the option is exercised will be considered a capital gain. In such a case, your employer would be entitled to deduct as a compensation expense the ordinary income portion of your gain.

2. For the entire time from the date the option is granted until three months before it is exercised, you must be an employee either of the corporation granting the option, a parent or subsidiary of that corporation, or a corporation that has assumed the option of another corporation as a result of a reorganization, liquidation, or similar transaction.

Nonstatutory Stock Options

Nonstatutory stock options (NSOs) are options that either fail to meet certain requirements or are specifically designated as NSOs. They are not afforded the special tax treatment given to ISOs (see the preceding paragraphs). Generally, these options are taxed at ordinary income rates. Depending on the particular characteristics of the option, it may be taxed (1) when the option is granted, (2) when it is exercised, (3) when it is sold, or (4) when restrictions on the stock lapse. Typically, most NSOs are taxed when exercised.

Tax Treatment at a Glance. This hypothetical example illustrates the tax treatment of nonstatutory stock options (NSOs) versus incentive stock options (ISOs):

Option Granted: 4/30/00	Nonstatutory Stock Option	Incentive Stock Option
Fair Market Value of Stock on 4/30/00:	$30	$30
Option Exercise Price:	$30	$30
Option Exercised: 10/30/00		
Fair Market Value of Stock on 10/30/00:	$50	$50
Option Spread:	$20	$20
Tax Treatment of Spread When Option Is Exercised:	$20 Taxed as Ordinary Compensation Income for Regular Tax Purposes	No Regular Tax Consequences (Spread of $20 Is Adjustment for AMT)
Regular-Tax Basis in Option Stock:	$50	$30
AMT Basis in Option Stock:	$50	$50
Stock Appreciates to $90		
Disqualifying Disposition (e.g., sale within 1 year of exercise)	$40 Short-term Capital Gain	$20 Ordinary Income $40 Short-term Capital Gain for Regular Tax and AMT

Non-Disqualifying Disposition $40 Capital Gain $60 Capital Gain
for Regular Tax
$40 Capital Gain
for AMT

E&Y FOCUS: When to Exercise Stock Options

In light of the substantial difference between the 20% long-term capital gain rate and the 39.6% maximum ordinary income rate, you should perform tax computations prior to making a decision to exercise an option or not and prior to making the decision to dispose of the stock received on exercise.

Incentive Stock Options. If you expect your company stock to appreciate over the long term, it generally makes sense to postpone exercising incentive stock options (ISOs) until their expiration date is imminent. By waiting, you can watch the stock appreciate as long as possible before having to pay the option price.

In the following situations, however, it may make sense to exercise ISOs before they expire:

- If you believe the company's stock price has peaked and you intend to sell the stock as soon as you can after exercising the options (i.e., before the required holding period);
- If the annual dividends paid on your company's stock exceed the carrying cost of the funds needed to exercise the options, that is, the option price plus any taxes due (this strategy would, of course, subject you to the risk that the stock price may fall); or
- If you have a need for cash now or in the near future that can be satisfied by exercising the options and subsequently selling the stock. You may not want to take the risk of a lower market price in the future.

Nonqualified Stock Options. Generally, if you expect the company stock to appreciate over the long term, it makes sense to postpone exercising NQSOs until their expiration date is imminent. By waiting, you can continue to benefit from the appreciation on all of the options without having to liquidate other assets or some of the stock. Remember, however, that when the options are exercised, you have to surrender cash (or, in some cases, stock) to pay the option price and the tax on the option spread. By deferring the exercise of the option, you can earn more appreciation before you have to cough up the option price and pay the tax bill.

In the following situations, however, it may make sense to exercise options before they expire:

- If you believe the company's stock price has peaked, and you intend to sell the stock as soon as you can after the exercise;
- If the annual dividends paid on your company's stock exceed the carrying cost of the funds needed to exercise the options; that is, the option price plus any taxes due (this strategy would, of course, subject you to the risk that the stock price may fall);

- If you have a need for cash now or in the near future that can be satisfied by exercising the options and subsequently selling the stock. You may not want to take the risk of a lower market price in the future;
- If you expect that ordinary income tax rates will increase in the future or you want to take advantage of lower capital rates on appreciation subsequent to exercise; or
- If you are subject to the alternative minimum tax but will not be entitled to a minimum tax credit carryover for the full amount of the AMT. The ordinary income from exercising the option will be subject to the AMT tax rate, which is substantially below the regular tax rate.

Prizes and Awards

Generally, contest prizes and awards are included in gross income. The value of an employee achievement award for length of service or safety performance can be excluded from your gross income to the extent your employer can deduct the expense. Special rules apply to limit the total awards you can exclude from your income in any one tax year. The maximum yearly exclusion is generally $400. However, if the awards received are under a plan that satisfies certain conditions specified by the tax law, you may be able to exclude from income up to $1,600 in total annual awards.

Reimbursements for Moving Expenses

Reimbursements for qualified moving expenses are not included in your gross income. Qualified moving expense reimbursements are those amounts received by an employee from the employer that would have been deductible moving expenses if paid by the employee. The same rule applies if the employer pays the expenses directly. (For a discussion of the qualified deductions allowed for employment-related moving expenses, see pages 49–50.)

Gifts and Inheritances

Your gross income does not include the value of property acquired by gift or inheritance unless you are an employee of the donor or decedent. (See Chapter 13 for a discussion of the gift and estate tax.)

Scholarships and Fellowship Grants

You can exclude from gross income the amount received as a qualified scholarship or fellowship grant provided you are a degree candidate and the monies are used strictly for qualified tuition, fees, books, supplies, and required equipment.

Cafeteria Plans

A cafeteria plan is an employee benefit plan under which a participant may choose between two or more benefits consisting of cash and qualified benefits. You may generally exclude from gross income employer contributions for nontaxable benefits selected under the plan (unless you are a "highly compensated participant" in a discriminatory plan). The exclusion from gross income does not apply to "key employees" where the statutory benefits provided to them exceed 25% of the total nontaxable benefits provided for all employees under the plan.

TaxSaver

Cafeteria plans can be used effectively to increase the tax benefits of certain deductions and credits. For instance, ordinarily only medical expenses in excess of 7.5% of your adjusted gross income can be deducted. However, if you contribute to your employer's cafeteria plan (in pre-tax dollars), you can then be reimbursed by the plan for certain medical benefits if the employer's plan provides this as an option. You will not be taxed on the reimbursement you receive. There are some risks for employees because money left over at the end of the year is forfeited, so consult your tax advisor.

Similarly, dependent care payments you make qualify you for the dependent care credit. Depending on your income level, you may get a tax credit for at least 20% of the payments you made. However, if your contribution to your employer's cafeteria plan is made in pre-tax dollars, the benefit of reimbursement of child care expenses from the plan can be as high as 39.6%, depending on your tax bracket.

Example: Assume you have medical expenses of $1,000. If your expenses are paid through a cafeteria plan, the cost to you will be $1,000 in reduced wages. If you are in the 31% bracket and pay the medical expenses after tax, you will have to earn $1,450 to have enough left over to pay the $1,000 of medical expenses.

2

What You Can Deduct: Exemptions, Adjustments, and Deductions

INTRODUCTION

This chapter discusses most of the deductions and exemptions that you can claim to lower your taxable income. Deductions include nonreimbursed medical and dental expenses, charitable contributions, nonbusiness casualty and theft losses, and home mortgage interest payments as well as amounts you pay for state and local income and property taxes, certain other interest payments, and a variety of miscellaneous items. Some of these deductions are subject to limits and thresholds. In addition, you are entitled to exemptions for yourself, for children, and for other dependents.

The amount of income tax you owe is figured by taking your gross income and subtracting allowable adjustments, deductions, and exemptions. The adjustment amounts reduce your gross income to arrive at a figure known as *adjusted gross income* (AGI). Then, deductions and exemptions are subtracted from your AGI to arrive at your taxable income, the amount on which income tax is imposed. You may subtract the greater of either the standard deduction, an amount determined annually by the federal government, or your itemized deductions, certain personal and investment expenses that the tax law specifies as deductible.

If your income level is above a specified amount, the tax benefits of some personal and dependent exemptions are phased out. In addition, certain deductions are only available to you if your expenses exceed a certain percentage of your income. This chapter will help you sort out those expenses you can deduct from those you can't. In the process, it will help you focus on possible ways to lower your tax bill.

STANDARD DEDUCTION

Individuals who do not itemize their deductions are entitled to a standard deduction amount. This amount varies according to your filing status. The standard deduction to which you are entitled is subtracted from your adjusted gross income in arriving at your taxable income. You can choose between itemizing your deductions or claiming the applicable standard deduction amount in figuring your taxable income, depending on which produces the greatest tax benefit.

The standard deduction amounts available to individuals are listed in Table 2.1, below.

For married individuals (filing jointly or separately where neither spouse itemizes) and surviving spouses, an "additional standard deduction" of $850 is allowed for each spouse over the age of 65 and for each spouse who is blind ($1,700 in the case of an elderly and blind taxpayer). The additional standard deduction is $1,100 for elderly or blind individuals who are unmarried and are not surviving spouses ($2,200 in the case of an elderly and blind taxpayer). These additional standard deductions are changed annually by a cost-of-living adjustment.

If you are eligible to be claimed as a dependent on another taxpayer's return, you may not claim the full standard deduction. Rather, your standard deduction would be limited to the greater of either $700 or your earned income plus $250. For taxpayers who are at least age 65 or blind and who are eligible to be claimed as a dependent on another taxpayer's return, the standard deduction is limited to the greater of either $700 or earned income, plus any additional standard deduction available because of age or blindness. In calculating the limitation, earned income includes taxable scholarship and fellowship funds you receive.

The following individuals are specifically excluded from using the standard deduction:

1. A married individual filing a separate return where the other spouse itemizes deductions;
2. A nonresident alien; or
3. An individual whose return covers less than 12 months due to a change in the annual accounting period.

TABLE 2.1 Standard Deductions

Filing Status	2000*
Single	$4,400
Head of household	6,450
Married filing jointly and surviving spouses	7,350
Married filing separately	3,675

These amounts are increased annually by a cost-of-living adjustment.

PERSONAL AND DEPENDENT EXEMPTIONS

Personal and dependent exemptions reduce your taxable income. For 2000, each exemption equals $2,800. (The amount is adjusted annually to reflect increases in the cost of living.) You are entitled to:

1. One exemption for yourself. (This exemption is not available to individuals who can be claimed as a dependent on another taxpayer's return.)
2. One exemption for your spouse if (a) a joint return is filed or (b) a joint return is not filed and your spouse has no gross income and is not the dependent of another.
3. One exemption for each dependent whose gross income is less than $2,800 or who is your child, if he or she is: (a) a full-time student under the age of 24 at the end of the year or (b) not yet 19 years old at the end of the year.

TAXSAVER

You may consider the option of taking a dependent exemption for your married child (if he or she so qualifies) and have the child file "married filing separately." In some cases, the benefit of claiming a dependent exemption may outweigh the benefit of having the child file a joint return with his or her spouse.

Personal and Dependent Exemption Phaseout

The tax benefits of the personal and dependent exemptions are phased out for taxpayers whose adjusted gross income exceeds specific amounts. The phaseout is accomplished by reducing the exemption amount allowed by 2% for each $2,500 (or fraction thereof) of AGI in excess of certain levels. In 2000, the phaseout of personal exemptions begins at an *adjusted gross income* of $193,400 for married taxpayers filing a joint return; $96,700 for married filing separately; $161,150 for head of household; and $128,950 for single taxpayers.

Example: Joe and Joan file a joint return. They have three dependent children. For 2000 they have adjusted gross income of $230,500. The dependency exemption amount for 2000, before any reductions, is $2,800. Because their AGI exceeds $193,400 by $37,100, each of their exemptions will be reduced by $840 [($37,100 ÷ $2,500 rounding up to the nearest whole number) × 2% × $2,800]. Thus, each exemption is only $1,960, or a total of $9,800 for their two personal exemptions and three dependency exemptions.

Children cannot claim a personal exemption for themselves if they are eligible to be claimed as an exemption on their parents' return. As discussed earlier, exemptions begin to phase out for parents with adjusted gross income in excess of $193,400 on joint returns, $96,700 on separate returns, $161,150 for heads of households, and $128,950 for single individuals. So there may be a point where your dependent child could recognize a greater tax benefit if he or she could claim a personal exemption rather than your taking the exemption on your own return. But to shift the exemption to your child, you will have to take steps to disqualify your child as your dependent. Generally, this can only be accomplished if your child receives less than half of his or her support from you.

Social Security Numbers. Taxpayers must report on their income tax return the Social Security number of any dependent claimed.

Definition of Dependents

A dependent is any person listed below who receives more than half of his or her support from the taxpayer and who does not file a joint return with his or her spouse:

1. A son or daughter of the taxpayer, or a descendant of either;
2. A stepson or stepdaughter of the taxpayer;
3. A brother, sister, stepbrother, or stepsister of the taxpayer;
4. A father or mother of the taxpayer, or ancestor of either;
5. A stepfather or stepmother of the taxpayer;
6. A son or daughter of the taxpayer's brother or sister;
7. A brother or sister of the taxpayer's father or mother; or
8. A member of the taxpayer's household, unless the relationship is in violation of local law.

Dependents of Divorced or Separated Parents. The dependent exemption for qualifying children of divorced or separated parents is generally allowed to the custodial parent (the parent who has custody of the child for the greater portion of the year) unless: (1) a multiple support agreement exists; (2) a pre-1985 divorce or separation agreement shifted the exemption to the noncustodial parent; or (3) the custodial parent releases the claim to the exemption to the noncustodial parent. To transfer the exemption, the custodial parent must sign a written declaration releasing the exemption to the noncustodial parent. The declaration may be made annually, for one or more calendar years, or permanently.

In giving up the exemption for a dependent child, the custodial parent does not forfeit the right to claim head-of-household status, the earned income credit, or the child and dependent care credit if the individual otherwise qualifies. These are discussed on pages 34 and 150.

The word "dependent" does not include any individual who is not a citizen or national of the United States, Canada, or Mexico. A legally adopted child need not be a U.S. citizen to qualify as a dependent if the child is a member of a household of a taxpaying U.S. citizen.

Multiple Support Agreements

An individual supported by several persons, none of whom alone furnishes more than one-half of his or her support, may qualify as a dependent. In this case, the dependency deduction may be claimed by any one individual (otherwise entitled to do so) contributing over 10% of the support, provided that:

1. over one-half of the support was contributed by persons who, except for the support test, would be entitled to claim the supported individual as a dependent, and
2. each other person described in (1) contributing over 10% of the dependent's support files a written declaration (Form 2120) with the return of the person who claims the exemption, stating that he or she will not claim a deduction for the same dependent for that year.

TaxSaver

If two or more individuals provide less than 50% but more than 10% of the support to a dependent (e.g., your parent), it may be more beneficial to give the right to claim the exemption to the supporter to whom it will yield the highest tax benefit.

TaxSaver

If your dependent maintains his or her own home and you paid the mortgage and real estate taxes, neither of you will be entitled to the mortgage interest or real estate taxes deduction. You may consider taking a partial interest in the property in order to secure the deductions subject to the mortgage interest limitation (page 76) on your return. Another option would be to give cash to your dependent so that he or she can pay the mortgage and real estate taxes directly. In turn, the dependent can deduct such payments on his or her own return.

INDIVIDUAL RETIREMENT ARRANGEMENTS (IRAS)

An individual retirement arrangement (IRA) is a personal savings plan that lets you set aside funds for your retirement, using pre-tax dollars. Subject to certain limitations, the amount you contribute to your IRA can be deducted from your taxable income. Another type of IRA, known as a

Roth IRA, provides for tax-exempt withdrawals under certain circumstances. (See Chapter 5 for details.)

SIMPLIFIED EMPLOYEE PENSIONS

A simplified employee pension (SEP) is a written plan that allows an employer to make contributions toward an employee's retirement without becoming involved in more complex retirement plans. If you are self-employed, you can contribute to your own SEP. Subject to certain limitations, the amounts you contribute to an SEP can be deducted from your taxable income. (For more information see Chapter 5.)

KEOGH (HR 10) PLANS

If you are self-employed and own your own business, you may set up a retirement plan, commonly known as a Keogh or HR 10 plan. You must have earned income from the trade or business for which the plan was established to take a deduction for a contribution to the plan. A Keogh plan may be either a "defined contribution plan" or a "defined benefit plan." Within limits, amounts you contribute to a Keogh plan can be deducted in calculating your taxable income. (For more information on this type of plan, see Chapter 5.)

SIMPLE RETIREMENT PLANS

Small businesses that normally employ 100 or fewer employees can establish a savings incentive match plan for employees (SIMPLE). If you are self-employed, you can contribute to a SIMPLE plan. See pages 96–97.

DIVORCE OR SEPARATION

Alimony

Alimony is an amount paid to a spouse or former spouse under a divorce or separation agreement. You are allowed a deduction for alimony payments you make. (See page 25 for an explanation of how alimony you receive is taxed.)

What Qualifies as Alimony. To qualify for a deduction as alimony, payments stipulated in the divorce or separation agreement should not be designated as something other than alimony. In addition, the parties to the divorce or legal separation must not be members of the same household at the time of payment, and there must be no liability for payments to continue after the death of the spouse receiving the money. Payments made under a divorce or separation decree executed after 1984 must be in cash or its equivalent. For example, transferring securities to satisfy payments due under a divorce or separation agreement does not qualify as alimony. Cash payments made to a third party, however—such as medical expenses paid to doctors or hospitals on behalf of the spouse or former spouse at his or her request—will qualify as alimony, assuming all other requirements are met.

TAXSAVER

If you pay medical expenses for your separated spouse (under a separation agreement) or your former spouse, you should deduct the payment as alimony, not as medical expenses. Alimony is fully deductible from your adjusted gross income (whether or not you itemize your deductions), whereas only the portion of your medical expenses that exceeds 7.5% of your adjusted gross income will be deductible.

Deductible alimony payments made under divorce or separation agreements executed after 1984 are subject to recapture rules when payments are "front loaded." In other words, if the payments decrease by more than a designated amount during the first three postseparation years, you may be required to recapture and include in your gross income some portion of alimony that you deducted in a prior tax year. On the other hand, if you received the payment, you deduct any recaptured amount from your income in the computation year.

Exceptions to the recapture rules apply when alimony payments end because either party dies, the spouse receiving the payments remarries before the end of the third postseparation year, or the payments are subject to fluctuation because they are tied to the payer's compensation or income from a business or property.

Child Support

Child support payments are neither deductible by the payer nor included as income by the spouse who receives them. If any portion of payments that were agreed to be alimony could be reduced because of circumstances relating to a child (e.g., the child's leaving school or the family household, becoming employed, getting married, or dying), that portion may be reclassified as nondeductible and nontaxable child support. This can occur even when the divorce or separation agreement specifically provides for separate child support payments.

Payments are presumed to be child support if a reduction is scheduled to occur within six months before or after a child reaches age 18, 21, or the local age of majority, or when two or more reductions are scheduled within one year of a child reaching an age between 18 and 24 that is designated in the agreement. Payments that represent property settlements or child support are not treated as alimony.

TaxSaver

Deciding whether payments should be classified as alimony, a nontaxable property settlement, or child support can affect the amount of tax paid if the spouse who will be making the payments will be in a higher tax bracket than the spouse receiving them. The spouse making the payment typically wants it to be tax-deductible alimony to minimize his or her out-of-pocket costs. At the same time, the spouse receiving the payment doesn't want to see it eaten up by taxes.

A reasonable way to resolve the problem is to share the overall tax savings realized by treating the payment as alimony. For example, if the spouse making the payment offered to "gross up" the payment to cover the taxes the recipient would owe, both on the amount of the payment originally expected and the "extra" alimony offered, the payer could wind up paying less out-of-pocket (after deductions) than if the initially agreed-to level of the payment was treated as a nondeductible property settlement.

Transferring Property

Generally, a transfer of property from one spouse to the other "incident to the divorce" is tax-free—no gain or loss is recognized by the transferor spouse. Such transfers can include sales or exchanges of property between ex-spouses within one year after the marriage ends and transfers pursuant to a divorce or separation agreement generally occurring within six years after the marriage ends. These transfers are treated as gifts for tax purposes even if there was actually a bona fide sale. That is, the transferor spouse's basis in the property carries over to the transferee spouse, who may be required to recognize gain or loss when the property is ultimately sold or otherwise disposed of. (See Chapter 4, Tax Planning and Your Home, for more details.)

TaxSaver

Remember, when dividing up appreciated property in a divorce settlement, that the value of a particular property may be overstated if it does not take into account potential taxes that would be due on the gain incurred on a subsequent sale. The spouse receiving the property should consider having the divorce or separation agreement provide for reimbursement when the property is actually sold or otherwise disposed of.

Medical and Dental Expenses

Deductible Expenses

You may claim as itemized deductions certain medical and dental expenses for yourself, your spouse, and your dependents. You may also deduct medical expenses that you pay for any person whom you could have claimed as a dependent on your return if that person had not received $2,800 or more of gross income or had not filed a joint return. A child of divorced parents is treated as a dependent of both spouses for the purpose of computing medical expenses. However, you may deduct only the part of your medical and dental expenses that is more than 7.5% of your adjusted gross income. Medical expenses are not subject to the reduction in itemized deductions for taxpayers with adjusted gross incomes in excess of $128,950 ($64,475 for married persons filing separately) under an overall limitation discussed on page 56.

Medical Savings Accounts

Beginning in 1997 and continuing for four years, self-employed individuals and individuals employed by "small employers" who are covered under a high-deductible health plan are able to deduct contributions to a medical savings account (MSA). Income earned in an MSA is tax-free, as are distributions to pay for medical expenses. To have an MSA, you cannot be covered under a health plan in addition to the high-deductible health plan, unless the additional coverage is for accidents, disability, dental care, vision care, long-term care, or if it is another type of "permitted" insurance. However, the number of eligible individuals who can set up MSAs is capped at a national level of 750,000.

What to Include as Medical and Dental Expenses

Medical expenses include the costs of related transportation, hospitalization insurance, Medicare supplemental insurance, certain capital expenditures if they exceed any increase in property value, and certain expenses incurred by a physically handicapped individual for removing structural barriers to accommodate the disability. You may also include the cost of hearing aids, dentures, eyeglasses, and so on, and wages you paid for nursing services. The cost of elective cosmetic surgery is not deductible. However, cosmetic or plastic surgery to correct a deformity or personal injury or to treat an illness or disease is a deductible medical expense. Prescription drugs and insulin are the only medications that are considered medical expenses.

TaxSaver

If you make a medically related capital improvement to your home, such as installing an elevator, you should request a written recommendation for the improvement from your doctor. In addition, obtain a reliable written appraisal from a real estate appraiser or a valuation expert. Be prepared to prove to what extent the value of your property was not increased by the expenditure of the improvement, because only that amount is deductible.

TAX*ORGANIZER*

Certain medical expenses may qualify for the dependent care credit. (See page 159.) However, the same expense may not be used for both benefits. You should analyze each benefit based on your marginal tax rate and your medical expense deduction limitation (7.5% of adjusted gross income) to determine how best to classify the expense.

When seeking medical care away from home, you can deduct lodging expenses of up to $50 per night per individual as a medical expense. Lodging can include the expenses for the person seeking treatment and other qualified individuals, such as a parent traveling with a sick child.

TAX*ALERT*

In 2000, self-employed individuals can deduct 60% of their health insurance premiums in calculating adjusted gross income rather than choose a medical deduction.

Separate Returns. If you and your spouse do not live in a community property state and you file separate returns, each of you may claim only the medical expenses you actually paid. Any medical expenses paid out of a joint checking account in which you and your spouse have the same interest are considered to have been paid equally by each of you unless you can show otherwise.

TAX*SAVER*

Because you may deduct only the part of your medical and dental expenses that is more than 7.5% of your adjusted gross income, you should consider filing separate returns whenever the medical expenses of either spouse substantially exceed those of the other spouse. Figure your tax filing jointly and separately before deciding which alternative to choose.

When to Deduct. You may deduct medical expenses only in the year you paid them. If you charge medical expenses to your credit card, deduct the expenses in the year the charge is made even if you pay the charge in a later year.

Reimbursements. You must reduce your total medical expenses for the year by the total reimbursements you receive from insurance or other sources for medical expenses during the year before you apply the 7.5% adjusted gross income limit. Reimbursements include payments received from Medicare.

TAX*SAVER*

If you are reimbursed in a later year for medical expenses you deducted in an earlier year, you must report the reimbursement as income in the later year. However, do not report more than the amount you previously deducted as medical expenses. In making the calculation, you may also exclude the amount of expenses in the previous year that did not reduce the amount of income taxes you paid. For example, if you had a taxable loss in the year of the deduction, you would not have had a tax benefit from your medical deductions and any subsequent reimbursement is not considered income. This same rule would apply if the expenses did not produce any benefit in the earlier year because they did not exceed 7.5% of your adjusted gross income in that year.

TAXES

Deductible Taxes

If you itemize deductions, you can deduct state, local, and foreign income taxes, real property taxes, and state and local personal property taxes. You can generally deduct property taxes only if you own the property.

You may deduct only those taxes paid during the calendar year for which you file a return. Deductible taxes are subject to the overall limit on itemized deductions for taxpayers with adjusted gross income in excess of $128,950; $64,475 for married persons filing separately. See discussion on page 56.

See page 157 for the discussion about how state, local, and foreign taxes affect your alternative minimum tax calculations.

Nondeductible Taxes

Taxes that cannot be deducted are: the federal income tax; state and local sales taxes; Social Security taxes; estate, gift, and inheritance taxes; gasoline, cigarette, and liquor taxes; automobile registration fees (unless based on the automobile's value); and driver's license fees. Certain taxes paid in connection with the acquisition or disposition of property, such as transfer taxes associated with a purchase, must be capitalized.

Half the self-employment taxes you pay may be deducted and treated as attributable to a trade or business that you conduct. Most otherwise nondeductible state, local, foreign, and excise taxes are deductible if incurred in a trade or business or in the production of income.

Deduction vs. Credit for Foreign Income Tax

You may elect to have foreign income taxes (including withholding) on dividends or other income credited directly against your U.S. tax liability (subject to a limitation based on the effective U.S. rate of tax). However, you cannot take a deduction or credit for foreign income taxes paid on tax-exempt income under the foreign earned income exclusion.

TAXSAVER

It is usually better to take a credit for foreign taxes than to deduct them as itemized deductions, because credits reduce your U.S. tax on a dollar-for-dollar basis, while a deduction just reduces the amount of income subject to tax. See Chapter 9 for more information about the foreign tax credit.

Refunds of Taxes

If you receive a refund of state or local (or foreign) income taxes in a year after the year in which you paid them, you may have to include all or part of the refund in income in the year you receive it. This includes refunds resulting from taxes that were overwithheld, not figured correctly, or decreased as a result of an audit. If you did not itemize your deductions in the previous year or if the portion of the claimed deduction that is refunded did not provide a tax benefit, you do not have to include the refund in income.

Example: In 1999 you have $4,000 in state income taxes withheld. You claim a $4,000 itemized deduction. In 2000 you file a state tax return and receive a $500 refund. That refund must be included in your 2000 income.

INTEREST EXPENSES

If interest paid during the taxable year is deductible, it will be as an itemized deduction, a passive activity deduction, or a business expense. However, several limitations apply. Deductions for personal interest are not allowed. There are also limitations on the deduction of passive activity interest and investment interest (page 44). Your deduction for interest paid during the year is limited to the amount that represents the cost of using the borrowed funds for that year or a preceding year. An exception to this rule applies for points paid to obtain a loan to purchase or to improve a principal residence as long as the payment of points is an established business practice in your area.

Interest expense, except for investment interest, is subject to the overall limit on itemized deductions for taxpayers with adjusted gross income in excess of $128,950; $64,475 for married persons filing separately. See discussion on page 56.

Personal Interest

Interest on personal loans is not deductible on your individual tax return. Personal interest generally includes all interest other than:

- Interest incurred in connection with a trade or business (other than the trade or business of performing services as an employee);
- Investment interest;

- Interest taken into account in computing your income or loss from a passive activity;
- Qualified residence interest; and
- Interest on certain estate taxes that have been deferred.

TAX*SAVER*

You should ordinarily pay off personal debts because the related interest expense, unless qualified residence interest, is not deductible. One way to accomplish this objective is to use a home equity loan to pay off your personal debt. This interest is fully deductible up to certain limits.

Home Mortgage Interest

Generally mortgage interest is any interest you pay on a loan secured by your home. This includes a mortgage, second mortgage, a line of credit, and a home equity loan. Most home mortgage interest is deductible, subject to limitations discussed in Chapter 4, Tax Planning and Your Home.

Investment Interest

There are specified limits on the deduction of investment interest by individuals. Investment interest is interest paid on indebtedness properly allocable to property held for investment. Property held for investment includes any property that produces interest, dividend, annuity, or royalty income not derived in the ordinary course of a trade or business, and any property held by a taxpayer in an activity involving the conduct of a trade or business that is not a passive activity (pages 11–15) and in which the taxpayer does not materially participate. Investment interest does not include qualified residence interest (see above) or interest taken into account in computing your income or loss from a passive activity.

The deduction for interest on investment indebtedness is limited to your net investment income—the excess of investment income over certain directly connected expenses.

Investment interest deductions that are disallowed solely by these provisions may, in most cases, be carried forward and deducted in subsequent years, subject to the annual limits.

TAX*ALERT*

A net capital gain attributable to the disposition of property held for investment is no longer includible in the definition of investment income for purposes of computing the investment interest deduction limitation. However, you may elect to include net capital gain amounts in investment income for this purpose if you also agree to reduce your net capital gain eligible for the 20% maximum capital gains rate by the same amount.

Deciding whether to make the election depends on how long you would otherwise have to wait to take your deduction. Here are some general guidelines:

■ *You may be better off waiting and carrying forward the investment interest deduction if your rate may soon increase, and you expect to have more noncapital gain investment income in the short term.*
■ *There is no substitute for running the numbers for your situation, especially considering the 20% capital gains rate.*

TAXSAVER

You should regularly review the mix of your investment portfolio to be sure that your assets generate enough investment income so you can deduct all the interest you incur on your margin account. A margin account loan is an amount you borrow from a broker to purchase additional securities.

Tax-Exempt Securities

Interest paid on money borrowed to purchase or carry tax-exempt securities or certain life insurance contracts is not deductible. In addition, the deduction of interest paid for money borrowed to purchase or carry investments in stock of certain regulated investment companies will be limited if the company makes a distribution of tax-exempt interest during the taxable year.

Other Interest

Below-Market Interest Rate Loans. If you are the recipient of an interest-free loan, you can deduct interest imputed on the loan, subject to the applicable interest expense limitations. The interest is calculated using specified rates based on the average market yields of U.S. Treasury obligations. With certain exceptions, interest is imputed on loans payable upon demand of over $10,000 outstanding after June 6, 1984, and on term loans made after June 6, 1984. (For further discussion, see pages 20 and 249.)

Interest to Carry Discount Bonds and Investments. Special rules limit your deduction for interest expense incurred to purchase or carry bonds that were acquired at a market discount (purchased at less than face value). For debt obligations issued after July 18, 1984, the interest expense deduction is limited to the sum of:
1. the interest income received from the bonds during the tax year, and
2. the interest expense that exceeds the sum of the interest income received in item (1) plus accrued market discount.

The disallowed interest is deferred until the bond is sold or matures, and is then deducted. If you elect to include the accrued market discount in your current income, you can fully deduct the interest instead of deferring it.

Example: Tom buys a $100,000, 9% interest-bearing bond for $90,000 on January 2, 2000. The bond was originally issued at face value in 1990. It matures in 2010, 10 years after Tom purchased it. Tom borrowed to acquire the bond. In 2000, Tom paid $10,200 in interest on the loan. The allowable interest deduction for 2000 is figured as follows:

(a) Interest expense	$10,200
(b) Interest income ($100,000 × 9%)	(9,000)
(c) Net interest expense	1,200
(d) Accrued market discount ($10,000 ÷ 10 yrs.)	(1,000)
(e) Net interest expense in excess of the interest income received	$ 200

The total allowable interest expense deduction is $9,200 [(b) + (e)]. The remaining $1,000 will be allowed as a deduction in the year the bond matures or is sold.

The same limitation applies to interest expense arising from the purchase of short-term obligations. The interest deduction for an amount equal to the daily accrual of the obligation's discount income will be deferred until the short-term obligation is redeemed or sold. If you elect to include the accrued discount in income, you can fully deduct the interest instead of deferring the interest deduction.

TAX*ORGANIZER*

How you characterize interest expense depends on how you used the debt proceeds. You must keep detailed records so that the IRS can trace the ultimate use of borrowed dollars that give rise to each dollar of interest expense.

Example: You purchase through your broker $40,000 worth of stock. Several months later you need $20,000 to purchase a car. You borrow the $20,000 by collateralizing your stock. The interest on that loan is considered to be consumer interest (generally nondeductible). On the other hand, if you had purchased the stock on margin for $20,000—that is, you borrowed the money for the purchase from your broker—and spent your remaining personal funds of $20,000 on the car, the interest attributable to the margin debt is investment interest and potentially deductible.

Qualified mortgage interest is deductible in full, regardless of how the loan proceeds are actually used.

Deduction for Student Loan Interest. You can claim a deduction for interest expenses on qualified education loans that include indebtedness incurred for your benefit or the benefit of your spouse, or any dependent at the time the indebtedness is incurred. Qualified loans also include refinancings or consolidations of the original loans. You can claim this deduction whether or not you itemize your deductions. The deduction is allowed only for interest paid on a qualified education loan during the first 60 months in which interest payments are required on each loan outstanding (the original loan or loans and subsequent refinancing of those loans are treated as one loan for purposes of counting the first 60 months). Months during which the qualified education loan is deferred or in forbearance do not count against the 60-month period. No deduction is allowed for individuals claimed as dependents on another taxpayer's return for the tax year.

The maximum deduction is phased in over several years. The maximum deduction will be $2,000 in 2000, and it will top out at $2,500 in 2001. The maximum deduction amount is not indexed for inflation.

The deduction is phased out for individual single taxpayers with modified adjusted gross income (AGI) of $40,000–$55,000 and for couples filing jointly with modified AGI of $60,000–$75,000. These income ranges will be indexed for inflation occurring after the year 2002, rounded down to the closest multiple of $5,000. Thus, the first tax year for which the inflation adjustment could be made will be 2003. For purposes of the deduction, modified AGI includes amounts excludable from gross income under Section 137 (qualified adoption expenses).

The deduction is effective for the first 60 months of interest payments due and paid after December 31, 1997, on any qualified education loan. Old loans entered into before the date of enactment qualify, but only for the first 60 months of payments under those loans.

Example: Tom went to college for his bachelor's degree from 1990–1994. Payments on his student loan began in January 1995 (six months after graduation). In addition, Tom received his master's degree in July 1999. Payments on that loan began in February 2000. Tom can deduct the interest for the next 24 months on his undergraduate loan (loan was already in pay status for 36 months) and for the first 60 months on his graduate loan—subject to the overall deductibility cap for the year of repayment ($2,000 in 2000, $2,500 in 2001, etc.).

Unlike the Hope and Lifetime Learning tax credits (see pages 163–165), education loans include loans covering both tuition and room and board. However, loans cannot include educational expenses that are paid through amounts from an employer educational assistance program or from amounts withdrawn from an education IRA. It is unclear how students or the IRS will be able to separate these expenses from the total loans received and payments made on those loans.

The U.S. Treasury is authorized to require lenders to report to borrowers the amount that constitutes deductible student loan interest. In this regard, the government is also to include a method for borrowers to certify to lenders that loan proceeds are being used to pay for qualified educational expenses.

As with the education tax credits, this deduction is another factor to consider in determining whether or not a working student should be claimed as a dependent. Parents with income above the income thresholds cannot claim this deduction.

Charitable Contributions

You are allowed to take a tax deduction for contributions you make to qualified charitable organizations, provided you satisfy detailed rules that require you to substantiate your gifts. (See Chapter 6.)

Casualty and Theft Losses

A casualty is the damage, destruction, or loss of property resulting from an identifiable event that is sudden, unexpected, or unusual. A sudden event is one that is swift, not gradual or progressive. An unexpected event is one that is ordinarily unanticipated and one that you do not intend. An unusual event is one that is not a day-to-day occurrence and one that is not typical of the activity in which you were engaged.

Defining a Loss. A deduction is allowed for losses of business property, investment property, or nonbusiness property caused by fire, storm, or other casualty, including theft. Generally, the deduction is the lesser of either the adjusted basis of the property before the casualty or the actual loss measured by its fair market value before and after the casualty. If you recover any amount of the loss by insurance, you must reduce the deduction you take accordingly. A special rule applies to business or income-producing property that is completely destroyed because of a casualty loss. Your loss is your basis in the property (without regard to fair market value), less any amount you receive from insurance payments. If your personal casualty losses exceed your personal casualty gains in a taxable year, your casualty loss deduction is limited to the sum of your personal casualty gains and any amounts that exceed 10% of your adjusted gross income.

Deductions for casualty losses of nonbusiness property are limited to the amount of each loss in excess of $100. A husband and wife filing a joint return are treated as one individual for purposes of the $100 limitation. If each spouse sustains a loss from the same casualty, only one $100 limitation will apply. After considering the $100 floor applicable to each separate loss, your total personal casualty losses are deductible in full to the extent they are offset against any casualty gains. A casualty gain occurs when your insurance reimbursement is more than your basis in the property, even if the decrease in the fair market value of the property is more than its basis.

Example:

Value of the property before the casualty	$100
Value after the casualty	75
Loss	25
Insurance reimbursement	20
Basis in property	15
Gain	$ 5

Any excess loss is deductible as an itemized deduction only for the amount that exceeds 10% of your adjusted gross income. If casualty gains exceed casualty losses, the 10% floor is not imposed, and the gains and losses are treated as arising from the sale of capital assets. You are not permitted to deduct nonbusiness casualty losses unless an insurance claim for the damage to the insured property is filed on a timely basis.

Casualty losses occurring in federally declared disaster areas at any time during the taxable year may be deducted on the tax return for the year preceding the year of the loss. This may enable you to get an immediate refund of taxes you already paid.

If you have a casualty or theft on nonbusiness property, you must use Section A of Form 4684, *Casualties and Thefts,* to figure and report your gain or loss. Be sure to attach Form 4684 to your return.

TAXORGANIZER

If you are going to claim a casualty or theft loss, it is important that you gather as much supporting evidence as possible. Newspaper clippings about a storm, police reports, and insurance reports may all be helpful in proving the nature of the casualty or theft loss and when it occurred. You have the burden of proof to establish that a casualty occurred and that your loss was a direct result of a casualty.

Establishing the amount of your loss may be difficult, but the time you spend documenting the loss may help reduce your tax. You should make a list of all lost, damaged, or destroyed items as soon after the disaster or casualty as possible. IRS Publication 584, Nonbusiness Disaster and Casualty Loss and Theft Workbook, may be useful. It has schedules to help you figure a loss on your home and its contents and on your car, van, truck, or motorcycle.

Casualty and theft losses are not subject to the overall 3% limit on itemized deductions for individuals with adjusted gross income in excess of $128,950; $64,475 for married persons filing separately. See discussion on page 56.

MOVING EXPENSES

Under certain circumstances, expenses you incur in connection with changing the location of your employment are deductible. The expenses can be deductible if the distance between your new job and your residence is at least 50 miles more than the distance between your old job and your residence. In addition, if you are an employee, you must work full-time during at least 39 weeks of the 12-month period after relocating. If you are self-employed, the standard is stiffer. You must work full-time at least 78 weeks during the 24-month period after relocating. In addition, you must work full-time for at least 39 weeks during the immediate 12-month period after relocating.

If you are fired or laid off, involuntarily lose your job (for other than willful misconduct), or are required to move again by your employer before the 39 weeks are up (or 78 weeks, if applicable), you can still deduct your moving expenses. You may also be exempted from the 39-week or 78-week requirement because of death or disability.

TaxSaver

If you file a joint return, the time test may be met by either spouse. However, weeks worked by both husband and wife cannot be added together to meet the time test.

The deduction for moving expenses is allowed for the following:
1. Travel expenses (including lodging) for an employee or self-employed person and his or her family to the new residence; and
2. Expenses for moving household goods and other personal effects.

The deduction for expenses that fall into categories (1) and (2) is unlimited. Expenses that qualify as moving expenses that are not paid or reimbursed by the taxpayer's employer are allowable as a deduction in calculating adjusted gross income (AGI). Thus, moving expenses are no longer an itemized deduction. Reimbursement or payment of moving expenses by an employer is excludable from gross income of the employee, and is not included in the employee's Form W-2.

Use Form 3903, *Moving Expenses,* to report your moving expenses if your move was within or to the United States or its possessions (e.g., U.S. Virgin Islands, Puerto Rico, American Samoa, etc.).

TaxAlert

Deductible moving expenses do not include the following:
- *the cost of meals;*
- *the cost of pre-move house-hunting trips;*
- *the cost of temporary living expenses;*
- *the costs incident to the sale or lease of the old residence, including settling of an unexpired lease; and*
- *the costs incident to the purchase or lease of a new residence.*

EMPLOYEE BUSINESS EXPENSES AND OTHER EXPENSES

This section covers a variety of expenses that you are allowed to deduct on your individual return. These personal business expenses can be broken down into three broad categories: deductible employee expenses, deductible expenses of producing income, and other deductible expenses. Business-related travel and entertainment expenses are discussed in Chapter 3.

The general rule is that you may deduct any business expense incurred by you personally that is related to your trade or business, connected with producing income, or paid to determine your tax. Expenses other than these are generally considered personal and typically may not be deducted. But, with careful and proper planning, you may be able to deduct more than you think.

Deductions Subject to the 2%-of-Adjusted-Gross-Income Limit

Most miscellaneous itemized deductions are deductible only to the extent that the total of all these deductions is more than 2% of your adjusted gross income. Miscellaneous deductions that are not subject to this limitation are discussed later in this chapter.

Your deduction is the excess of the total of the allowable deductions over 2% of your adjusted gross income. The 2% limit is applied after any other deduction limit (such as the 50% limit on meals and entertainment) is applied.

Unreimbursed employee business expenses are also subject to the overall limit on itemized deductions for taxpayers with adjusted gross income in excess of $128,950; $64,475 for married persons filing separately. See discussion on page 56.

Employee Business Expenses

If you are an employee, including an outside salesperson, you may deduct as an adjustment to *gross* income only the amount reimbursed by your employer for work-related business expenses. Any expenses that are not reimbursed by your employer are deductible only as a miscellaneous deduction (subject to the 2% limit) on Schedule A, Form 1040.

If you claim a deduction for any employee business expenses, you must complete Form 2106 and attach it to your Form 1040. You do not have to complete the form if your business expenses were equal to the reimbursements you received from your employer, the reimbursements were not included in your W-2 form, and you adequately accounted to your employer for those expenses. If none of your employee business expenses are reimbursed by your employer, however, and you are not claiming any meal, entertainment, travel, or transportation expenses, you do not have to complete Form 2106. Instead, list your employee business expenses on Schedule A.

TAXSAVER

If you can get your employer to reimburse you for what would otherwise be unreimbursed business expenses in lieu of an equal amount of salary, you should do so. You gain at no additional cost to your employer. Reimbursed employee business expenses are not subject to the 2% floor that might otherwise limit their deductibility.

Business Gifts

Deductions for business gifts are limited to $25 per individual recipient per year.

TAXSAVER

When there is an overlap, in fact, it is usually to your advantage to treat a particular item as an entertainment expense rather than as a gift. Although entertainment expenses are subject to a 50% limitation and must be considered ordinary and necessary, there is no fixed dollar limitation on the deduction.

Club Dues

No deduction is allowed for dues or assessments paid for membership in a business, social, athletic, luncheon, sporting, hotel, or airport club, including dues and fees paid to a country club. However, dues paid to professional or service organizations, such as the ABA, AICPA, Kiwanis, or Rotary clubs, are deductible if paid for business reasons and the organization is not principally an entertainment organization. Specific business expenses, such as meals and entertainment that may occur at a club, are deductible to the extent that they otherwise satisfy the standard for deductibility.

Educational Expenses

In general, educational expenditures, such as tuition, books, supplies, lab fees, and certain travel and transportation costs, are deductible (whether or not the education leads to a degree) if the education (1) maintains or improves skills required in your employment or business or (2) meets the express requirements of your employer, or applicable law, imposed as a condition of employment. However, educational expenditures that are made to meet minimum educational requirements or that qualify you for a new trade or business, such as a law degree, are not deductible. Therefore, only expenses for education relating to your present work are deductible.

Employer-Provided Educational Assistance. Up to $5,250 of employer-provided tuition reimbursement for *undergraduate* education is excludable from an employee's income each calendar year.

Home Office Expenses

A home office qualifies as the "principal place of business" if (1) the taxpayer uses the office to conduct administrative or management activities of a trade or business, and (2) there is no other fixed location of trade or business where the taxpayer conducts substantial administrative or management activities of the trade or business. Deductions are also allowed for a home office if the taxpayer uses the office exclusively on a regular basis as a place of business and, in the case of an employee, only if such exclusive use is for the employer's convenience. (For more on home office expenses, see Chapter 4, Tax Planning and Your Home.)

Computers. You may be able to claim an accelerated depreciation deduction and a Section 179 first-year expensing deduction (page 254) for your home computer provided you use the computer over 50% of the time for business (in your work as an employee) and the computer was placed in your home for the convenience of your employer, as a condition of your employment, so that you can properly perform your duties as an employee. Your employer does not have to explicitly require you to buy the computer provided its purchase spares the employer the cost of providing suitable equipment with which to perform your job responsibilities.

Expenses to Produce Income and Other Expenses

You may deduct certain other expenses as miscellaneous itemized deductions to the extent that the total amount of these deductions exceeds 2% of your adjusted gross income. These include expenses you pay:
1. To produce or collect income,
2. To manage, conserve, or maintain property held for producing income, or
3. To determine, contest, pay, or claim a refund of any tax.

These expenses must be ordinary and necessary and bear a reasonable and proximate relation to the income or income-producing property, and the income must be taxable to you.

Indirect Deductions of Partnerships and S Corporations. Deductions of pass-through entities, such as a partnership or S corporation, are passed through to the partners or shareholders. If the deductions are miscellaneous itemized deductions, they are usually deductible only to the extent that they exceed 2% of your adjusted gross income.

Investment Advisory Fees. Amounts paid for managing your investments are deductible subject to the 2% limit if they relate to investments that produce taxable income.

Trustee's Administrative Fees. Fees that are billed separately and that you paid in connection with your Individual Retirement Account or Arrangement (IRA) are deductible, subject to the 2% limit, provided that they are ordinary and necessary.

TaxSaver

If the trustee of your IRA takes his or her fee out of your $2,000 contribution, there will be less money in your IRA account that can be invested. You should consider paying the fee separately from your IRA contribution. For more about IRAs, see Chapter 5.

Legal Expenses. Legal fees that you pay to produce taxable income are usually deductible subject to the 2% limit. You may deduct legal expenses for tax advice related to a divorce if your lawyer's bill specifies how much is for tax advice and if the amount is determined in a reasonable way. Generally, legal expenses of a personal nature are not deductible.

Safe Deposit Box Rent. If you use a safe deposit box to store taxable income-producing stock, bonds, or investment-related papers or documents, the rent is deductible subject to the 2% limit.

Tax Preparation Fees. Amounts paid for tax preparation are usually deductible in the year you pay them. Thus, you may deduct, subject to the 2% limit, your fees paid in 2000 for preparing your 1999 return.

Deductions Not Subject to the 2% Limit

Some expenses can be deducted as miscellaneous itemized deductions whether or not the total of your miscellaneous expenses exceeds 2% of your adjusted gross income. Some of the expenses not subject to the 2% limit include the following:

Federal Estate Tax on Income in Respect of a Decedent. You may deduct the federal estate tax attributable to "income in respect of a decedent" that is ordinary income and that you, as a beneficiary, include in your gross income. Income in respect of a decedent is gross income that the decedent had a right to receive and could have received had death not occurred, and that could not have been properly included in the decedent's final income tax return.

The deduction for federal estate tax attributable to income in respect of a decedent is subject to the overall limit on itemized deductions for high-income taxpayers.

Gambling Losses to the Extent of Gambling Winnings. While gambling losses are not subject to the overall limit on itemized deductions, you may not deduct more gambling losses than the gambling winnings you report.

Other Adjustments to Income

Early Withdrawal from Savings Accounts. Penalties paid because of the premature withdrawal of funds from time savings accounts or certificates of deposit are allowed as a deduction against your total income in figuring your adjusted gross income.

Forestation/Reforestation Amortization Expenses. If you can claim an amortization deduction for the costs of forestation or reforestation but you do not have to file the *Business Income Form* (Schedule C) or *Farm Income Form* (Schedule F), you can claim such deductions as an adjustment to income in figuring your adjusted gross income.

Supplemental Unemployment Benefits. If, during the tax year, you paid supplemental unemployment benefits that you have previously reported as income because you became eligible for payments under the Trade Act of 1974, you can deduct the repayment as an adjustment to your gross income. Alternatively, if the amount you repay is more than $3,000, a tax credit is available.

Net Operating Loss Deduction

The net operating loss (NOL) deduction permits a taxpayer to use a loss from one year against income from another year. A net operating loss is determined by making specific adjustments to eliminate certain nonbusiness items in the loss year.

NOLs incurred in taxable years beginning on or before August 5, 1997, may be carried back 3 years and then forward 15 years. You may also elect to forgo the carryback period for NOLs incurred in taxable years ending after 1975 and only carry the loss forward for 15 years. NOLs arising in taxable years beginning after August 5, 1997, may be carried back 2 years and forward 20 years. Special rules apply to farmers and small businesses and to the determination of the NOL deduction under the alternative minimum tax. (See page 154.) Net operating loss for businesses is discussed in Chapter 15.

Overall Limit on Itemized Deductions

Itemized deductions—i.e., deductions claimed on your return—are reduced by 3% of the excess of your adjusted gross income over $128,950 (married filing separately, $64,475), adjusted annually for inflation. This means, for example, that a taxpayer with AGI of $195,617 would lose $2,000 [($195,617 − $128,950) × 3%] of itemized deductions.

This overall limitation is imposed *after* any other limitations affecting specific categories of itemized deductions are applied. For example, miscellaneous itemized deductions will be subject to both the 2% floor discussed on page 51 and the additional 3% phaseout.

Medical expenses, casualty, theft, and gambling losses, and investment interest expenses are not subject to this limitation. And in no case can the reduction be more than 80% of your otherwise allowable deductions. Also, the limitation does not apply if you are subject to the alternative minimum tax.

TaxSaver

If you can reduce your 2000 AGI to below $128,950 you will avoid having your itemized deductions reduced at all. For every $1,000 of AGI in excess of $128,950 your itemized deductions are reduced by $30.

3

Travel and Entertainment Expenses

INTRODUCTION

Travel and entertainment expenses that are directly related to your business and income-producing activities are usually deductible whether you are an outside salesperson or an employee.

Travel expenses include transportation fares, automobile expenses, costs of meals and lodging, baggage charges, and miscellaneous business expenses (e.g., telephone charges) incurred while away from home. The cost of transportation (including automobile expenses) between your home and your regular place of business is not deductible, but the cost of local transportation between business locations during the day is generally deductible. You cannot deduct travel expenses when the sole purpose of the travel is educational.

There are limits, however, on the deductibility of certain expenditures for travel, business meals, entertainment activities, and entertainment facilities. In addition, special record-keeping requirements are imposed on taxpayers claiming deductions for these items. Additional special rules apply to deductions for cars and other property used for transportation, foreign travel, and attendance at foreign conventions. This chapter spells out what is deductible and what isn't and the limits that apply.

THE 50% DEDUCTION LIMITATION

Your allowable deduction for business-related meals, entertainment, and entertainment facilities is limited to 50% of the amount spent, including taxes and tips.

Example: A self-employed individual pays $50 for a business meal, plus $4 in tax and $10 in tips for a total of $64. The allowable deduction after the 50% deduction limitations will be $32 ($64 × 50%).

Expenses subject to the 50% rule include: cover charges, room rentals for a dinner or a cocktail party, and parking for an entertainment activity.

The 50% limitation generally applies to any deduction for food or beverages, including meals an employee consumes while traveling "away from home" on business. However, the 50% rule does *not* apply to the otherwise deductible costs of transportation to and from a business meal (e.g., cab fare).

Exceptions: The 50% deduction limitation does *not* apply in the following cases:

- Reimbursed expenses (in which case the person making the reimbursement is generally subject to the 50% limitation).
- Ticket packages for certain charitable fundraising sports events.
- Expenses excludable from employees' incomes as *de minimis* fringe benefits (e.g., a holiday turkey, ham, or fruitcake).
- Meals provided to employees for the convenience of the employer at an employer-provided eating facility.

TaxAlert

Employers who provide no-cost meals to employees and impose a stay-on-premises requirement for legitimate business reasons are entitled to deduct 100% of the cost of providing the meals. For example, a casino that requires its employees to eat meals on the premises for security purposes can deduct 100% of the cost.

TaxAlert

Under the 1997 Tax Act, the deductible percentage for meals consumed while away from home gradually increases to 80% for individuals in certain industries. The taxpayers to whom this change applies are: certain air transportation employees; certain interstate truck operators and interstate bus drivers; certain railroad employees; and certain merchant mariners. The increase in the deductible percentage is phased in under the following schedule:

Taxable years beginning in	Deductible percentage
1998 and 1999	55%
2000 and 2001	60%
2002 and 2003	65%
2004 and 2005	70%
2006 and 2007	75%
2008 and thereafter	80%

Conventions and Investment Seminars

You can deduct travel expenses for attending conventions, seminars, sales meetings, or similar meetings in connection with the active conduct of a trade or business. However, you cannot deduct such expenses if the purpose of attending investment seminars, conventions, or similar meetings is for the production or collection of income, or the management, conservation, or maintenance of property held for the production of income.

Unreimbursed Employee Travel and Transportation Expenses

Unreimbursed employee travel and transportation expenses are deductible only as a miscellaneous itemized deduction (with an exception for certain performing artists). Total miscellaneous itemized deductions are deductible only to the extent they exceed 2% of your adjusted gross income. See Chapter 2, What You Can Deduct, for a further discussion of unreimbursed business expenses.

Example: Your adjusted gross income is $75,000 and your reimbursed travel and entertainment expenses total $2,300. You figure your deduction as follows:

Adjusted gross income	$75,000
Unreimbursed T&E expenses	$ 2,300
Other miscellaneous itemized deductions	$ 200
Total miscellaneous expenses	$ 2,500
2% of adjusted gross income floor	$ 1,500
Deductible amount	$ 1,000

TaxAlert

An expense item exempted from the travel and entertainment rules still must meet the regular tax requirements to be deductible. This means that the item must be an "ordinary and necessary" expense in carrying on a trade or business, or qualify for a deduction under some specific provision of the IRS code.

TRAVEL AND TRANSPORTATION

Domestic Travel (Away from Home Overnight)

Expenses incurred in traveling away from home overnight on business are generally deductible. Travel expenses include fares, meals, and lodging. However, expenses incurred for meals and entertainment while away from home are subject to the 50% deduction limitation discussed above. To be deductible, domestic travel must be primarily related to business, and certain record-keeping requirements must be satisfied. *If you fail to properly substantiate your expenses, they may be disallowed.*

TaxAlert

A deduction is allowed for travel expenses paid or incurred with respect to a spouse, dependent, or other individual accompanying a person on business travel only if the spouse, dependent, or other individual is a bona fide employee of the person paying or reimbursing the expenses and the following apply:

- *The travel of the spouse, dependent, or other individual is for a bona fide business purpose.*
- *The expenses incurred would otherwise be deductible.*

__Example:__ Mrs. Smith, an employee of an investment advisory firm, is accompanied on a business trip by her husband, Mr. Smith, who is not a firm employee. Because Mr. Smith assisted his wife on the trip by entertaining clients, helping her conduct a seminar, and performing other substantial business services, Mr. Smith's presence on the trip had a bona fide business purpose. The firm paid all of Mrs. and Mr. Smith's travel expenses. Under the new law, the company may not deduct the costs of Mr. Smith's travel because he is not a company employee. Alternatively, the company could treat the value of Mr. Smith's travel as compensation to Mrs. Smith and take the deduction. Under the prior law, the firm may have been able to deduct the costs of Mrs. and Mr. Smith's travel as an ordinary and necessary business expense.

Travel by Water

Your allowable deductions for travel by ocean liner, cruise ship, or other form of "luxury water transportation" cannot be more than twice the highest federal *per diem* amount for travel in the United States multiplied by the number of days of such transportation. (For example, the highest federal *per diem* amount at the time of travel was $253 for 2000. Consequently, your allowable deduction for travel by luxury water transportation in 2000 cannot exceed $506.) The cost of on-board meals and entertainment, if separately stated (or clearly identifiable), would be subject to the 50% deduction limitation discussed above (before applying the *per diem* limitation).

The luxury water travel limitation does not apply to expenses of a convention, seminar, or other meeting held on a cruise ship.

Conventions on Cruise Ships

No deduction is allowed for the expenses of a convention, seminar, or other meeting held on a cruise ship, unless:

- The meeting directly relates to the active conduct of the taxpayer's trade or business.
- The ship is registered in the United States.
- All ports of call are in the United States or its possessions.

Deductions for such cruises are also subject to a special $2,000-per-year limitation.

TAX*ALERT*

If you claim a deduction for the expense of attending a convention on a cruise ship, you must attach two statements to your tax return. One statement, signed by the person attending the convention, must include the total number of days on board the ship, total number of hours per day devoted to meetings of the convention, and a schedule of the meeting program. The other statement, signed by an officer of the sponsoring organization, must include a program schedule detailing each day's activities and a statement of attendance detailing the number of hours each day you attended program activities. Be aware that these statements function as a red flag to the IRS in selecting returns for audit.

Foreign Business Travel

If your travel outside the United States is devoted to business activities (for more than 75% of the time), or if the business trip is for seven days or less, all related expenses generally are deductible (subject to the 50% deduction limitation on meals). However, foreign conventions are subject to special rules, which are discussed in the following section. If nonbusiness activity accounts for 25% or more of the total time spent out of the United States, or the trip is for more than seven days, the expenses allocable to the nonbusiness activity will not be deductible. However, these limitations will not apply if either:

- You had no substantial control over arranging the trip.
- You can establish that a personal vacation was not a major consideration in making the trip.

You are considered to have no substantial control over the arranging of the trip if you travel under a reimbursement or other expense allowance arrangement and are neither a managing executive of, nor related to, the employer.

Example. Assume an executive attends a business negotiation in London for six days and sightsees for six more days. His employer reimburses the executive for all airfare and for six days of meals, lodging, and incidental costs related to the business portion of the travel. Unless an exception is met, one-half of the airfare cost is allocable to the personal portion of the trip and must be reported on the executive's tax return as an excess reimbursement. (*Note:* The employer, however, can claim the entire reimbursement as a deduction, subject to the 50% deduction limitation.)

Foreign Conventions

With certain exceptions, the expenses of attending a foreign convention are deductible only when the meeting is directly related to the active conduct of a trade or business and it is as reasonable for the convention to be held in a foreign country as in the North American area. Among the factors to be considered in determining the reasonableness of a foreign convention are:

- The purpose of the meeting and the activities being conducted.
- The purpose and activities of the sponsoring organization.
- The residences of active members of the sponsoring organization and where these meetings have been or will be held.

Any convention, seminar, or similar meeting held outside the United States, its possessions, Trust territories, Canada, Mexico, and certain Caribbean countries is generally considered a foreign convention.

Meetings of Stockholders, Employees, Directors, Business Leagues

Certain types of business meetings are subject to less restrictive rules than those that apply to foreign conventions. Deductions are generally allowed (subject only to the record-keeping requirements) for:

- Business meetings of your employees, stockholders, agents, or directors.
- Meetings of tax-exempt business leagues, chambers of commerce, real estate boards, boards of trade, and professional football leagues.

However, any meal or entertainment expenses would be subject to the 50% deduction limitations.

Special Rules

Here are some special rules for deducting certain travel expenses.

- *Educational travel:* No deduction is allowed for travel as a form of education.
- *Travel of a charitable organization:* No deduction is allowed for travel expenses (including meals and lodging) incurred in performing services "away from home" on behalf of a charitable organization unless *no* significant element of personal pleasure, vacation, or recreation is involved in the travel. The limitation applies whether the expenses are paid directly by the individual or indirectly by the charitable organization (e.g., through reimbursement).

TAXALERT

Travel expenses incurred with the primary purpose of engaging in deductible business-related education are deductible. For instance, a high school English teacher's costs for travel and room and board to attend a university extension course held overseas can be deducted. However, an English teacher could not deduct costs of a trip through Europe to visit famous literary sights.

Automobile Expenses

The deduction for automobile expenses can be calculated in one of the following two ways:

- *Actual expenses:* Automobile depreciation is added to the actual expenses related to use of the automobile. Depreciation deductions for certain luxury automobiles may be limited. For automobiles first placed in service in 2000 and for which business use exceeds 50%, the depreciation deduction is limited to $3,060 in the first year, $4,900 in the second year, $2,950 in the third year, and $1,775 for each succeeding year. These amounts are indexed annually for inflation.

Maximum Depreciation Deduction Allowed (business use >50%)

Year placed	Tax Year			
into service	1st	2nd	3rd	4th +
1988	$2,560	$4,100	$2,450	$1,475
1989	2,560	4,100	2,450	1,475
1990	2,660	4,200	2,550	1,475
1991	2,660	4,200	2,550	1,475
1992	2,660	4,300	2,550	1,575
1993	2,760	4,400	2,650	1,575
1994	2,860	4,600	2,750	1,675
1995	2,960	4,700	2,850	1,675
1996	3,060	4,900	2,950	1,775
1997	3,160	5,000	3,050	1,775
1998	3,160	5,000	2,950	1,775
1999	3,060	5,000	2,950	1,775
2000	3,060	4,900	2,950	1,775

These amounts are further limited if the auto is used for both business and personal use. If a vehicle is used for business 50% or less of the time, the alternative depreciation system (ADS) must be used.

TaxAlert

Electric Cars. *Under the 1997 Tax Act the maximum depreciation deduction allowed for a passenger vehicle propelled primarily by electricity and built by an original equipment manufacturer is approximately tripled. For electric automobiles placed in service after August 5, 1997, and before January 1, 1998, the depreciation limitations are: $9,480 for the first year; $15,100 for the second year; $9,050 for the third year; and $5,425 for each succeeding year. For electric automobiles placed in service in 1998, the depreciation limitations are: $9,380 for the first year; $15,000 for the second year; $8,950 for the third year; and $5,425 for each succeeding year. For electric automobiles placed in service in 1999, the depreciation limitations are: $9,280 for the first year; $14,900 for the second year; $8,950 for the third year; and $5,325 for each succeeding year. For electric automobiles placed in service in 2000, the depreciation limitations are: $9,280 for the first year; $14,800 for the second year; $8,850 for the third year; and $5,325 for each succeeding year.*

■ *Standard rate:* The deduction is computed using the standard mileage rate of 32.5 cents per mile for all miles of business use. The basis of the vehicle must be reduced (but not below zero) by 14 cents per mile for all miles for which the standard mileage rate is used.

If you own a luxury business car, the standard mileage rate is probably inadequate to cover your operating costs. You should keep detailed records of your total expenses so that you may claim a larger deduction than you would be able to by using the standard mileage rate.

Car Loans. *Interest paid on loans to purchase a car—even if used by an employee for business—is considered personal interest and is not deductible. However, if you finance the car by taking out a home equity loan, the interest will be fully deductible as home mortgage interest. The after-tax cost of home equity payments will often be lower than the best car loan available. If you don't own a home or have enough equity available, consider leasing because to the extent the car is used for business, the deductible portion of your lease payments includes the implicit financing costs as well as depreciation.*

E&Y FOCUS: Leasing a Car

If you lease a car, you can deduct the part of each lease payment that is for the use of the car in your business or work. Normal operating costs and maintenance may also be deducted. Special rules apply to reduce the annual lease deduction for leased cars similar to the limitations of depreciation that apply to luxury automobiles.

Should you buy or lease a car?

Here are some of the things you would need to know before deciding:

1. What are the costs of buying a car including the financing cost and monthly payments on a loan? (Can you finance with a home equity loan and deduct the interest? See TaxSaver above.)
2. The monthly payments on the lease.
3. How many miles you expect to drive the car and the additional charges at the end of the lease term if your actual mileage exceeds the amount set out in the contract. How much more would your monthly payment be if you increased the annual mileage allowance?
4. An estimate of the car's value when you would normally sell or trade it in.
5. What you think you could earn on your payments if it were available for investment.

You would then compare the costs of buying versus leasing a car in today's dollars. To do that you need to calculate the present value of the payments on the lease or on a loan if you decide to borrow some or all of the purchase price. Present value is the financial term for what a dollar paid or received in the future is worth to you today ($1,000 paid five years from today effectively costs you less than if you paid the $1,000 today. That's because you could earn money with that $1,000 during the five years before you pay it.)

A few other points should be noted:

- Know your obligations under a lease contract for early termination and wear and tear to the car. Leasing car companies will generally make you pay dearly if you want out of your lease early, or if you don't return the car in good shape.
- Know whether insurance will cover your remaining contract obligation if the car were totally destroyed during the lease term.

Most often the purchase price of a car is negotiable, and so are the lease terms. Shop around.

Purchasing a car outright should be the least expensive way to go if you can't earn more on your money than you would have to pay in finance charges. Purchasing the car with financing is usually next, and leasing (other than a lease with a single, front-end payment) is generally the most expensive. However, these generalizations will vary depending on dealer incentives, interest rates, and other factors applicable to your situation.

Record-Keeping. You must meet the same record-keeping requirements for automobiles as for other travel and entertainment expenses.

TAXORGANIZER

Adequate records include a written log, diary, account book, expense statement, trip sheet, or similar record maintained for each expenditure or use. However, in some cases, you may substantiate the business and investment use of automobiles (except pooled vehicles) by keeping records on a sample basis.

You can substantiate the business use of a car by keeping an adequate record of business use during the first week of each month. If this sampling method is used, you must be prepared to demonstrate that the periods for which an adequate record is maintained are representative of the use for the year.

A record should be kept of *each* separate expenditure or use. However, certain expenditures such as fuel or repairs for automobiles may be aggregated. For these costs, only the date and amount (and not the business purpose) need be recorded. These expenditures are then prorated based on the total business use of the property. Similarly, multiple uses that are part of a single business use (such as an uninterrupted business trip) may be recorded by a single record.

Example: A salesperson's use of a car during a business trip away from home over several days can be accounted for by a single record of miles traveled.

Exceptions: Certain vehicles, because of their nature—a hearse, for example—are not likely to be used more than minimally for personal reasons. These vehicles are exempt from the record-keeping requirements. Other examples include vehicles designed to carry cargo with a loaded gross vehicle weight over seven tons, police and fire vehicles, and certain buses and delivery trucks.

Employer-Provided Cars: Employees need to keep the necessary records to substantiate the property's business use for their employers. However, in some situations, the record-keeping burden may be eliminated. If your employer has a written policy generally prohibiting personal use of the car, for example, or includes the full annual value of the automobile in your wages, records do not have to be kept.

> ### *TaxOrganizer*
>
> *If you claim a deduction for automobiles, you must answer certain questions and provide specific information regarding their use (on Form 2106). For automobile expenses claimed by employees, requested information includes personal, business, and total mileage; total commuting miles and average commuting distance; and a "yes" or "no" response as to whether written evidence exists supporting the deductions or credits. Special rules and questions apply to employers providing vehicles to employees. These information reporting requirements highlight the importance of maintaining adequate written records.*

Entertainment Activities

Though there are some notable exceptions, you are not allowed a deduction for any expense item relating to an entertainment activity unless:

- The expenditure is *directly related* to the active conduct of your trade or business or
- The expenditure directly precedes or follows a substantial and *bona fide* business discussion, and it is *associated with* the active conduct of your trade or business.

For this purpose, "entertainment" means any activity generally considered entertainment, recreation, or amusement. An activity may be considered entertainment even though it could be otherwise characterized as something else—advertising, for example.

Examples: Entertaining includes activities at nightclubs, cocktail lounges, theaters, country clubs, and sporting events.

In addition, in order for the expenditure to be deductible, the purpose of the entertainment has to be to obtain income or some other specific business benefit (other than goodwill). Of course, all entertainment expenditures are subject to the 50% deduction limitation, discussed above.

> ### *TaxOrganizer*
>
> ***Additional Substantiation Requirements.*** *If the business discussion took place before or after a meal or entertainment, the following information about the discussion is required in addition to the general record-keeping requirements for the expenditures:*

- *Date and duration of the business discussion.*
- *Nature of the discussion and the business reason for the entertainment, or nature of the business benefit derived or expected to be derived.*
- *Identification of the persons entertained.*

Tickets

The deduction for the cost of a ticket for an entertainment activity (before applying the 50% rule described above) is limited to the face value of the ticket.

Example: A payment to a "scalper" or ticket agency is *not* deductible to the extent the cost of the ticket exceeds its face value.

This limitation does not apply, however, to any ticket to a sports event organized primarily to benefit a tax-exempt charitable organization if all net proceeds are donated to the organization and substantially all work performed in carrying on the event is provided by volunteers. An example would be a golf tournament that donates all net proceeds to charity.

Luxury Skyboxes

Deductions for the cost of leasing private luxury boxes ("skyboxes") *for more than one event* at the same arena are limited to the face value of the highest price non-luxury box seats offered for sale to the general public multiplied by the number of seats in the box. This limitation does not apply if you rent a skybox for only one event at the arena. Rentals by related parties are taken into account in applying these rules. Separate meal and beverage charges are normally not covered by the skybox limitation, but they are subject to the business meal deduction limitations.

TaxAlert

The IRS has ruled that these limitations do not prevent an otherwise allowable charitable deduction for a portion of a payment made to a university for the right to buy stadium seating.

Business Meals

No deduction is allowed for the portion of any business meal considered lavish or extravagant under the circumstances. Business meal deductions are restricted in a number of other ways:

- To be deductible, expenditures for business meals (like other entertainment expenses) must meet either the "directly related to" or "associated with" tests discussed on page 66. However, if you eat alone while away from home overnight on business, you will not fail the "directly related to" or "associated with" tests solely because of the absence of a business discussion.

■ Business meals are deductible only if either you or your employee is at the meal. For this purpose, an independent contractor who performs significant services for you is treated as an employee if he or she attends the meal in connection with performance of such services.

After the above determinations are reached, only 50% of business meal expenses is allowed as a deduction.

TaxAlert

Congress has instructed the IRS to adopt stricter substantiation requirements for business meals to ensure that they clearly serve a business purpose.

Entertainment Facilities

Deductions for expenses paid or incurred for a facility used for entertainment, amusement, or recreation are generally not allowed. Entertainment facility expenses include depreciation and operating costs such as rent, utilities, and maintenance, and salaries or other compensation paid to caretakers. Interest, taxes, and casualty losses relating to an entertainment facility are, however, deductible.

Any real or personal property—whether owned or leased—may be considered an entertainment facility if used during the year for entertainment. Entertainment facilities can include country clubs, athletic clubs, yachts, hunting lodges, fishing camps, swimming pools, tennis courts, bowling alleys, automobiles, airplanes, hotel suites, apartments, and vacation homes. However, a facility is not considered an entertainment facility if used only incidentally for entertainment, and such use is insubstantial in relation to its other business use, or if such facility is used exclusively by one's employees.

TaxAlert

An employer may deduct 100% of the cost of entertainment or an entertainment facility provided to employees to the extent the expense is reported as compensation to the employee. Also, if the employer provides free vacation flights to employees on the corporate jet, the cost of providing the flight is fully deductible if the value of the flight is included in the employee's compensation. In this case, the employer may deduct the full cost of providing the flight even if the cost exceeds the amount required to be included in employee income.

Club Dues

Dues paid for membership in professional organizations such as the AICPA (the American Institute of Certified Public Accountants), AIA (the American Institute of Architects), or the ABA (American Bar Association), or public service organizations such as the Rotary or Kiwanis, are deductible if paid for business reasons and the organization's principal purpose is not to conduct entertainment activities. Dues or assessments paid for membership in a social, athletic, or sporting club, including dues and fees paid to a country club, are not deductible.

General Travel and Entertainment Record-Keeping Requirements

Travel and entertainment expenses are an ordinary and necessary part of doing business, but they may not be deducted unless you meet specific substantiation requirements, some of which have already been described above. The law specifically disallows any deduction for travel and entertainment expenditures unless you substantiate these expenses through (1) "adequate records" or (2) "sufficient evidence corroborating the taxpayer's own statement." This rule also applies to deductions for entertainment facilities. Maintaining "adequate records" is clearly the preferable approach.

To claim a deduction under either method, you must substantiate the following:

Required Elements
- The *amount* of such expense or other item.
- The *time and place* of the travel, entertainment, amusement, recreation, or use of the facility or property; or the *date and description* of the gift.
- The *business purpose* of the expense or other item.
- The *business relationship to the taxpayer* of the person or persons entertained, using the facility or property, or receiving the gift.

Adequate Records

A diary, log, statement of expense, account book, or similar record of the necessary information should be maintained. Canceled checks, credit card receipts, hotel bills, and other documents must be kept to corroborate any expenditure for lodging and any other expenditures of $75 or more (except transportation charges for which such documentary evidence is not readily available). However, such documents by themselves—without a diary noting business purpose and business relationship of the person entertained—may not adequately support a deduction.

The records must be prepared or maintained so that each entry is recorded "at or near the time of the expenditure or use." A log maintained on a weekly basis will normally be adequate.

TAXSAVER

Any expenditure or use not documented by adequate records must be substantiated by "sufficient evidence corroborating" your own written or oral statements. Such evidence may ultimately be accepted by the IRS, but at-

tempting to substantiate T&E expenditures in this manner is not recommended because it may cause unnecessary and time-consuming disputes.

TaxAlert

Claiming a credit or deduction without adequate records (or sufficient corroborating evidence) may result in a negligence or fraud penalty in certain cases.

TaxOrganizer

An IRS agent might request the following information when examining your travel and entertainment deductions in connection with a business meeting:
- *The exact nature of business conducted.*
- *The time actually spent on business.*
- *The social events included in the agenda.*
- *Whether the site and time of the meeting were primarily vacation-oriented (such as at a resort area in season).*

Expense Account Allowances

If your reimbursements for travel and entertainment expenses from your employer equal your expenses, and you are required to make an adequate accounting to your employer, then neither the reimbursement nor the expenses need to be reported on your tax return. (Your employer, however, will be subject to the 50% deduction limitation unless an exception applies.)

If reimbursements exceed your deductible expenses, the excess must be included in your taxable income. If expenses exceed your reimbursements, and you wish to deduct the excess expenses on your tax return, you must substantiate to your employer all the expenses and show the reimbursed portion on IRS Form 2106. You will be subject to the 50% deduction limitation, and excess expenses will be allowable only as a miscellaneous itemized deduction subject to the 2%-of-adjusted-gross-income floor, discussed in Chapter 2.

Adequate Accounting

To adequately account for your expenses you should submit to your employer a written account book, diary, expense statement, trip sheet, log, or similar record—along with receipts and other supporting documentation—sufficient to substantiate each element of an expenditure. You must also account for all amounts received as advances or reimbursements, including amounts charged directly to the employer through credit cards.

An employee who has adequately accounted to the employer will not be required to substantiate business expenses to the IRS unless (1) the employee claims deductions for business expenses in excess of reimbursements, (2) the employee is "related" to the employer, or (3) the IRS determines that the employer's accounting procedures are inadequate. (Generally, an employee is considered to be related to the employer if he or she is more than a 10% shareholder or a member of a family owning more than 10% of the stock of the employer.)

Standard Reimbursement Arrangements

According to IRS rules, you do not have to document incurring certain expenses if you are reimbursed for these expenses at (or below) a standard *per diem* rate. However, the time, place, and business purpose of the expenses still must be substantiated. Standard reimbursement rates have been established for (1) overnight travel (including meals and incidental expenses); (2) meals and incidentals only; and (3) mileage.

If the standard federal *per diem* rate exceeds your actual deductible business expense, the excess need not be reported as income. If the standard reimbursement rate is less than your deductible business expenses, and you wish to deduct the excess, you must claim deductions for the expenses on Schedule A of Form 1040. The unreimbursed expenses will be treated as a miscellaneous itemized deduction subject to the 2%-of-adjusted-gross-income floor and the 50% deduction limitation rule (for meals and entertainment).

If your employer's *per diem* rate exceeds the allowable amount and the reimbursement plan does not require employees to return any amount in excess of the substantiated expenses to the employer, you may have to report the full reimbursement as income and deduct any expenses as a miscellaneous itemized deduction. If the plan does require repayment of the excess *per diem* amount to the employer, but you do not return such amount, you also may have to report the excess amount as income.

Overnight Travel Allowances. You can satisfy the "adequate accounting" requirements for overnight travel expenses if your employer reimburses you for not more than (1) the maximum *per diem* rate established periodically by the federal government for "subsistence" in the travel locality or (2) the high-low substantiation rate. "Subsistence" for purposes of this rule means expenses for meals and lodging, laundry, and tips, but not taxicab fares or telephone costs, which can be separately reimbursed. The high-low substantiation rate is a simplified method of computing the federal *per diem* rate. It eliminates the need to keep a current list of the *per diem* rate in effect for each city. Under the high-low method, areas eligible for the high rate are listed in IRS Publication 1542.

TaxAlert

The IRS has indicated it will generally require the entire amount of subsistence for meals, lodging, laundry, and tips to be treated as an expense for food and beverages, and thus subject to the 50% deduction limitation.

Meal Allowance. An employer may wish to use a flat allowance for meals only to reimburse you for these expenses. Under a special meal allowance rule, an employer can presently reimburse an employee not more than $34 or $42 per day (depending on the locality of travel) for meals and certain incidental expenses for a "full day of travel." The amount deductible by the employer is subject to the 50% deduction limitation.

Mileage Allowance. If you are reimbursed by your employer for local travel and transportation costs at no more than the standard mileage rate determined periodically by the IRS, the "adequate accounting" requirement may be satisfied. The rate for 2000 is 32.5 cents per mile for *all miles of use for business.* The rate for the charitable use of an automobile is 14 cents per mile, and the rate for using an automobile for medical and moving purposes is 10 cents per mile. Additional amounts can be deducted for tolls and parking expenses incurred for business purposes.

However, some related rules and limits apply. The standard mileage rate cannot be used if (1) you did not claim the mileage allowance in the first year you used the car for business; (2) the car has been depreciated using a method other than straight-line; or (3) additional first-year depreciation has been claimed. Deductions are not allowed for commuting to a "regular" place of business. However, if you are an employee with a regular place of business, you may deduct daily transportation expenses incurred while working at a "temporary" business location. However, if your reimbursements from your employer exceed the standard mileage rate multiplied by the number of business miles you substantiate, the excess may be considered income to you, unless you are required to return it.

Fixed-Amount Reimbursement Arrangements

If your employer does not require you to account for your travel and entertainment expenses, you can deduct reimbursements received only as a miscellaneous itemized deduction, subject to the 50% deduction limitation rule for meals and entertainment expenses and the 2%-of-adjusted-gross-income floor. Reimbursed expenses that do not exceed the standard-mileage and *per diem* rates set by the IRS may be deducted directly from your gross income.

TAX**A**LERT

Disallowed Expenses. *If an employer bears the cost of travel or entertainment expenses reimbursing you for your expenses, the rules governing the deduction of these expenses generally apply to the employer, not the employee. However, if you are reimbursed for an entertainment expense, and that expense is subsequently disallowed by the IRS on a subsequent audit of your employer, you may have to treat the reimbursed amount as income paid to you on which you will owe tax. Your employer will not, however, automatically be able to deduct the amount paid to you as compensation. Regulations provide that, to be regarded as deductible compensation, the disallowed expenditure must have been treated as compensation on your employer's income tax return as originally filed.*

Payments to reimburse expenses of shareholder-employees may be treated as dividends if the corporation's deduction is disallowed. In this situation, the reimbursed shareholder would have to include the amount in income, and the employer corporation would not be allowed a deduction. However, if a preexisting agreement requires the shareholder-employee to repay the amount of any nondeductible item to the employer, the shareholder-employee then can deduct the amount repaid and the corporation is restored to the position it was in before making the disallowed payment. There's one catch: the IRS could view such an agreement as an indication that the company may have taken some questionable deductions.

Entertainment Expenses Treated as Compensation or Income. An employer is not subject to travel, entertainment, and record-keeping rules if the expenses of providing goods, services, or facilities to an employee are treated as compensation to the employee on the employer's tax return as originally filed and income tax is withheld on the compensation.

Expenses for goods, services, or facilities provided to nonemployees are exempt from the special travel, entertainment, and record-keeping rules to the extent that the expenses are includible in the income of the nonemployee recipient either as compensation or as a prize or award. However, this exemption applies only if the taxpayer includes the amount on an information return (Form 1099), if such a return is required.

4

Tax Planning and Your Home

Introduction

Your home is often your most significant asset. For this reason, if no other, you will want to do everything you can to maximize your after-tax return on this investment. Fortunately, your home can also be your biggest tax shelter. The tax code allows you to deduct interest paid on a home mortgage, within certain limits, from your adjusted gross income. This chapter discusses numerous tax-saving strategies that involve your home. It discusses ways you can maximize your deduction for home mortgage interest; ways to minimize the gain and recognize loss when you sell your residence; and what tax deductions you may be able to take if you own a second home. It suggests different methods by which you may divide jointly owned property because of a divorce, what you can deduct if you have an office at home, and ways you may generate charitable contributions using your home.

Rules for Selling Your Home

You generally are able to exclude up to $250,000 ($500,000 if married filing a joint return) of gain realized on the sale or exchange of a principal residence. The exclusion is allowed each time you sell or exchange a principal residence that meets the eligibility requirements, but generally no more frequently than once every two years.

To be eligible for the exclusion, you must have owned the residence and occupied it as a principal residence for at least two of the five years prior to the sale or exchange. If you fail to meet these requirements by reason of a change of place of employment, health, or other unforeseen circumstances, you are able to exclude the fraction of the $250,000 ($500,000 if married filing a joint return) equal to the fraction of two years that these requirements are met. For example, if you used property as a principal residence for 18 months in the five years prior to sale, up to 75% of the $250,000 or $500,000 limitation would be excludable.

The home sale exclusion rule should allow you to base future housing decisions on personal and nontax financial considerations following the sale of a current residence. For example, under the old law, you would be taxed on any part of your gain from a sale that was not reinvested in a new residence. Now, if you are planning a postretirement move to a "lower-cost" area, you can "trade down" to a less expensive residence rather than feeling pressured to reinvest the sales proceeds in a new home of equal or greater value simply to reduce taxes. You will then be able to put some of your home equity to a different use by, say, reinvesting a portion of the sales proceeds in higher-growth or income-producing assets.

The exclusion should also ease record-keeping requirements by eliminating the need to document minor home improvements. (*Note:* records documenting the original acquisition cost of the residence should still be maintained.) However, record-keeping may become more important if you expect to realize gains in excess of the exclusion allowances, since you will no longer be able to indefinitely defer gains through a series of rollovers until death.

TaxOrganizer

Selling expenses and any home improvements you've made over the years will reduce the amount of gain that is taxable, thereby reducing any taxes you might owe. You need to keep good records of such expenses in order to figure the lowest taxable gain you must report.

Losses on the sale of a personal residence are nondeductible personal losses. In addition, gain will be recognized to the extent of any depreciation allowable with respect to the rental or business use of such principal residence for periods after May 6, 1997.

TaxSaver

If you believe your home will decline in value before you sell it, you may want to convert it to rental property before the value declines so that the loss, if any, may be deducted. The built-in loss as of the conversion date is not deductible.

Real Estate Taxes. The deduction for real estate taxes on any real estate sale is apportioned between the seller and the buyer based on the number of days in the real-property tax year that the property is owned by each.

Below-Market Interest. In certain instances the seller of a personal residence may be required to acknowledge additional interest income for debt obligations issued with a below-market interest rate. (See page 21.)

Penalty-Free IRA Distribution for the Purchase of a First Home

Generally, a 10% additional tax applies to distributions from an IRA prior to age 59½. The 10% early withdrawal penalty does not apply to distributions from an IRA if the taxpayer uses the money to pay qualified acquisition costs for a principal residence of a "qualified first-time homebuyer" who is the taxpayer, the taxpayer's spouse, or a child, grandchild, or ancestor of the taxpayer or taxpayer's spouse. A qualified first-time homebuyer is someone who has had no ownership interest in a residence during the past two years. The term "qualified acquisition costs" means the costs of acquiring, constructing, or reconstructing a residence. Such term includes any usual or reasonable settlement, financing, or other closing costs.

The aggregate amount of the distribution for first-time home purchase cannot exceed a lifetime cap of $10,000. The $10,000 lifetime ceiling on the new exception, together with the ordinary income tax rates on IRA distributions that would still apply to such distributions, is likely to minimize the impact of the new exception, even in starter home markets.

Home Mortgage Interest

Generally, mortgage interest is any interest you pay on a loan secured by your home. This includes a mortgage, a second mortgage, a line of credit, and a home equity loan. Most home mortgage interest is deductible, subject to the following limitations.

Deductions for interest on home mortgage loans are generally allowed only if the loans are secured by your principal residence or second residence and only for loan principal up to $1 million. Acquisition indebtedness is debt incurred in acquiring, constructing, or substantially improving a qualified residence. Acquisition indebtedness is reduced by principal payments made on such debt. If you have repaid some of your "acquisition debt" (most commonly by making mortgage payments), it cannot be restored through refinancing. You can refinance your mortgage up to the balance remaining on the old mortgage and still deduct the interest. If you refinance in an amount in excess of the balance remaining on the old mortgage, the interest allocable to the excess is not deductible unless the excess was used to substantially improve your home or it qualifies as home-equity indebtedness.

Acquisition indebtedness that was incurred prior to October 14, 1987, is not subject to the $1 million limitation. However, the amount of such debt reduces (but not below zero) the $1 million limitation on subsequent acquisition debt. Such debt includes that which was incurred on or before October 13, 1987, and was secured by a qualified residence as of that date and at all times thereafter.

Home mortgage interest is also deductible on a home-equity loan to the extent that the loan does not exceed $100,000. The home-equity debt must not exceed the fair market value of a qualified residence, reduced by the amount of acquisition indebtedness for that residence. Home-equity loans may provide you with deductible interest on debt incurred for personal purposes, such as the purchase of a family car. (See Chapter 2, page 44.)

TaxSaver

If you own more than two homes, you may not deduct the interest on more than two of these homes as home mortgage interest during any one year. You must include your main residence as one of the homes. You may choose any one of your other homes as a qualified residence and may change this choice in a different tax year.

However, you cannot choose to treat one home as a second residence for part of a year and another home as a second residence for the remainder of the year if both of these homes were owned by you during the entire year and neither was your main residence during that year.

TaxSaver

Generally, costs for your children's dormitory space at college are not deductible. However, if you purchase a condominium in which your college-age dependent child lives while at school, you may be able to generate a deduction. This is possible because the interest expense for a qualified second residence is deductible. The interest portion of the mortgage and any related property taxes would be deductible. Obviously, appreciation or depreciation potential and other factors must be considered when looking at this idea, but under the right circumstances it could make sense.

E&Y FOCUS: Before You Refinance

Here are some questions you should consider when you are thinking about refinancing your mortgage:

1. What will it cost to refinance the mortgage?
2. How much longer do I plan to own my home?
3. Will my financial condition in the future allow me enough cash flow to continue paying the mortgage?
4. Should I consider an adjustable-rate mortgage (ARM) or a fixed-rate mortgage? ARMs generally may require smaller monthly payments than a fixed-rate mortgage. However, monthly payments on an ARM will increase if interest rates go up and could, at some time, exceed the amount of a fixed-rate mortgage.

   If the rates stay low you can be ahead with an ARM. However, if you are on a fixed income, there is always a risk that rates will go up beyond what you can afford.

Points

"Points" are certain charges sometimes paid by a borrower. They are also referred to as loan origination fees or premium charges. If the payment of any of these charges is only for the use of money, it is interest.

Because points are, in effect, interest paid in advance, generally you may not deduct the full amount for points in the year paid. Points that represent prepaid interest generally must be deducted over the life of the loan.

Exception: You may deduct the entire amount you pay as points in the year of payment if the loan is used to buy or improve your principal residence and is secured by that home. (You may, if you wish, still elect to deduct the points over the life of the loan if that is more advantageous for you, e.g., when you're claiming the standard deduction in the year of purchase.) This exception will apply only if:

1. The payment of points is an established business practice in the area where the loan was made, and
2. The points paid do not exceed the amount generally charged in this area.

Furthermore, the points charged on a mortgage obtained to purchase your principal home are immediately deductible whether paid out of separate funds or, if the following additional conditions are satisfied, incorporated into the mortgage note. These additional requirements are:

1. Your lender prepares a Form HUD-1, *Uniform Settlement Statement*, that explicitly states the points incurred on the loan. Points may be identified as "loan origination fees," "loan discount," "discount points," or simply, "points."
2. The points must be computed as a percentage of the principal amount of the loan.
3. The total of your down payment plus other cash paid by the time you close is at least as much as the amount of points charged.

To be immediately deductible, points paid on home improvement loans must be paid from separate funds at closing—that is, they cannot be included in the borrowed amount.

Points paid on a loan to purchase or improve your second home do not qualify for full, immediate deduction. Generally, points paid on the refinancing of a principal residence must be spread over the life of the loan.

TaxAlert

If a buyer does not have enough cash to close the purchase of a house and pay points, the mortgage lender will very likely require a higher interest rate. But, the purchaser might not be able to afford payments with the higher interest, so the seller pays the points. The question then is "if there is a deduction, who gets it?"

TaxSaver

A borrower may deduct points paid by the seller if the following conditions are satisfied.

- *The rule only applies to points—that is, to financing costs described on the HUD-1 or similar settlement statement as "loan origination fees," "loan discount," "discount points," or "points."*

- *Points must be described as a percentage of the loan amount.*
- *The amount of the points must be reasonable for the local market.*
- *Points are only deductible to the extent of the amount of funds brought to the table by the buyer. Furthermore, the buyer's basis in the home must be reduced by the amount of seller-paid points deducted.*

TaxSaver

Generally, each point subtracts about 1/8% from the interest rate on a 30-year mortgage. However, the effect is much greater if the loan is for a shorter period of time. Therefore, if you expect to sell your property well before the mortgage is paid off, it could be better to pay a higher interest rate and fewer points.

Alternative Minimum Tax Consequences. Home mortgage interest is allowed as a deduction for AMT purposes. However, the definition of such interest is narrower than that of "qualified residence interest" for regular tax purposes. Refinanced home mortgage interest that is applicable to any mortgage in excess of the outstanding mortgage before refinancing is not deductible for AMT purposes. (See page 154 for further discussion.)

Second Homes

Vacation Homes and Other Dwellings. Benefits may be derived from the ownership of a second home. You may significantly reduce your taxable income by increasing your home mortgage interest deduction, subject to certain limitations (see pages 43–48). If you rent your property, you may reduce your taxable income further through the deduction for rental expenses (see page 81).

Residence and Domicile. Residence and domicile are different concepts. They may be the same or they may be different. Your residence is where you currently live. Your domicile is where you are permanently established. The home you are residing in may be your vacation home while your domicile is somewhere else. You can have many residences but only one domicile. Where your domicile is located can have a significant effect on your income and estate taxes. For a further explanation see below.

TaxSaver

When considering retirement, you should try to establish your domicile in a state where the income and estate taxes will be the lowest.
   Example: A New Yorker who has a residence in New York City retired to Florida for five years before his death. The man kept an office in New York but spent most of his time (more than six months a year) in Florida. New York claimed that the man was a resident of New York because he died there and was buried there. The New York estate taxes would have equaled $4 million.

However, the man had arranged his will through a Florida attorney and took numerous steps to declare Florida as his new domicile. It was determined that he was, indeed, a resident of Florida and a nonresident of New York. As a nonresident, his estate taxes in New York were less than $20,000.

E&Y FOCUS: Establishing Your Domicile

Where you actually establish domicile can have a tremendous impact on your tax bill. For example, New York and Massachusetts have significant state income taxes while Florida and Texas have none. States also have differing rules governing certain estate matters, such as the division of property when someone dies without a will.

To Establish Your New Domicile

- Register and vote in your new state. Advise the Board of Elections where you formerly voted that you have moved, and cancel your old registration.
- File a declaration of domicile. Some states, such as Florida, have a special form you can file to establish permanent residency.
- File, as a resident, all state and local tax returns required by your new state—and use your new address on all future tax returns.
- Change your car's title and registration.
- Obtain a driver's license in your new state.
- Take advantage of homestead exemptions if your state offers them—they're an excellent way to help establish a change of domicile and reduce real estate taxes.
- Open bank accounts in your new state.
- Become a member of organizations in the new state rather than continue memberships in the old state.
- Execute a new will in which you refer to your domicile.
- Spend more time in your state of domicile than in any other state.
- Declare your new state as your domicile on all forms that require a statement of residence. Examples are passports, contracts, credit applications, and hotel registrations.
- Use your new address in all formal agreements.
- Register securities at your new address.
- Change insurance policies that do not relate specifically to property located outside your new state.
- Change your address with the Social Security Administration.
- Change credit cards, particularly those that are national in scope.

Rental Income and Expenses

Rental income includes any payment you receive for the use or occupation of property. For example, if you rent the loft above your garage or a room in your house, you will have rental income. If you receive property or services as rent, the fair market value of the property or services you receive is rental income.

Deductible Rental Expenses. Repairs, advertising, janitorial and maid service, rental of equipment, utilities, fire and liability insurance, taxes, interest, commissions for the collection of rent, and travel and transportation expenses—all of these expenditures, if they are incurred in renting property, may be deductible. Repairs are expenses incurred to keep your property in good operating condition. Repair expenses include repainting property inside or out, fixing gutters or floors, and fixing leaks. Repairs are different from improvements. Improvements must be "capitalized" and depreciated—that is, the cost of the item is written off as a business expense over a period of years. (See the discussion of depreciation later in this chapter.) Improvements are expenditures that either add to the value of your property or prolong the property's useful life. Improvements include such items as building an addition, putting in new plumbing or wiring, and installing a new roof. If you make improvements for a tenant and, at the termination of the lease, you dispose of the improvements, you are able to take the basis adjusted for depreciation into account for purposes of determining your gain or loss.

TAX*SAVER*

You may deduct expenses on your rental property during a period in which it is not being rented as long as it is actively being held out for rent. This rule applies to a period between rentals as well as to the period during which a property is being marketed as a rental property for the first time. The IRS can disallow these deductions if you are unable to show that you were actively seeking a profit and had a reasonable expectation of achieving one. However, the deduction cannot be disallowed merely because your property was difficult to rent.

Rental of Vacation Homes and Other Dwellings. If you rent out part or all of a vacation home or other dwelling unit, and you also use any part of the unit for personal purposes during the year, you must divide your expenses between the rental use and the personal use.

TAX*SAVER*

When Rental Income Isn't Taxed. *If a residence is rented out for fewer than 15 days during the taxable year, the rental income is not taxable. This is one of the few instances in which rental income is nontaxable. Consequently, if you live near the site of a major annual sporting event—say, The Masters Golf Tournament in Augusta, Georgia—and you rent out your residence only during the event (for 14 days or less), any income you receive will be tax-free. However, expenses attributable to the rental of your residence, such as depreciation, insurance, and so on, are not deductible except for interest, taxes, and casualty losses that are deductible on Schedule A, Form 1040, if you itemize.*

Figuring Rental Expenses. If you rent out a dwelling unit for 15 days or more, the income you receive is taxable. Expenses related to the property rental are deductible, subject to certain limitations based on the number of days you personally use the dwelling unit. Generally, your deductions can be found by applying this formula: Expenses × rental days ÷ total days used for all purposes.

Example: You own a ski chalet that is used only during the winter ski season. During the year, the dwelling unit is rented out for 80 days and used personally by you for another 10 days. Total utility expenses are $1,800. You can deduct $1,600 of the utility expenses against rental income ($1,800 × 80 ÷ 90). The remaining $200 is considered a nondeductible personal expense.

If You Use a Rental Property for More Than 14 Days. When you use a dwelling unit for personal purposes for more than the greater of 14 days or 10% of the number of days that the dwelling unit was rented at a fair market rate during the year, a further restriction applies to the deduction for rental expenses. In this case, the dwelling unit is treated as a residence. The rental expense deductions are limited to the amount of gross rental income, reduced first by any allocated expenditures that would otherwise be deductible, such as interest and taxes, and then by other deductible expenses, such as allocated utilities and depreciation.

Generally, a dwelling unit is used for personal purposes only on days that it is:

- used by you or by any other person who has an interest in it;
- used by a member of your family or by a family member of any other person who has an interest in it, unless that family member uses the dwelling unit as his or her main home, pays a fair rental price, and arranges the rental pursuant to a shared equity financing agreement. For purposes of this rule, your family includes only brothers and sisters, spouses, ancestors (parents, grandparents, etc.), and lineal descendants (children, grandchildren, etc.);
- used by another under an arrangement that lets you use some other dwelling unit; or
- used by anyone at less than a fair rental price.

TaxSaver

The rule relating to personal use does not apply to use by an in-law of the taxpayer who owns the property. Thus, a son-in-law could lease property at a fair value to his mother-in-law, and it would not be treated as personal use.

Some days that you spend at the dwelling unit are not counted as days of personal use. For example, any day that you spend repairing and maintaining your property on a full-time basis is not counted as a day of personal use. In addition, the fact that family members used the dwelling for personal purposes on the same day that you are repairing or maintaining it does not make the day a personal day. You also do not have to count days on which you used the property as your main home as days of personal use, if you used the property as your main home before or after renting it or offering it for rent, and either (1) you rented or tried to rent the property for 12 or more consecutive months, or (2) you rented or tried to rent the property for a period of less than 12 consecutive months and the period ended because you sold or exchanged the property.

TaxSaver

The IRS method for allocating expenses between personal and rental use requires a strict allocation between the total number of days the unit was used during the year and the number of rental days. Taxpayers, however, have successfully challenged this method in a number of Tax Court cases. Using the Tax Court method, you can allocate interest and taxes based on the number of days in the year rather than the number of days rented as prescribed by the IRS. Depending upon the method you choose for allocating expenses between personal and rental use, you may be able to increase your total expense deductions.

Vacation Homes and the Passive Activity Rules

Vacation homes and other rental properties considered rental activities are subject to the passive activity rules discussed on page 11. Consequently, when making decisions regarding renting, financing, and selling properties, you must consider the impact of rental losses being disallowed and the $25,000 rental loss limitation deduction that is applicable to certain taxpayers. (See discussion of exception for active real estate participation in Chapter 1.) Losses that are not deductible as a result of the passive activity rules can be carried forward to later years and, subject to the same income limitations, deducted in those years.

TaxSaver

When the cash flow from your rental property is not enough to meet your operating costs, you should reconsider your reasons for owning the property. You should determine if the expected growth in the value of the property will make up for the losses you are incurring each year. Remember, what has to be made up includes what you could earn on the net after-tax proceeds from the sale if the property were sold today.

Depreciation

Depreciation is the annual deduction you are entitled to take to cover the cost of certain capital expenditures for property held for business or investment purposes. The depreciation deduction is claimed over "the recovery period" of the property, which varies depending upon the type of property. For example, the recovery period for the cost of a new roof on a rental home is longer than the recovery period for furniture bought for the home. Depreciation is calculated in the same way whether you report income on the cash or accrual method.

Several factors determine how much depreciation you can deduct. The main factors are: (1) your cost basis in the property and (2) the recovery period for the property.

The total of all your annual depreciation deductions cannot be more than your cost or other basis in the property. For this purpose, the total depreciation must include any depreciation that you were allowed to claim, even if you did not claim it.

For more information about depreciation see Chapter 15, Determining Income, Deductions, and Taxes for Your Business.

Contributions to Charitable Organizations

Contribution of Property. A transfer of an undivided interest in property qualifies as a charitable contribution and may be deducted. You may deduct the fair market value of the property at the time of contribution if the property would qualify for long-term capital gain treatment if sold. Generally, the contribution of your residence will qualify for such treatment. However, if you have owned your residence for less than a year, your deduction is limited to its fair market value minus the amount that would be ordinary income or short-term capital gain. See Chapter 6, Charitable Contributions, for a complete discussion of charitable contributions.

Contribution of Property Subject to a Mortgage. If you contribute your residence to a charity and it is subject to a mortgage, you will be allowed a partial deduction. In determining the amount of the contribution, the contribution will be treated as a bargain sale—the amount of the charitable deduction is the difference between the fair market value of the property and the amount of the mortgage. Further, you must treat as taxable gain any excess of the full amount of the mortgage over your basis in the property allocable to the amount of the mortgage.

Partial Interest in Property. Generally, no deduction is allowed for a charitable contribution of less than your entire interest in property. For example, the owner of property will not get a deduction for giving a "life estate interest" in a property to charity. (A life estate interest is an interest in property that terminates upon the death of the life estate's owner.) A contribution of the right to use property is a contribution of less than your entire interest in that property and is not deductible.

Exceptions: There are some situations in which you may claim a deduction for a charitable contribution that is less than your entire interest in the property:

1. *Undivided part of your entire interest.* A contribution of an undivided part of your entire interest in property must consist of a part of each

and every substantial interest or right you own in the property. It must extend over the entire term of your interest in the property.

2. *Remainder interest in a personal residence or farm.* You may take a charitable deduction for an irrevocable gift to a qualified organization of a remainder interest (i.e., the donor retains an interest for his or her lifetime) in a personal residence or in a farm.

TaxSaver

If you give a remainder interest in a personal residence (or a farm) to a qualified charity, the present value of the remainder interest is deductible as a charitable contribution. One significant advantage of such a gift is that you suffer no loss of income or increase in expense from the gift, but you still gain a current income tax deduction. The gift may be made without the use of a trust. In addition, you continue to use and enjoy the home for life.

To qualify for the deduction, the gift must be a gift of your personal residence. The home does not have to be your principal residence. Thus, the gift may be your vacation home.

The charity receives no immediate benefit; however, the opportunity for future benefits can be substantial.

Example: *A 62-year-old woman owns a personal residence with a fair market value of $162,000. The land on which the residence is located is valued at $42,000. The residence has a remaining useful life of 35 years and an estimated salvage value of $30,000. According to IRS tables, the value of the remainder interest in the home and the land is approximately $40,000, which is currently deductible as a donation of the interest. Besides a substantial income tax deduction, the donor will receive an estate tax deduction for the value of the interest that passes to charity at her death.*

Divorce and Separation

The tax effects on the sale or transfer of one's residence incident to a divorce can vary substantially depending on whether the couple retains ownership, sells, or transfers the property.

If title is given to your spouse or former spouse, incident to divorce, no gain or loss is recognized on the transfer. A transfer of property is incident to divorce if the transfer occurs within one year after the date on which the marriage ends, or if the transfer is related to the ending of the marriage. The spouse receiving the property takes the basis of the transferring spouse. This result occurs even if the spouse who retains the residence pays cash and the transaction is made in the form of a sale.

An alternative is to retain your interest in the residence even though you no longer live there. This option may be attractive if there are not enough assets to compensate you for your interest in the residence. Under this alternative, you and your spouse could agree, pursuant to the settlement, that the residence subsequently will be sold (for example, when the children no longer live there) and the proceeds from the sale divided between the two of you. Your spouse could then use the $250,000 exclusion. Or, alternatively, couples may decide to sell the house to a third party and split the proceeds.

TaxSaver

If you decide to retain your interest in the residence, you should consider transferring it to your spouse and as part of the divorce settlement require him or her to divide the proceeds upon sale. Consequently, any applicable exclusions may be used toward the entire proceeds.

Home Office Expenses

To qualify for a deduction for home office expenses, you must use the home office exclusively as an office and it must be: (1) your principal place of business; (2) used by patients, clients, or customers in the normal course of your business; or (3) used in connection with your business if the office is a separate structure not attached to the dwelling unit. In determining whether you meet this standard, you must look at: (1) the relative importance of the activities performed at each business location; and (2) the amount of time spent at each location. The IRS has indicated that it will first look to the "relative importance" test. If this test does not produce a definitive answer, then the amount of time spent at each location is the determining factor. This test may result in a taxpayer having no specific office that can be deemed the principal place of business and, thus, being denied a deduction for home office expenses.

The allowable deduction is limited to the gross income generated from the use of the residence, reduced first by any expenditures otherwise deductible, such as taxes and interest, and then reduced by other deductible trade or business expenses, such as prorated utilities and depreciation. Any disallowed expenses can be carried forward to future years, subject to the gross income limitation in those years.

You are not entitled to home office deductions for expenses attributable to the rental of all or part of your home to your employer for performing services as an employee. An independent contractor is treated as an employee under these rules.

Clarification of Definition of Principal Place of Business

Beginning in 1999, a home office qualifies as the "principal place of business" if both: (1) the office is used by the taxpayer to conduct administrative or management activities of a trade or business and (2) there is no other fixed location of the trade or business where the taxpayer conducts substantial administrative or management activities of the trade or business.

As under old law, deductions will be allowed for a home office meeting the two-part test only if you use the office on a regular basis as a place of business and, in the case of an employee, only if such exclusive use is for the convenience of the employer. The fact that a taxpayer also carries out administrative or management activities at sites that are not fixed locations of the business, such as a car or hotel room, will not affect the taxpayer's ability to claim a home office deduction. You are still eligible to claim a deduction even if you conduct an insubstantial amount of administrative or management activities at a fixed location outside the home.

5

IRAs, 401(k) Plans, and Other Retirement Plans

As this book was being prepared in September 2000, Congress was still considering legislation that could affect individuals' tax planning for the coming year. We strongly encourage you to consult with your tax advisor for the most updated information.

INTRODUCTION

Ask a financial planner what's the best way to save money for your retirement, and chances are he or she will recommend that you contribute as much as you can to a 401(k) plan, an individual retirement account or annuity (IRA), a Keogh plan, a Simplified Employee Pension (SEP), a savings incentive match plan for employees (a SIMPLE plan)—or some combination of the five, if you're eligible. Congress has expanded IRA options for retirement and family education savings with the addition of the Roth IRA and the Education IRA. This chapter will explain what these savings plans are and how they operate. In addition, it will suggest strategies you can use to make the most of your long-term savings.

IRAs

An IRA is a personal savings plan that lets you set aside funds for your retirement. An individual's deductible IRA contribution is limited to the lesser of $2,000 or 100% of compensation (or earned income from self-employment). Alimony is treated as compensation for this purpose. The amount you can contribute to your IRA is determined on an individual basis. Therefore, if you and your spouse each receive compensation over $2,000 or meet the requirements for a spousal IRA (discussed below), then each of you can contribute $2,000 to your respective IRAs. Earnings in your IRA are not taxable until they are distributed to you. Contributions must be in cash to be deductible, although nondeductible rollover contributions from qualified plans or other IRAs can be made in the form of property.

Although you may contribute to an IRA if you are under age 70½ and you have compensation or earned income at least equal to the amount contributed, you may not deduct any part of your IRA contribution on your 2000 return if:

1. You are single and an active participant in a qualified retirement plan provided by your employer during the year, and your adjusted gross income (AGI) exceeds $42,000.
2. You are married filing jointly and an active participant in a qualified employer retirement plan, and your AGI exceeds $62,000.
3. You are married filing separately and you or your spouse is an active participant in a qualified employer retirement plan, and your AGI exceeds $10,000. For married couples filing separately, if one spouse is an active participant in a qualified retirement plan, then the other spouse will also be treated as a participant in the plan, unless the couple has lived apart throughout the entire year.

You may claim a reduced deduction if you are an active participant in an employer plan and your AGI is less than the dollar amounts above but more than $52,000 for joint filers ($32,000 for single filers and $0 for married filing separately). These income phaseout limits for deductible IRA contributions are scheduled to increase gradually until the limits reach $50,000–$60,000 in 2005 for single filers ($80,000–$100,000 in 2007 for joint filers). See the discussion below.

TaxSaver

Contributing before-tax earnings to an IRA account can make a big difference in your retirement savings. For example, assume you are in the 28% tax bracket and that you are earning 6% interest on your savings. You can earn approximately 1.2 times more money after paying taxes on the distribution (payable at the time of withdrawal) on a $2,000 IRA contribution held for 20 years than if you did not make that before-tax contribution. If your tax rate drops after your retirement because you have less income, your savings could amount to an even bigger nest egg.

Example: If you contributed $2,000 a year to an IRA for 20 years and the IRA earned 6% each year, at the end of 20 years you would have about $73,600. If you deposited $1,440 ($2,000 less $560 in tax) each year in an account earning 6% and paid tax on the interest you earned each year, you would have about $44,300 in the account at the end of 20 years. Even if the entire $73,600 were distributed and taxed at 28%, you would still be ahead by $8,700 by investing in an IRA. As Table 5.1 illustrates, the compounding effect in your IRA increases your balance disproportionately as the return on your investments increases.

The relative advantage of a deductible IRA investment over a comparable after-tax investment may be less if you invest in capital assets such as stocks that produce capital gains rather than in income-producing investments that produce interest. This is because the favorable 20% tax rate on capital gains and the ability to deduct capital losses from ordinary income (within limits) does not apply to investments held in an IRA. All distributions from an IRA attributable to deductible contributions are taxed at ordinary income rates. Nevertheless, over time you will probably still be better off with an IRA in-

vestment because of the advantages of tax-free compounding of dividends and realized capital gains combined with the lower ordinary income tax rate on IRA distributions you take in retirement.

Nondeductible IRA Contributions. Even if you do not qualify for a tax-deductible contribution to your IRA, you can still make an after-tax contribution. The earnings on these contributions accumulate tax-deferred until you withdraw the money from your IRA. The maximum nondeductible contribution is the lesser of your taxable income or $2,000 ($4,000 for married filing jointly) minus the amount of any deductible contribution you may make. See Table 5.2. If you're also eligible for a Roth IRA (described later, page 92), you'll always be better off contributing to a Roth IRA rather than making a nondeductible IRA contribution.

TABLE 5.1 Investing in Your IRA

	6% Annualized Return		12% Annualized Return	
	IRA Account	Savings Account	IRA Account	Savings Account
Annual Contribution	$2,000	$2,000	$2,000	$2,000
Less Tax @ 28%	$0	$560	$0	$560
Net Contribution	$2,000	$1,440	$2,000	$1,440
Amount after 20 Years	$73,600	$44,300	$144,100	$70,450
Less Taxes Paid on Withdrawal @ 28%	$20,600	$0	$40,350	$0
Amount Remaining	$53,000	$44,300	$103,750	$70,450

TABLE 5.2 IRA Deductions

Adjusted Gross Income Allowable Deduction

Married Filing Jointly*	Single	Not an Active Participant	Active Participant
$0–$51,999	$0–$31,999	$2,000	$2,000
$52,000–$60,999	$32,000–$40,999	$2,000	$200–$2,000**
$61,000–$61,999	$41,000–$41,999	$2,000	$200***
$62,000 and over	$42,000 and over	$2,000	$0

A married couple filing separately is subject to a special limitation (see above).
**The $2,000 amount is reduced by a percentage equal to your adjusted gross income in excess of the lower adjusted gross income limits divided by $10,000. For example, a single individual with an adjusted gross income of $38,000 is allowed an IRA deduction of $600.*
***The IRA deduction will not be reduced below $200 until it is reduced to $0 at $62,000 (married filing jointly) and $42,000 (single) of adjusted gross income.*

Spousal IRAs. If you are married and file jointly, you can contribute to an IRA for a nonworking spouse. The spousal IRA may be contributed to a deductible or nondeductible IRA or a Roth IRA (explained below), or a combination of the two, but the maximum contribution to a spousal IRA is $2,000. This means the total combined contribution that can be made to your IRA and your spouse's IRA can be as much as $4,000 for the year, provided you have at least $4,000 in earned income. If neither you nor your spouse participates in an employer retirement plan, you may deduct the full $4,000. If you are covered by an employer plan, but are eligible for an IRA contribution as a joint filer, you can deduct the full $4,000. You may be able to deduct a $2,000 contribution to a spousal IRA even if you are an active participant in an employer plan and ineligible to make a deductible IRA contribution on your own. A nonactive participant spouse of an active participant can make a fully deductible IRA contribution if their combined AGI is below $150,000. This deduction is phased out between $150,000 and $160,000 of AGI.

When to Make Your IRA Contributions. Contributions to an IRA can be made starting from the first day of the tax year through the due date (without extensions) of your tax return for that tax year. This means that IRA contributions can generally be made until April 15 of the year following your tax year.

TAXSAVER

You can maximize your savings by funding your IRA as early as possible for any given tax year. By contributing to your IRA at the beginning of a tax year instead of waiting until April 15 of the following year, your contribution can earn as much as 15½ months' worth of additional tax-deferred interest.

IRA Custodial Fees. Annual custodial fees paid to maintain an IRA, as well as the initial fee to establish an IRA, may be deductible if you pay the fees separately rather than having the costs charged to the IRA account itself. Such IRA expenses are only deductible as miscellaneous itemized deductions subject to the 2%-of-adjusted-gross-income floor.

TAXALERT

The 1997 Tax Act created an Education IRA and a Roth IRA and modified the rules relating to deductible IRAs. While most of the changes or additional IRAs are significant, many high-income taxpayers remain eligible only for nondeductible IRAs if they participate in a qualified plan.

In considering these new or modified IRAs, you should pay particular attention to the interactions between these different types of accounts. In general, you can contribute a maximum of only $2,000 in total for any year for yourself to any of the IRAs available for retirement, plus a similar amount for your spouse. Education IRAs have separate interactions with the education tax credits and qualified state tuition programs.

Depending on your individual circumstances, you have a choice of four types of tax-favored IRA accounts: the Education IRA and Roth IRA are now available in addition to the existing deductible IRA and nondeductible IRA.

ROTH IRAS

Roth IRAs (named after the senator who sponsored the legislation) are a type of individual retirement-savings vehicle. Unlike deductible IRAs, contributions to a Roth IRA are not deductible from taxable income. However, qualified distributions from a Roth IRA are not includible in your gross income. By permitting tax-free withdrawals, contributions made early in the taxpayer's working life receive the greatest tax benefit.

Contributions. You can make an annual nondeductible contribution to a Roth IRA of the lesser of $2,000 ($4,000 for married couples filing jointly) or 100% of your earned income. As with regular IRAs, the Roth IRA contribution may be made for a tax year up until the due date of your tax return (without extensions). The maximum contribution to a Roth IRA is reduced by any contributions that you make to non-Roth IRAs, with the exception of Education IRAs. Unlike "traditional" IRAs, contributions to a Roth IRA can be made even after you reach age 70½, as long as you or your spouse has sufficient earned income.

> **TAXALERT**
>
> *If you or your spouse is over age 70½, you should consider making a nondeductible contribution to a Roth IRA. You can contribute as much as $2,000 ($4,000 for a couple filing jointly) as long as you have at least that much in earned income. You are not required to take distributions from a Roth IRA during your lifetime, and Roth IRAs pass tax-free to your heirs.*

Income Limits. The maximum contribution that can be made to a Roth IRA is phased out for single filers with AGI between $95,000 and $110,000 ($150,000 and $160,000 for couples filing jointly). Unlike deductible IRAs, the same income limitations apply to all individuals contributing to a Roth IRA, regardless of whether they are active participants in an employer retirement plan.

Distributions. Qualified distributions from a Roth IRA are not includible in income if the distribution is made after the five-tax-year period beginning with the first tax year for which a contribution was made to a Roth IRA and is:
1. On or after the date on which you attain age 59½;
2. To a beneficiary on or after your death;
3. Attributable to you becoming disabled; or
4. For first-time home-buyer acquisition costs up to $10,000.

The Roth IRA includes a special ordering rule that allows early withdrawals (before the five years have passed). This rule provides that amounts withdrawn are first considered to come from contributions. After all original contributions have been withdrawn, remaining amounts are considered to be income earned within the IRA. Distribution of these amounts would be taxable and could be subject to an early withdrawal penalty. Early withdrawals from the Roth IRA, therefore, are tax-free and penalty-free as long as you are withdrawing contributions, not accumulated earnings.

TaxAlert

Distributions made from a Roth IRA within five years of a conversion from a traditional IRA are subject to the 10% penalty tax on early withdrawals from a retirement plan. Congress added this change to close an apparent loophole whereby a taxpayer could convert an existing IRA to a Roth IRA and liquidate the Roth IRA immediately after conversion without being exposed to the early withdrawal tax, even if under age 59½.

Special Rules. Taxpayers with AGI of less than $100,000 (determined without regard to amounts that are included in income as a result of the conversion) are eligible to roll over or convert an existing IRA into a Roth IRA. Income taxes are imposed on the taxable amounts converted (which represent earnings and contributions), but no 10% excise tax for early withdrawal would apply.

TaxSaver

Converting your regular IRAs to Roth IRAs can be an excellent long-term tax-saving opportunity. However, eligibility for Roth IRA conversions is limited to tax payers whose AGI (exclusive of the amount converted) is less than $100,000 in the year of the conversion. If you think your AGI may exceed the $100,000 limit, it may be possible to control the timing and amount of income—and "above-the-line" deductions—to qualify for a Roth IRA conversion. For example, you might consider contributing more to a 401(k) plan at work, delaying the sale of appreciated property, delaying the exercise of stock options, or shifting investments to tax-exempt securities or low- or non-dividend-paying stocks. If you misjudge your income and make a Roth IRA conversion in a year when your AGI exceeds the $100,000 threshold, you can "undo" the conversion before the extended due date of your return for the year of the conversion.

TaxAlert

If you convert a traditional IRA to a Roth IRA, you can generally undo the transaction and restore the original IRA without tax liability if you do so within the same tax year. The approach of subsequently "reconverting" back to a Roth IRA in the same tax year has attracted attention because of the potential to minimize tax liability by timing the Roth IRA conversion to catch a low point in the value of the IRA. The IRS has recently clamped down on the use of Roth IRA reconversions in this manner. In 1999, an individual who con-

verted a traditional IRA that had not been previously converted to a Roth IRA and then transfered the converted amount back to a traditional IRA could reconvert that amount to a Roth IRA only once on or before December 31, 1999. For 2000 and beyond, reconversions are generally not permitted until the following tax year.

EDUCATION IRAS

The purpose of the new Education IRAs is to create a trust or custodial account exclusively for paying qualified higher education expenses.

Contributions. You can make a nondeductible contribution of up to $500 per year per beneficiary into an Education IRA. Eligible contributions must be in cash and made before the beneficiary reaches age 18.

The contributor need not be related to the beneficiary, and there is no limit on the number of individual beneficiaries for whom one contributor could set up an Education IRA (provided the contributor has modified AGI within the established limits, and that each contribution for each individual does not exceed $500 annually). Multiple Education IRAs could be created for one beneficiary, but the contribution limit of all contributions for a single beneficiary is $500 in any one tax year.

No contribution may be made by any person to an Education IRA during any year in which any contributions are made by anyone to a qualified state tuition program on behalf of the same beneficiary.

Example: If grandparents contribute to a qualified state tuition program on behalf of a child, and the parents establish an Education IRA for the same child, the parents cannot make the $500 annual contribution to the Education IRA in any tax year in which the grandparents have made a contribution to the state tuition program on that child's behalf.

Income Limits. The $500 annual contribution limit for Education IRAs is phased out for single contributors with modified AGI between $95,000 and $110,000 ($150,000 and $160,000 for couples filing jointly). Individuals with modified AGI above the phaseout range cannot make contributions to an Education IRA established on behalf of any other individual.

Distributions. Distributions from an Education IRA are excludable from your gross income to the extent that the distribution does not exceed qualified higher education expenses (postsecondary tuition, fees, books, supplies, equipment, and certain room and board expenses) incurred by the beneficiary during the year the distribution is made. The beneficiary can be enrolled at an eligible educational institution on a full-time, half-time, or less than half-time basis. However, certain room and board expenses are qualified higher education expenses only if the student incurring such expenses is enrolled at an eligible educational institution on at least a half-time basis.

Special Rules. Any balance remaining in an Education IRA at the time a beneficiary becomes 30 years old must be distributed, and the earnings portion of such a distribution will be included in the gross income of the beneficiary and subject to an additional 10% penalty tax because the distribution was not for educational purposes. The law allows tax-free (and penalty-free) transfers and rollovers of account balances from one Education IRA benefiting one beneficiary to another Education IRA benefiting a different beneficiary (as well as redesignations of the named beneficiary), provided that the new beneficiary is a member of the family of the old beneficiary and that the transfer or rollover is made before the old beneficiary reaches age 30.

If a beneficiary's interest in an Education IRA is rolled over to another beneficiary, there are no transfer tax consequences as long as the two beneficiaries are in the same generation. If a beneficiary's interest is rolled over to a beneficiary in a lower generation (e.g., parent to child or uncle to niece), the five-year averaging rule described in connection with qualified state tuition programs may be applied to exempt up to $50,000 of the transfer from gift tax.

401(k) Plans

If your employer has a 401(k) plan or another plan that allows you to set aside income (e.g., a tax-sheltered annuity or 403(b) plan, which is generally available to employees of tax-exempt and educational organizations), you can elect to defer a certain amount of your salary on a before-tax basis. Such amounts are withheld from your salary and are not reported as income until withdrawn from the plan. Income earned on your 401(k) investment is also tax-deferred. Unlike an IRA, you may be able to borrow from your 401(k) plan without penalty. Subject to nondiscrimination tests that apply to 401(k) plans, you can elect to defer your wages up to a maximum of $10,500 in 2000. Also, many employers provide a matching contribution in their 401(k) plans. For example, a 401(k) plan may provide that, for each $1 you contribute, the employer will contribute 50¢. (With this kind of plan, you would receive an immediate return on your investment of 50%.)

Because funds in a 401(k) plan accumulate tax-free, it is usually a good idea to make as large a contribution to your 401(k) plan as possible. In addition, because contributions to your 401(k) plan are made on a before-tax basis, any contributions made to the plan reduce your adjusted gross income.

TAXSAVER

Although the funds in your 401(k) plan are meant to be set aside for your retirement, you may still have access to them if you need money at an earlier time. Your plan may permit you to borrow from your account, subject to strict rules. Despite the restrictions, you may be better off borrowing from your retirement fund than getting a loan from your bank. If the loan from the bank is for personal purposes, it will result in nondeductible interest. Although a loan from your 401(k) plan does not generate deductible interest, you may get a better rate and the interest you pay is allocated directly back to your account.

In addition to the general qualified plan distribution rules discussed below, 401(k) plans are also subject to special rules regarding certain distributions. Specifically, employee deferrals cannot be distributed prior to one of the following events:

- retirement
- death
- disability
- separation from service with the employer
- attainment of age 59½
- termination of the plan
- disposition of corporate assets or disposition of subsidiary
- hardship

SIMPLE PLANS

Employers with 100 or fewer employees earning at least $5,000 and who do not maintain another employer-sponsored retirement plan are eligible to set up Savings Incentive Match Plan for Employees of Small Employers (SIMPLE) plans. These plans, which are not subject to some of the complicated rules that apply to other types of retirement plans, can be adopted as an IRA or as a part of a 401(k) plan. All employees who earn more than $5,000 a year must be eligible to participate, and self-employed individuals may also participate in SIMPLE plans. In general, contributions to a SIMPLE plan are not taxable until withdrawn.

The employer generally must either match elective employee contributions (limited to $6,000 annually) dollar-for-dollar up to 3% of compensation or make a "nonelective" contribution of 2% of compensation on behalf of each eligible employee. No other contributions may be made to a SIMPLE account. Contributions to a SIMPLE account generally are deductible by the employer; however, matching contributions are deductible only if made by the due date (including extensions) of the employer's tax return.

Employers are given a two-year grace period to maintain a SIMPLE plan once they are no longer eligible to participate.

TAXSAVER

If you earn limited amounts of self-employment income, a SIMPLE IRA may allow you to shelter the maximum amount from taxes. Although employee *elective contributions to SIMPLE IRAs are capped at $6,000 per year, contributions are not subject to a percentage-of-compensation limitation as they are in a Keogh plan. Thus, if you received $10,000 in self-employment income, you could deduct a contribution of $6,000 (or 60%) to a SIMPLE IRA, plus any matching contributions.*

DISTRIBUTIONS FROM IRAS AND 401(K) PLANS

The rules governing the taxation of distributions from IRAs and 401(k) plans are very complex. Not only can the tax rules for ordinary retirement withdrawals be confusing, but the tax law also provides for complicated penalty taxes if distributions are received too early (generally before age 59½), or if distributions begin too late (generally after April 1 of the year following the year you turn age 70½).

Tax Rules for Ordinary Withdrawals. In general, distributions from IRAs and 401(k) plans are taxed as ordinary income. If nondeductible contributions have been made to an IRA, however, distributions are taxed in much the same way as an annuity. The portion of each distribution that is attributable to nondeductible contributions, if any, is excluded from your taxable income. The ratio of each distribution to be excluded is determined by dividing undistributed nondeductible contributions by your total IRA account balance. If no nondeductible contributions have been made, then the entire distribution is considered ordinary income. (Nondeductible contributions to IRAs have only been allowed since 1987.) Premature distributions from Roth IRAs are considered to come from nondeductible contributions. Other distributions are tax-free if you meet the requirements.

Lump Sum Distributions. A lump sum distribution is the distribution within a single tax year of an employee's entire account balance made on the occurrence of certain events (e.g., attainment of age 59½). Formerly, individuals who received lump sum distributions could lower their tax by taking advantage of five-year income averaging. Congress repealed five-year averaging for post-1999 tax years. However, individuals who were at least age 50 on January 1, 1986, remain eligible for 10-year averaging and capital gains treatment on the portion of a lump sum distribution attributable to pre-1974 service. Taxpayers using 10-year averaging must use the tax rates in effect in 1986, which were generally higher than current rates.

Distribution of Employer Securities. If you receive a distribution consisting of employer securities, you may be able to defer tax on the "net unrealized appreciation" until you sell the securities. This treatment is available for lump sum distributions of employer securities from a tax-qualified employer retirement plan that are attributable to employer contributions. The "net unrealized appreciation" is the price increase in the distributed securities during the period they are held by the plan.

Penalty Tax for Early Distributions. Most distributions from qualified retirement plans made to employees before they reach age 59½ are subject to an additional tax of 10% on the taxable part of the distribution. For this purpose, a qualified retirement plan means: (1) a qualified employee retirement plan (including a 401(k) plan); (2) a qualified annuity plan; (3) a tax-sheltered annuity plan for employees of public schools or tax-exempt organizations; or (4) an IRA (including a SEP or a SIMPLE IRA).

Exceptions: This additional tax does not apply, under the following circumstances, to distributions that are:
1. Made to a beneficiary or to the estate of the participant on or after his or her death;
2. Made because the participant is totally and permanently disabled;
3. Made as part of a series of substantially equal periodic (at least annual) payments over the participant's life expectancy or the joint life expectancies of the participant and his or her beneficiary. (This exception does not apply to non-IRA distributions unless the distribution begins after you've left your job);
4. Made to an employee who left his or her job in or after the year in which he or she reached age 55;
5. Paid to the employee, to the extent the employee has deductible expenses for medical care (whether or not the employee itemizes deductions for the tax year);
6. Paid to another person designated in a qualified domestic relations order; or
7. Made to an employee who, as of March 1, 1986, left his or her job and began receiving benefits from the qualified plan under a written election designating a specific schedule of benefit payments.
   Exceptions 4 and 6 above do not apply to IRAs.

TaxAlert

Congress has eased restrictions for preretirement IRA distributions for educational and home-buying expenses. Under the new rules, the 10% early withdrawal penalty does not apply to distributions from retirement IRAs if you used the amounts to (a) pay qualified higher education expenses (including those related to graduate-level courses) for you, your spouse, or any child or grandchild, or (b) pay acquisition costs of a principal residence for the purchase of a first-time home for you, your spouse, or any child or grandchild. A qualified first-time home-buyer is someone who has had no ownership interest in a residence during the past two years. The aggregate amount of the distribution for first-time home purchase cannot exceed a lifetime cap of $10,000.

Penalty Tax for Late Distributions. Qualified plan distributions can generally be deferred until after an employee retires without regard to the employee's age. However, non-Roth IRA distributions must begin by April 1 of the year following the calendar year in which the IRA holder attains age 70½ to avoid incurring a minimum distribution penalty.

As a minimum distribution, the individual must either (1) receive his or her entire interest in the plan by the required beginning date or (2) begin to receive regular partial distributions by the beginning date in an amount large enough to use up the entire interest over the employee's life expectancy or over the joint life expectancies of the employee and a designated surviving beneficiary. The payout can also be over a period that is less than the employee's life expectancy.

If the required minimum distribution is not made, an excise tax equal to 50% of the amount required to be (but not actually) distributed is imposed. This excise tax may be waived if you establish that the shortfall in distributions was due to reasonable error and that reasonable steps are being taken to remedy the shortfall.

TaxSaver

One significant advantage of the Roth IRA over the traditional IRA is that the Roth IRA is not subject to the minimum distribution rules when the taxpayer turns age 70½. In addition, unlike a traditional IRA, contributions can be made to a Roth IRA even after the taxpayer turns 70½. Consequently, the Roth IRA offers potential for a large buildup of the taxpayer's estate that can be passed on to heirs.

TaxSaver

Distributions from Pension Plans. *The Small Business Job Protection Act of 1996 changed the requirements concerning when distributions from pension plans must be made. Beginning after December 31, 1996, distributions from qualified pension, profit-sharing (including 401(k)), stock bonus, and tax sheltered annuity plans must begin by April 1 of the calendar year following either (1) the calendar year in which the employee attains age 70½ or (2) the calendar year in which the employee retires, whichever occurs later. (The law has not changed for IRAs.)*

Individuals who are 5% owners of the employer are required to begin receiving qualified plan distributions no later than April 1 of the calendar year that follows the year in which the 5% owner reaches age 70½.

Participants in qualified plans who currently receive distributions, but who do not have to receive distributions under the new law, may, if the plan allows, be able to stop receiving distributions until required to do so under the new law.

Nontaxable Distributions. Some distributions from an IRA or 401(k) plan are not taxed. These include: (1) rollovers (discussed below), (2) withdrawals of IRA contributions by the due date (including extensions) of the return for the year the contributions are made, and (3) withdrawals of excess IRA contributions.

Rollovers. A rollover is a tax-free transfer of cash or other assets from a qualified retirement plan to an eligible retirement plan. An eligible retirement plan is an IRA, a qualified employee retirement plan, or a qualified annuity plan. A rollover may also include a distribution from one IRA and a contribution to another. You cannot roll over a distribution from an employee retirement plan directly to a Roth IRA. You must roll over to a traditional IRA and then convert to a Roth IRA if you are eligible.

The rollover must be completed not later than the 60th day following the day on which you receive the distribution. Generally, only one rollover is allowed per year for rollovers between IRAs. If you transfer funds directly between trustees of your IRAs and you never actually control or use the account assets, however, this is not considered a rollover and you may transfer your account as often as you like.

TaxSaver

Mandatory Withholding on Rollovers. *A mandatory withholding of 20% is imposed on distributions eligible for rollover unless the plan making the distribution directly transfers the payout to the IRA or other qualified plan that is designated to receive the rollover. Traditionally, distributions have been paid directly to retiring or terminating employees who in turn decided how much of the proceeds should be kept or rolled over. This rule, however, sets a trap if the distribution check is made out to you. On a $100,000 distribution, for example, you would receive only $80,000 after withholding. If you plan to roll over the entire $100,000 to your IRA, you would have to come up with an additional $20,000 in order for the total amount deposited in the IRA within 60 days of receiving the $80,000 check to equal the original $100,000 distribution. Otherwise, the $20,000 withheld would be treated as a taxable distribution subject to ordinary income tax and, if applicable, the 10% early distribution tax (discussed above). Note that the $20,000 withheld is refundable, but only after you file your Form 1040 after the close of the year. However, a check merely delivered to you will not present a problem, so long as it is not negotiable by you. For example, a check made payable to "ABC Bank as trustee of the IRA of John Q. Smith" is okay. Mandatory withholding does not apply to distributions from an IRA.*

TaxSaver

Because of the mandatory withholding rules, if you are going to receive a payment from a qualified plan that is to be rolled over to an IRA, make sure that the plan transfers the funds directly to the IRA through a trustee-to-trustee payment.

You can roll over the otherwise taxable portion of a distribution of any part of your account balance into a qualified retirement plan, annuity plan, or IRA. A distribution that is required for an individual who is over age

70½ or that is part of a series of substantially equal periodic payments for life or a term of 10 or more years is ineligible for tax-free rollover.

TAX*ALERT*

For tax years beginning after 1996, a tax-free rollover may also be made between SIMPLE plans. In addition, after two years of participating in a SIM-PLE plan, your account can be rolled over to an IRA tax-free. If you stop participating in a SIMPLE account, such as when you leave your employment, your SIMPLE account will be treated as an IRA.

TAX*SAVER*

If you need money for no longer than 60 days, consider withdrawing the money from your IRA if you are sure you will have the cash to put into another IRA within 60 days. You will not incur any tax or penalties, and you will have the cash for 60 days. You can do this only once in a 12-month period.

SIMPLIFIED EMPLOYEE PENSIONS

A simplified employee pension (SEP) is a written plan that allows an employer to make contributions toward an employee's retirement without becoming involved in more complex retirement plans. If you are self-employed, you can contribute to your own SEP.

The SEP rules permit an employer to annually contribute to and deduct from each participating employee's SEP up to 15% of the employee's compensation or $25,500, whichever is less. (The $25,500 is based on compensation being limited to $170,000. This amount is adjusted annually for inflation, but the amount contributed can never exceed $30,000 in any one year.) If you are self-employed, special rules apply when figuring the maximum deduction for these contributions. In determining the percentage limit on contributions, compensation is net earnings from self-employment, taking into account the contributions to the SEP.

TAX*SAVER*

Even if your employer makes contributions to a SEP for your account, you can make contributions to your own IRA. The IRA deduction rules, previously discussed, apply to any amounts you contribute to your IRA.

TAX*SAVER*

A self-employed person can claim a deduction to a SEP as long as the contribution is made by the due date of the return, including extensions. Even if you failed to set up a plan by December 31, you can still establish a SEP after the end of the year and make a timely payment.

TaxAlert

SEPs permitting salary reduction contributions cannot be established after 1996, although SEPs that allowed elective deferrals before 1997 can continue to do so.

Keogh (HR 10) Plans

If you are self-employed and own your own business, you may set up a retirement plan, commonly known as a Keogh or an HR 10 plan. You must have earned income from the trade or business for which the plan was established to take a deduction for a contribution to the plan. A Keogh plan may be either a "defined contribution plan" or a "defined benefit plan."

Under a defined contribution plan, such as a profit-sharing plan or a money purchase pension plan, the benefit you eventually receive is based solely on the contributions credited to your account and the earning attributable to those contributions. Typically, contributions to a profit-sharing plan are made out of a company's profits, and therefore can vary from year to year. Contributions to a money purchase pension plan are usually calculated as a percentage of self-employed income and must be made whether the company had a profit or loss for the year.

Under a defined benefit plan, you are promised a fixed benefit and the annual contributions are based on the amount that is actuarially needed to provide you that benefit at a normal retirement age.

Contribution Limits. Deductible contributions to a profit-sharing plan are generally limited to the lesser of $25,500 (the $25,500 is based on compensation being limited to $170,000; this amount is adjusted annually for inflation, but the amount contributed can never exceed $30,000 in any one year) or 15% of earned income for the year; deductible contributions to a money purchase pension plan are generally limited to the lesser of $30,000 or 25% of earned income for the year. If you maintain a combination of a profit-sharing Keogh plan and a money purchase Keogh plan, the maximum combined deductible contributions are limited to $30,000 or 25% of earned income per year.

The current maximum benefit that can be promised at retirement age under a defined benefit plan is generally the lesser of 100% of earned income (determined on a three-year average basis) or $135,000. This dollar limit is adjusted annually for cost-of-living increases. The $30,000 defined contribution plan limit will also be adjusted for cost-of-living increases in $5,000 increments.

Note that, for purposes of these limitations, "earned income" must be reduced by an amount equal to one-half of your self-employment taxes for the year and by your Keogh contribution.

Three Key Keogh Rules:

1. A Keogh plan must be established before the end of your tax year. Contributions can be deducted if made by the due date for your tax return (including extensions).
2. The plan must be written. Prototype plans can frequently be obtained from banks and other financial institutions.
3. A summary description of the plan must be provided to your employees. There are specific definitions of employees who must be covered and specific rules on such items as discrimination and vesting.

COMPANY RETIREMENT PLANS

For a discussion of how company retirement plan benefits are taxed, see Chapter 12, Retirement Planning.

TaxSaver

If you are employed and attained age 70¹/₂ in 1997 or after, you may be able to defer distributions from your employer retirement plan until you retire, if the plan allows. The old rule, changed by the 1997 Tax Act, required all employer plans to begin distributions to employees the year after they attained age 70¹/₂. Delaying distributions, if allowed by your plan, may be advantageous because you can continue to benefit from tax-deferred earnings in the plan.

TaxAlert

States Can't Tax Former Residents' Pensions. *A state is prohibited from imposing income tax on any retirement income collected by an individual who is not then a resident or domiciliary of that state. Retirement income from a broad range of plans and trusts is covered, including:*

- *qualified pension, profit-sharing, and stock bonus plans (such as 401(k) plans),*
- *simplified employee pensions (SEPs),*
- *Code Section 403(b) tax-sheltered annuity arrangements (often available to teachers),*
- *individual retirement account or individual retirement annuities,*
- *eligible deferred compensation plans as defined in Code Section 457 (plans set up by state and local governments and tax-exempt organizations),*
- *any federal government retirement program, and*
- *special employee-funded trusts set up before 1959, as described under Code Section 501(c)(18).*

In addition, the law exempts from state taxation certain income received from nonqualified deferred compensation plans in the form of an annuity over 10 or more years. It also protects any distribution received from a nonqualified ERISA "excess" plan after termination of employment.

6

Charitable Contributions

INTRODUCTION

You are generally entitled to a tax deduction for charitable contributions you make. How you make your contributions and even the type of property used—cash, stock, or whatever—can affect whether you get the maximum tax benefit from your contribution. This chapter discusses some of the tax strategies you can use so that contributions you make can have the most impact on both the charities you're benefiting and the taxes you're paying.

A charitable contribution for which a tax deduction may be available is a contribution or gift to, or for the use of, *a qualified organization* (see below). In many cases, the tax benefit can lower the cost of making a gift, perhaps enabling you to give even more generously.

Making the most of your contributions will depend on:

- Who is the recipient—a public charity or a private foundation?
- When will you make the gift—now or later?
- What will you give—cash or property?
- How will you make the gift—outright or deferred?

WHO IS THE RECIPIENT?

Qualified Organizations. Only gifts to organizations recognized by the IRS as charities are deductible. You *cannot assume* that an organization to which you want to contribute is officially recognized as a charitable organization and that your contribution will be deductible for federal income tax purposes. Many tax-exempt organizations are not qualified to receive tax-deductible contributions. IRS Publication No. 78, which is periodically supplemented, contains a list of qualified organizations. A listing of qualified organizations is also available on the IRS Web site, www.irs.gov.

You may deduct a contribution you make to, or for the use of, the following organizations:

- A state, a U.S. possession (including Puerto Rico), a political subdivision of a state or possession, the United States, or the District of Columbia, if the contribution is made only for public purposes
- A community chest, corporation, trust, fund, or foundation organized and operated only for charitable, religious, educational, scientific, or literary purposes, or to sponsor national or international amateur sports competition, or for the prevention of cruelty to children or animals
- War veterans' organizations, including posts, auxiliaries, societies, trusts, or foundations organized in the United States or its possessions
- Domestic fraternal societies operating under the lodge system, if the contribution is to be used only for charitable, religious, scientific, literary, or educational purposes, or for the prevention of cruelty to children or animals
- Nonprofit cemetery companies, if the contribution can be used only for the perpetual care of the cemetery as a whole, and not for a particular lot or mausoleum crypt

Examples of Qualified Organizations. Qualified organizations include the following:
- Nonprofit volunteer fire companies
- Public parks and recreation facilities
- Nonprofit hospitals and medical research organizations
- Churches and other religious organizations
- Most nonprofit educational institutions
- Most nonprofit charitable organizations, such as the Boy Scouts, CARE, Gifts in Kind, Girls and Boys Clubs of America, Girl Scouts, Goodwill Industries, Red Cross, Salvation Army, United Way, and Volunteers of America.

Deductible Contributions. Only individuals who itemize deductions may deduct charitable contributions. Even then, deductions for charitable contributions are subject to the overall limit on itemized deductions discussed on page 56.

Your total deduction for charitable contributions is limited to 50% of your contribution base, an amount generally equal to your adjusted gross income, but in some cases you may be limited to 20% or 30% of your contribution base. See "Limits on Deductions" later in this chapter, especially the section on "When Contributions Are More Than 20% of Your Income."

Benefits Received. If you make a contribution to a charitable organization and also receive a benefit from that organization, you may deduct only the amount that exceeds the value of the benefit you receive. If you pay more than fair market value to a qualified organization for merchandise, goods, or services, the amount you pay that is more than the value of the item may be a charitable contribution.

Example: If you contribute $100 to a symphony orchestra and receive a pair of tickets worth $25, your deduction is limited to $75. Generally, the charity will advise you of the value of the benefit and how much you can deduct. The discussion beginning on page 118 explains what is needed to document these types of contributions.

Dues, fees, or assessments are deductible if you pay them to qualified organizations. However, you may deduct only the amount that is more than the value of the benefits you receive. You may not deduct dues, fees, or assessments paid to country clubs and other social organizations.

Athletics Tickets.   If you make a payment to or for the benefit of a college or university that would be deductible as a charitable contribution but for the fact that you receive (directly or indirectly) the right to purchase seating for a sporting event at the school's stadium, only 80% of your payment is treated as a charitable contribution. But there's a catch: the 80% limitation does not apply if you receive tickets or seating (rather than merely the right to purchase tickets) in return for the payment. In that case, the deduction must be reduced by the value attributable to the tickets.

Out-of-Pocket Expenses.   You may deduct certain amounts you pay in the course of providing volunteer services to a charitable organization. You may not, however, deduct the value of your time or services.

Car Expenses.   You may deduct unreimbursed out-of-pocket expenses, such as the cost of gas, that are directly related to the use of your car in giving services to a charitable organization. You may not deduct any part of general repair and maintenance expenses, depreciation, or insurance.

If you do not want to deduct your actual expense, you may use a standard rate of 14 cents a mile to figure your contribution deduction for the use of your car in providing services to the charitable organization. You may deduct parking fees and tolls in addition to the standard mileage rate. However, depreciation and insurance are not deductible.

Travel Expenses.   You may deduct your transportation and other travel expenses while you are away from home performing services for a charitable organization. Deductible travel expenses include: air, rail, and bus transportation; out-of-pocket expenses for your car; parking fees and tolls; taxi fares and other costs of transportation between the airport or station and your hotel; lodging cost; and the cost of meals. Travel expenses are only deductible if there is no significant element of personal pleasure, recreation, or vacation in the travel.

When Deductible.   To deduct your contributions, you must make them in cash or other property before the close of your tax year. If you make a contribution with borrowed funds, a deduction is allowed in the year you make the contribution, regardless of when you repay the loan. Contributions charged on your credit or charge card are deductible in the year you make the charge, not when you pay the bill.

TAXORGANIZER

Documents and Records. A volunteer who incurs unreimbursed expenses while performing services for a charity will be treated as having sufficient substantiation for the deduction if he or she has: a written record showing the name of the charity, the date and amount of the expense, and a letter or other communication from the charity describing the services provided by the taxpayer and stating whether the charity provided any goods or services in consideration, in whole or in part, for the unreimbursed expenses.

Gifts of properly endorsed stock certificates are deductible in the year you mail or personally deliver the certificates to the charity or to the charity's representative. However, if you give the certificates to your broker or the issuing corporation for transfer to the charity, a deduction is not allowed until the stock is transferred on the corporation's books. If you plan to give stock to a charity, plan far enough in advance to assure yourself of having the certificates or of having the broker or issuing corporation complete the transfer on the corporation's books. A note or a pledge to a charity is not deductible until it is paid.

TAXSAVER

Planning Your Charitable Gifts. For most people, the simplest approach to gift-giving is to give an outright gift. Even then, proper planning can pay surprising dividends for you.

Consider your tax rates in planning charitable contributions. A $1,000 contribution reduces taxes by $150 for a taxpayer in the 15% bracket, $280 for a taxpayer in the 28% bracket, $310 for a taxpayer in the 31% tax bracket, and so forth. The after-tax cost of a contribution decreases as your tax rate increases. Thus, if you can control the timing of your charitable contributions, you should consider making larger contributions in years in which you are subject to high marginal tax rates.

Consider also when your contribution is made. A deductible contribution reduces the tax due April 15 of the year following the contribution. A contribution made on December 31 reduces the tax due by as much as the contribution made on the prior January 1, except you have the use of the money from January 2 to December 30. While it is not always practical to defer your giving until the last day of the year, you should consider the time value of money when planning substantial gifts.

PRIVATE FOUNDATIONS

A private foundation is an entity that can be formed and controlled by you or your family to support your charitable activities or to make charitable grants according to your wishes. Once the foundation qualifies for tax-exempt status, your charitable contributions to it are deductible, subject to the limitations discussed later.

TAXSAVER

You don't have to be inordinately rich to consider setting up your own private foundation. Private foundations afford you a good deal of flexibility in determining how your charitable contributions will be spent, may be controlled by a single individual or family, and provide some tax benefits, too. The foundation has to be set up according to specific IRS rules, and you will need professional advice.

__Example:__ Suppose you want to commit to making a contribution of $20,000 a year to a charity for the next five years. Assuming you are in the 39.6% tax bracket and can realize an 8% rate of return on your investments, (1) you could contribute about $80,000 to your private foundation, which would make the payments in each of the five years, or (2) you could make these contributions out of your current income. Choosing (2) would cost you more because the tax savings would be spread out over the five-year period as the contributions were made. By choosing (1), you could claim an $80,000 deduction the year you contributed the money to your foundation.

TAXALERT

Deductions for donations of appreciated capital gain property (which has been held for more than 12 months) donated to a private nonoperating foundation are limited to your basis in the property unless the property contributed constitutes qualified appreciated stock, in which case you can claim a deduction for the appreciated value of the stock—not just your basis. Qualified appreciated stock is stock that has been held for more than one year and for which market quotations are readily available on an established securities market.

TAXSAVER

The tax benefits from creating a private foundation can also be achieved by contributing to a community trust, foundation, or donor-advised fund. Community trusts, community foundations, and donor-advised funds are public charities in which you may establish a segregated account, thus avoiding the costs of setting up your own private foundation as well as the percentage limitations of a private foundation. However, because they are public charities, you will not have the same degree of control over the use of the contributed funds as you would with your own private foundation.

NONDEDUCTIBLE CONTRIBUTIONS

Some organizations are not qualified to receive tax-deductible contributions. For example, contributions to the following organizations are not deductible:

- Chambers of commerce and other business leagues or organizations
- Civic leagues

- Country clubs and other social clubs
- Homeowners' associations
- Political organizations (and candidates)

In addition, contributions used to influence legislation are not deductible. Even if an organization is a qualified organization, no deduction is allowed for contributions to the organization that are earmarked for use in, or in connection with, attempting to influence the general public on legislative matters, elections, or referenda.

Direct contributions to needy or worthy individuals are not deductible. The contributions must be made to, or for the use of, a qualified organization and not earmarked by you for the use of a specific person.

GIFTS OF PROPERTY

If you donate property to a qualified organization, you generally may deduct the fair market value of the property at the time of the contribution. However, if the property increased in value while you owned it, you may have to make some adjustments. (See "Giving Property That Has Increased in Value," below.)

Determining Fair Market Value. Fair market value is the price at which property would change hands between a willing buyer and willing seller, neither having to buy or sell, and both having reasonable knowledge of all the necessary facts.

Used Items. The fair market value of used items is ordinarily far less than their original cost. You should claim as the value the price that buyers of used items actually pay in stores where such property is for sale, such as consignment or thrift shops. (See IRS Publication 561, *Determining the Value of Donated Property,* for further details.)

Giving Property That Has Increased in Value. As noted above, if you donated property to a qualified organization, you generally may deduct the fair market value of the property at the time of the contribution. The exception to this rule is when the property you donate has increased in value. In this case, the amount of the deduction is the fair market value of the property minus the amount that would have been ordinary income or short-term capital gain had the property been sold at its fair market value on the date of the gift. (Ordinary income property would include items such as inventory; any property held one year or less is short-term capital gain property.) The following are two examples of these rules.

Example: You donate stock that you held for five months to your church. The fair market value of the stock is $20,000, but you paid $16,000 (your basis). Because the $4,000 of appreciation would be a short-term capital gain if you sold the stock, your deduction is limited to $16,000 (fair market value less the appreciation).

Example: You donate 300 shares of stock to your local charitable hospital on December 15, 2000. The stock has a fair market value of $30,000 on the date of contribution. You acquired the stock in the following three transactions:

Date of Acquisition	Number of Shares	Total Cost
January 15, 1999	100	$5,500
February 1, 1999	100	7,000
January 15, 2000	100	8,500

Your deduction is $28,500. If the stock had been sold for $30,000 on the date of the contribution, the gain from the first two purchases would have been long-term capital gain. However, a sale of the third 100 shares would have generated $1,500 in short-term capital gain. This latter gain must be deducted from the $30,000 fair market value to arrive at the amount of your deduction.

TaxSaver

Donating Appreciated Securities. *If you donate appreciated securities that you have held for the required long-term holding period, you benefit in two ways. First, you are entitled to a deduction based on the fair market value of the securities. Second, you avoid paying tax on the appreciation. Consequently, the real cost to you of your contribution is reduced by the tax benefit of the contribution deduction you claim and the tax you avoided by not selling the appreciated property.*

Example: You have adjusted gross income of $190,000 and are in the 36% tax bracket. If you give stock that cost you $20,000 but is now worth $50,000 directly to a public charity, your taxable income will be reduced by $50,000 and you will have a tax savings of about $18,000 (provided you are not subject to the alternative minimum tax). If you sell the stock first and give the proceeds to the charity, you will still have a $50,000 deduction, but you will also pay tax on the entire $30,000 of capital gain, probably at the maximum capital gain rate of 20%—$6,000. This will reduce your overall tax savings to $12,000 ($18,000 less $6,000). And this simple example does not take into account the fact that the additional capital gain income will increase your overall limit on itemized deductions (see page 56)—reducing your tax savings even more. Thus, the best approach in this example is to give the appreciated stock to charity. You get a $50,000 deduction and recognize no gain.

On the other hand, if the property value has decreased below your cost, it usually is better to sell the property and donate the proceeds. By selling it you will realize a capital loss that may be used to offset other capital gains or—within limits—other income.

TaxSaver

To ensure that you get the maximum tax benefit from a contribution of appreciated property, be sure that the property qualifies as "long-term capital

*gain property.'' For this purpose, property held for more than one year con-
stitutes long-term capital gain property.*

Bargain Sales

A bargain sale of property to a qualified charitable organization—that is,
a sale at less than the property's fair market value—is partly a charitable
contribution and partly a sale. The part that is considered a charitable
contribution is the difference between the fair market value at the time of
sale and the amount realized. The part that is considered a sale is the
amount realized. It may result in a taxable gain. To determine the amount
of the gain, you must allocate your adjusted basis in the property between
the part that is considered a charitable contribution and the part sold. The
adjusted basis of the part sold is figured as follows:

$$\text{Adjusted basis of entire property} \times \frac{\text{Amount realized}}{\text{Fair market value of entire property}}$$

TaxSaver

*Suppose you own a piece of real estate that your town would like to have
for a park. It has a fair market value of $125,000 and you paid $50,000 for
it 10 years ago. Naturally, the town would like you to donate the property.
While you are willing to make a contribution to the town, that's a little more
than you had in mind. You would like to recoup your original cash investment.*

*If you sell the property to the town for $50,000, here is what happens:
you get a $75,000 charitable deduction ($125,000 [fair market value] −
$50,000 [amount realized]). But because the transaction is treated as part
sale, you incur a capital gain tax computed as follows:*

*The basis for the property sold is $20,000 ($50,000 [basis of entire prop-
erty]) ×*

$$\frac{\$50,000 \; [amount \; realized]}{\$125,000 \; [FMV \; of \; entire \; property]}$$

*$50,000 [amount realized] − $20,000 [basis of property sold] = $30,000
[taxable gain]*

$30,000 [gain] × 20% [Long Term Capital Gain tax rate] = $6,000

*However, the $75,000 deduction will reduce your taxes by $29,700 (as-
suming a 39.6% marginal tax rate).*

*So you will actually net $73,700 from the transaction: $50,000 (amount
realized) + $23,700 (net tax savings).*

Limits on Deductions

Provided your contributions for the year otherwise qualify, and they are
20% or less of your adjusted gross income, they will not be subject to
percentage limitations; there are other limitations, however.

Future Interest in Tangible Personal Property. You may deduct the value of a charitable contribution of a future interest in tangible personal property only after all intervening interests and rights to the actual possession or enjoyment of the property have either expired or been turned over to someone other than yourself or a related party or organization.

A future interest is any interest that is to begin at some future time, regardless of whether it is designated as a future interest under state law. The amount of the deduction is the value of the future interest when you and a related person no longer have an interest in the tangible personal property. When these interests end, you may still claim the deduction even if there are other outstanding interests that must end before the future interest is realized by the qualified charitable organization.

Example: You transferred a sculpture in 2000 to your son to use and enjoy for life. When your son dies the sculpture will go to the local museum of art. If your son irrevocably transfers his life interest to a local college or any other unrelated person in a later year, you may take a charitable deduction in that year, but not sooner. The amount of your deduction is the value of the future interest in the sculpture at the time of the transfer to the unrelated person.

When Contributions Are More Than 20% of Your Income. If your contributions are more than 20% of your adjusted gross income, the amount of your deduction may be limited to 20%, 30%, or 50% of your adjusted gross income.

How much you can deduct depends on three main factors: the type of charity to which the contribution is given—a public charity or a nonoperating private foundation; the nature of the contribution—cash or property; and the manner of the contribution—to the charity or for the use of the charity. Sometimes the use to which the property will be put also needs to be considered. In addition to the percentage limitation, ordering rules apply. These may limit deductions if multiple contributions are made during the year. You should consult with your tax advisor.

Partial Interest in Property. Generally, no deduction is allowed for a charitable contribution of less than your entire interest in property. For example, the owner of property will not get a deduction for giving a "life estate interest" in the property to charity. (A life estate interest is an interest in property that terminates upon the death of the life estate's owner.) A contribution of the right to use property is a contribution of less than your entire interest in that property and is not deductible.

Exceptions: There are some situations in which you may claim a deduction for a charitable contribution that is less than your entire interest in the property:
1. *Undivided part of your entire interest.* A contribution of an undivided part of your entire interest in property must consist of a part of each

and every substantial interest or right you own in the property. It must extend over the entire term of your interest in the property.

2. *Remainder interest in a personal residence or farm.* You may take a charitable deduction for a gift to a qualified organization of a remainder interest in a personal residence or in a farm, if the gift is irrevocable. A remainder interest in an asset is an interest that takes effect after a specified period of time—often the lifetime of the person giving the interest.

TAXSAVER

Giving a Remainder Interest in Your Personal Residence. *If you give a remainder interest in a personal residence (or a farm) to a qualified charity, the present value of the remainder interest is deductible as a charitable contribution. One significant advantage of such a gift is that you suffer no loss of income or increase in expense from the gift, but you still gain a current income tax deduction. The gift may be made without the use of a trust. In addition, you continue to use and enjoy the home for life.*

To qualify for the deduction, the gift must be a gift of your personal residence. The home does not have to be your principal residence. Thus, the gift may be your vacation home.

The charity receives no immediate benefit; however, the opportunity for future benefits can be substantial.

Example: *Assume a 62-year-old individual owns a personal residence with a fair market value of $162,000. The land on which the residence is located is valued at $42,000. The residence has a remaining useful life of 35 years and an estimated salvage value of $30,000. According to IRS tables, the value of the remainder interest in the home and the land (based on the donor's life expectancy) is approximately $40,000—which is currently deductible on a donation of the interest. Besides a substantial income tax deduction, the donor will receive an estate tax deduction for the value of the interest that passes to charity at his or her death.*

---

3. *Partial interests comprising your entire interest given to different charities.* A contribution of a life estate to one charity and the remainder interest to another charity will constitute a deductible even though the interests given to each charity are partial interests.

4. *A qualified conservation contribution.* A "qualified real property interest" such as a perpetual restriction on the use that may be made of the real property, made to a qualified organization exclusively for conservation purposes will constitute a deductible interest even though it is a partial interest.

5. *Interest transferred in trust.* A charitable deduction is available for the transfer of an income or remainder interest in property if the property is held in a qualifying charitable trust.

TaxSaver

Deferred Giving. You may want to make a contribution to charity but you need all your income for current expenses. You have two alternatives. You can either leave the property to charity when you die or give the property to charity now, subject to a retained income interest. Deferred giving, as the latter technique is known, simply involves a present gift to charity of the future use and employment of property. It offers one big advantage: you can get an income tax deduction now. Deferred giving also allows you to satisfy your charitable goals now while continuing to receive needed income. Moreover, you may even be able to enhance your cash flow in retirement years. Following are some deferred giving techniques.

CHARITABLE REMAINDER TRUSTS

You can transfer cash or income-producing property into a charitable remainder trust and receive an immediate tax deduction. The trust needs to provide that at least annual payments be made to you or any other designated beneficiary that is not a charity either over a term not exceeding 20 years or over the lifetime of the beneficiary or beneficiaries. When the term or lifetime interest ends, the charity will have full use of the entire property. Although actual receipt of the charity's interest is deferred, you receive an *immediate* income tax deduction for the present value of the interest that passes to charity. Later, the trust assets will be included in your taxable estate, but you will also receive an estate tax charitable deduction for the value that passes to charity.

The lifetime gift or the charitable bequest must be in the form of a charitable remainder annuity trust, a charitable remainder unitrust, or a pooled income fund. See explanations below.

Charitable Remainder Annuity Trust. A charitable remainder annuity trust must pay the income beneficiary a fixed *dollar amount* of at least 5% of the initial value of the assets placed in the trust.

Charitable Remainder Unitrust. A charitable remainder unitrust, another type of remainder trust, differs from an annuity trust in that it must pay the income beneficiary a fixed *percentage* of the fair market value of the trust's assets, valued annually. Payments from a unitrust can be limited to trust income with any unpaid amounts carried over to future years, when the trust has sufficient income to pay its current and past obligations. Thus, a charitable remainder unitrust may also be used as a retirement planning vehicle.

Example: Suppose a 55-year-old donor who intends to work for 10 more years transfers $100,000 of appreciated stock to a trust in exchange for annual payments for life equal to 7% of the trust's value. The donor would receive an immediate contribution deduction of about $24,000, the present value of the interest passing to charity. The trust could sell the stock tax-free and invest the proceeds to maximize growth. After 10 years of minimal or zero payout, the trust reinvests its assets to maximize its yield. Payments to the donor could be made of the entire income of the trust until the trust has made up for the 10 years of missed payments. As an added benefit, the donor who, say, is in the 36% income tax bracket could take the $8,640 (36% × $24,000) of tax savings from the deduction and purchase life insurance that would be owned by and payable to his or her children. The insurance proceeds paid to the children would partially replace the stock transferred to the trust and, with appropriate planning, would not be taxed in the parent's estate.

Restrictions. There are some restrictions with respect to transfers to a trust made after June 18, 1997. A trust *cannot* be a charitable remainder annuity trust if the annuity payout for any year is greater than 50% of the initial fair market value of the trust's assets. Likewise, a trust cannot be a charitable remainder unitrust if the percentage of assets that are required to be distributed at least annually is greater than 50%.

More important, however, for transfers to a trust made after July 28, 1997, the value of the remainder interest passing to charity must be *at least 10%* of the net fair market value of the contributed property. If that requirement is not met, the trust cannot be a charitable remainder annuity trust or charitable remainder unitrust. Note that this test is performed at the time the property is contributed to the trust. Thus, the trust will not fail the 10% test merely because the value of the property has declined between the time of the contribution and the time at which the remaining trust assets pass to the charitable remainderman.

TaxALERT

These restrictions, described above, were enacted because a growing number of taxpayers were creating charitable remainder unitrusts with "negligible" charitable interests. The new rules will deny certain individuals the ability to create a qualified charitable remainder trust because of the preexisting rule requiring a minimum 5% payout rate.

For example, the retention of a 5% unitrust for life by a 24-year-old will result in a charitable interest of less than 10%. Furthermore, a couple aged 60 could not create a qualified charitable remainder unitrust with a payout rate as high as 10%. Nevertheless, charitable remainder trusts are still a viable planning technique for those individuals with sufficient charitable motives.

TaxSAVER

The Advantages of a Charitable Remainder Unitrust (CRUT). *The table below compares the sale of $300,000 of stock ($50,000 basis) with the transfer of stock to two different 20-year unitrusts—one with a 6% payout rate and the other with a 10.5% payout rate. The table assumes a 10% pretax total return on the reinvestment of the stock sale proceeds, a 36% combined marginal tax rate on current income, and a 25% combined tax rate on capital* *gains. For comparison, the table assumes that the after-tax portion of the unitrust distributions are reinvested to achieve the same 10% pretax total return earned without a CRUT.*

	No CRUT	20-Year CRUT 6% Payout	20-Year CRUT 10.5% Payout
Current Value of Stock	$ 300,000	$ 300,000	$ 300,000
Tax Basis	50,000	50,000	50,000
Capital Gains Reportable	$ 250,000	—0—	—0—
Capital Gains Tax	62,500	—0—	—0—
Remaining to Invest	$ 237,500	$ 300,000	$ 300,000
Present Value of Charitable Remainder (Tax Deduction)[1]	—	87,032	32,635
Tax Benefit of Deduction	—	31,331	11,749
Net Assets Received by Beneficiary after 20 Years[2]	1,007,748	909,575	1,025,012
Future Value of Charity's Interest at End of Trust Term	—	587,346	220,686
Combined Value Received by Donor and Charity	$1,007,748	$1,496,921	$1,245,698

1. Assumes an IRS interest rate of 7.6%, and annual trust payments made at year-end.
2. The CRUT scenarios incorporate tax savings from the charitable deduction and assume the entire amount is deductible without carryover.

Pooled Income Fund. A pooled income fund is a large trust maintained by a charity to which you may donate the remainder interest in property while retaining an income interest for the rest of your life. The amount of income you receive depends on the fund's rate of return. The tax consequences are similar to those for charitable remainder unitrusts.

The Charitable Lead Trust. A charitable lead trust is somewhat the mirror image of a charitable remainder trust. If you set up a charitable lead trust, the charity gets the *income* or *lead* interest, and the remainder interest returns to you or passes to beneficiaries of your choice.

If the remainder interest reverts to you, you may claim a current charitable income tax deduction equal to the present value of the income stream. However, the trust income will be included in your income as the charity receives it, and the remainder will be included in your estate. If the remainder interest passes to beneficiaries other than a charity, there may be no up-front charitable deduction, but usually (1) the income will not be included in your taxable income and (2) the remainder will not be included in your estate.

CARRYOVERS

If you cannot deduct all of your contributions in the current year because they exceeded your adjusted gross income limit, you may carry them over to subsequent years. You may deduct the excess in each of the next five years until it is used up, but not beyond that time. Contributions limited in the original contribution year will be subject to the same limitation in the carryover years. Excess contributions cannot be carried back and deducted in previous tax years.

TAXSAVER

You make a gift of long-term capital gain property and the amount of your deduction is limited to 30% of your adjusted gross income. If, for some unforeseen reason, the deduction cannot be used entirely in the current year or in carryover years, you may elect to reduce its value by 100% of the gain and deduct the lower basis on the gift under the 50% limitation.

Example: John Smith makes a contribution of long-term capital gain property that cost him $40,000 and now has a fair market value of $50,000. John dies during the taxable year. His adjusted gross income on his final return is $80,000.

Without the election to reduce the deduction mentioned above, John's deduction would be limited to $24,000 (30% × $80,000). However, if the value of the property is reduced by $10,000 (the appreciation in the value of the property), the deduction is subject to the 50% limit (50% × $80,000) and is increased to $40,000, his basis in the property.

TAXSAVER

If you anticipate a decline in your future adjusted gross income and you are subject to the 30% limitation for long-term capital gain property, you may want to consider electing to deduct the property's basis rather than its fair market value.

RECORD-KEEPING AND HOW TO REPORT CHARITABLE CONTRIBUTIONS

You are required to keep records to prove the amount of the cash and noncash contributions you make during the year. The kind of records you must keep depends on the amount of your contributions and whether they are cash or noncash contributions.

CASH CONTRIBUTIONS

Cash Contributions of Less Than $250. For each cash charitable contribution that is less than $250, you must keep one of the following:
1. A canceled check,
2. A receipt (or a letter or other written acknowledgment) from the charitable organization showing the name of the organization, the date of the contribution, and the amount of the contribution, or

3. Other reliable written records that include the information described in (2). Records may be considered reliable if you keep contemporaneous records, or if, in the case of small donations, you have items such as buttons, tokens, or emblems that have been given to contributors.

Cash Contributions of $250 or More. You must obtain a contemporaneous written acknowledgment from any charitable organization to which a contribution of $250 or more is made in order to deduct that contribution. A canceled check no longer constitutes substantiation for a contribution of money. You must obtain the written acknowledgment on or before the earlier of the date on which your return is actually filed or the due date for the return, including extensions.

The written acknowledgment must contain the following:
1. The amount of cash contributed;
2. Whether the charitable organization provided any goods or services in consideration, in whole or in part, for the contribution; and
3. A description and good faith estimate of the value of goods or services provided by the charity.

If the goods or services provided as consideration for the contribution consist solely of *intangible religious benefits,* a statement to that effect must be included in the written acknowledgment.

If you make multiple contributions to a charity, as long as there is no separate payment of $250 or more, written acknowledgment is not required even if the sum of separate payments is $250 or more.

You are not required to obtain substantiation for a donation if the charitable organization files a return with the IRS which includes the same information otherwise required from the taxpayer. However, the primary responsibility for requesting and maintaining the required substantiation rests with you, not the charitable organization.

Payroll Deduction Contributions. The IRS allows taxpayers who make contributions to charities through deductions from their paychecks some relief from the strict substantiation requirements for other cash contributions. You may substantiate payroll deduction contributions by a combination of:
(a) A paycheck stub, W-2, or other document from your employer showing the amount withheld from your wages; and
(b) A pledge card or other document from the charity stating that it doesn't provide goods or services in exchange for your contribution.
This substantiation requirement only applies to contributions in excess of $250 withheld from a single paycheck.

CONTRIBUTIONS TO CHARITY DINNERS, ETC.

For any contribution over $75 for which the charity provides goods or services (such as a charity dinner), the charity must provide a statement to the donor that reports the estimated value of the goods or services received by the donor in exchange for the contribution. As under prior law, a payment to a charity is deductible only to the extent that it exceeds the value of any goods or services received in return.

TAXSAVER

Raffle Tickets or Door Prizes. *If you purchase a ticket to a fundraising dinner, generally you can deduct the cost of the ticket that exceeds the value of the meal and any entertainment you receive at the event. However, if you are also given the chance to win a prize (say, a trip or car), the IRS will not allow you to deduct any portion of the purchase price of the ticket. If you decline to participate in the raffle by notifying the charity that you do not want to participate, you should be able to deduct the purchase price of the ticket less any value of the dinner and entertainment.*

NONCASH CONTRIBUTIONS

For a contribution not made in cash, the records you must keep depend on whether your deduction for the contribution is:
1. Less than $250,
2. At least $250 but not more than $500,
3. Over $500 but not more than $5,000,
4. Over $5,000.

Deductions of Less Than $250. If you make any noncash contribution, you must get and keep a receipt from the charitable organization showing:
1. The name of the charitable organization,
2. The date and location of the charitable contribution, and
3. A reasonably detailed description of the property.

A letter or other written communication from the charitable organization acknowledging receipt of the contribution and containing the information in (1), (2), and (3) will serve as a receipt.

You are not required to have a receipt if it is impractical to get one (for example, if you leave property at a charity's unattended drop site).

You must also keep reliable written records, including information regarding the fair market value of the property at the time of contribution and how you determined the fair market value (with a copy of an appraisal, if one was obtained), and the cost or other basis of the property.

Deductions of At Least $250 but Not More Than $500. If you claim a deduction of at least $250 but not more than $500 for a noncash charitable contribution, you must get and keep an acknowledgment of your contribution from the qualified organization. This acknowledgment must contain the information in items (1) through (3) listed under "Deductions of Less Than $250," above.

The acknowledgment must also meet these tests:
1. It must be written;
2. It must include:
   (a) An indication as to whether the qualified organization gave you any goods or services (other than token items of little value) in return for your contribution,
   (b) A description and good faith estimate of the value of any goods or services described in (a), and
   (c) If the only benefit received was an intangible religious benefit (such as admission to a religious ceremony), the acknowledgment must explain this and it does not need to describe or estimate the value of the benefit;
3. You must get it on or before the earlier of the due date, including extensions, for filing the return, or the date you file your return for the year you make the contribution.

Deductions Over $500 but Not More Than $5,000. In addition to the substantiation requirements listed above under "Deductions of At Least $250 but Not More Than $500," Form 8283 must be attached to your return if total noncash charitable contributions exceed $500. This form must contain the following information:
- Name and address of the organization receiving the gift;
- A description of the property contributed;
- The date of the contribution;
- The date the property was acquired;
- How you acquired the property (e.g., gift, purchase); and
- Fair market value of the property and the method used to determine such value.

Deductions Over $5,000. The substantiation requirements listed earlier under "Deductions Over $500 but Not More Than $5,000" also apply to deductions in excess of $5,000. In addition, individuals are required to obtain independent qualified appraisals for donations of noncash property if the claimed value of the property exceeds $5,000 or if the claimed value of all similar items donated to one or more charitable organizations exceeds $5,000. Nonpublicly traded securities must be appraised if they are valued at over $10,000. Publicly traded securities are not subject to this requirement.

7

Capital Gains
and Losses

INTRODUCTION

If you are looking for a tax break, generating capital gains could be one of your biggest opportunities. The top tax rate applicable to most long-term capital gains is 20%, while the rate applicable to ordinary income can go up to 39.6%. That's a 19.6% difference. If you can generate net capital gains instead of ordinary income, you will save considerably on your taxes. Also, with capital assets you usually have the flexibility to control when you recognize the income or loss, because in most cases you determine when to sell your assets.

Because of the lower long-term capital gains tax rates, investment strategies that emphasize capital appreciation over current income can significantly enhance after-tax portfolio returns. If you are a "buy-and-hold" investor, you should keep growth-oriented investments outside of tax-deferred accounts to benefit from the capital gains tax relief.

HOW CAPITAL GAINS ARE TAXED

Generally, capital gains are taxable, whether the underlying asset is held as an investment or for personal purposes. On the other hand, capital losses are only deductible if the assets were held for investment purposes.

If you incur losses from the sale of investment assets, you can deduct those losses to the extent they equal your capital gains. But if your losses exceed your capital gains, you can only deduct up to $3,000 of those losses in a given tax year against ordinary income. Any excess will be carried over until it can be offset against future capital gains or be deducted as a loss against your ordinary income up to $3,000 a year. (See "Deducting Capital Losses" on page 124 for more details.)

TaxSaver

Generally, it is preferable to defer gains and accelerate losses for the simple reason that the later the taxes are paid, the longer you have the use of the money.

TaxSaver

The price of a stock typically reflects accumulated corporate earnings. Thus, selling shares before a dividend is paid can produce capital gains, as opposed to ordinary income, for the portion of the stock's value attributable to the pending dividend.

Defining a Capital Asset

For the most part, everything you own and hold for personal or investment purposes is a capital asset. Examples of capital assets include stocks and bonds, your house or other residence, household furnishings, automobiles and boats, jewelry, and gold, silver, or other metals. Capital assets do not include inventory; notes and accounts receivable acquired in the ordinary course of a business for services rendered or from the sale of inventory; or, in certain cases, copyrights or literary, musical, or other artistic compositions. Letters and memorandums prepared by or for you also are not classified as capital assets. Gains on sales of certain assets used in a trade or business are taxed at capital gains rates; however, you may have to pay ordinary income tax rates on a portion of the gain resulting from the sale of such property.

Capital Gains Tax Rates

Several different capital gains tax rates apply, depending on the type of property sold, the holding period prior to sale, and your overall income level.

1. Gains on property held for 12 months or less are treated as *short-term* capital gains, subject to tax at the same rates as ordinary income.
2. Gains on the sale of property held for more than 12 months are considered long-term capital gains. Long-term capital gains are subject to the 10% (for gains in the 15% tax bracket) or 20% (for gains in the 28% tax bracket or higher) tax rates.

TaxSaver

You should attempt to incur capital losses only in years in which you have no capital gains or only short-term capital gains. If you are in the highest tax bracket, capital losses are better used to offset ordinary income rather than long-term capital gains, which are taxed at 20%.

The above rules are summarized in Table 7.1.

TABLE 7.1

Holding Period/ Marginal Tax Rate	10%	20%	Ordinary Income Rate
• ≤ 12 months			✕
> 12 months/ • 15% tax bracket	✕		
> 12 months/ • > 15% tax bracket		✕	

TAXALERT

When calculating capital gains, all long-term gains are first netted by long-term losses and short-term gains by short-term losses. Net losses in one category then offset net gains in the other. Net gains in each category are then subject to the rates shown in Table 7.1.

Rules Applicable Starting in 2001

Effective for taxable years beginning after December 31, 2000, the maximum capital gains rates for assets that are held more than five years are 8% and 18% (corresponding to the 10% and 20% rates for property held between 12 months and five years). The 18% rate only applies to assets the holding period for which begins after December 31, 2000. For this purpose, if you have an option to buy property, the date you received the option will start the holding period. For example, if you receive an option before the year 2001, the property will not qualify for the 18% rate. For capital assets held on January 1, 2001, you may elect to treat the asset as having been sold on such date for an amount equal to its fair market value, and as having been reacquired for an amount equal to such value. If you make such an election, any gain will be recognized (and any loss will be disallowed).

Collectibles and Depreciable Real Estate

Attention art lovers and real estate owners: long-term capital gains from sales of collectibles are still subject to tax at a maximum rate of either 15% or 28%, depending on the tax bracket in which the gains fall. The portion of a gain of real estate that relates to previous depreciation deductions will be taxed at a 25% rate.

Example: You purchased a rental property for $100,000 in 1994 and sold it in July 2000 for $125,000 (net of expenses), after having claimed depreciation deductions totaling $18,000. Your total gain would be $43,000 ($125,000 − [$100,000 − $18,000]). However, only amounts relating to price appreciation ($25,000) would be taxed at the 20% rate. The $18,000 of "depreciation recapture" would be taxed at 25%.

Calculating a Gain or Loss

You calculate the gain or loss on a sale or trade of property by comparing the amount you realize with the adjusted basis of the property. The adjusted basis of a property is your original cost or other basis, such as "carryover basis" if the property was acquired by gift, or a "stepped-up" basis if the property was acquired by inheritance—properly increased or decreased for items such as purchase commissions, legal fees, capital improvements, and depreciation. "Carryover basis" is the basis of the donor whereas "stepped-up basis" generally is the fair market value of the property on the date the person from whom the property was inherited died. The amount you realize from a sale or trade is the total of all money you receive, plus the fair market value of all property or services you receive. An indebtedness against the property, or against you, such as a mortgage, that is paid off as a part of the transaction or that is assumed by the buyer must be included in the amount realized.

Deducting Capital Losses

Capital losses are deductible to the extent that they do not exceed certain limitations. If your capital losses are more than your capital gains, up to $3,000 ($1,500 if you are married and file a separate return) of losses may be deducted provided your taxable income is at least equal to the amount of the deduction.

Carrying Forward Capital Losses

If your capital loss is more than the yearly limit, you may carry over the unused part to the next tax year and treat it as if it occurred in that year. A net loss may be carried forward until it is exhausted or until you die.

This carryforward may be used to reduce your tax when you have a capital gain in the future. If you do not have future capital gains, you may nonetheless use the carryforward loss to offset taxable income up to $3,000 per year.

TAX*SAVER*

You may save taxes by carefully planning major sales and exchanges. It may be better to wait until after the end of the year before finalizing a sale so that a gain may be deferred until the next year or so that more losses may be realized in the current year. Remember, too, capital gains increase your adjusted gross income (AGI). If your AGI is above $128,950 in 2000 (on a joint return), a portion of your itemized deductions will not be allowed. Fur-

thermore, if your AGI is above $193,400 in 2000 (on a joint return), your personal exemptions are decreased.

Worthless Securities. Stocks, stock rights, and corporate or government bonds with interest coupons or in registered form, which became worthless during the tax year, are treated as though they were capital assets sold on the last day of the tax year if they were capital assets in your hands. To determine whether they are long-term or short-term capital assets, you are considered to have held the stocks or securities until the last day of the year in which they became worthless.

TaxSaver

The deduction for a worthless security must be taken in the year in which it becomes worthless, even if it is sold for a nominal súm in the following year. If you do not learn that a security has become worthless until a later year, you should file an amended return for the year in which it became worthless. Since it may be difficult to determine exactly when a stock becomes worthless, the capital loss deduction should be claimed in the earliest year in which such a claim may be reasonably made. Because of this difficulty, a seven-year statute of limitations applies to the filing of such an amended return.

TaxOrganizer

You should keep any documents indicating the date on which the security becomes worthless. Examples of sufficient documentation are bankruptcy documents and financial statements.

Strategies for Selling Securities

Specify Shares to Be Sold

If your broker holds your securities that you purchased at different prices and dates, you must tell him or her which shares you are going to sell. You can do this by giving your broker a standing order to use securities with the highest basis when you sell. The same goes for your mutual fund shares. If you don't, the shares you purchased first generally will be considered the shares sold. This rule can result in a different gain or loss than you intended. See Chapter 11, Investment Planning, for further discussion.

TaxSaver

Identifying shares with greater-than-12-month holding will make you eligible for the lower rates—but may also force you to swallow larger capital gains if the stock appreciated steadily while you held it. To take advantage of the lower tax rates, written instructions must be delivered prior to sale. You should keep confirmation of the instructions in your personal tax files.

> **TAX SAVER**
>
> *If you have excess gains over losses, you can sell property on which you have losses to offset your gains and eliminate the tax on them. But be aware of how holding periods from these losses will match up with your gains.*
>
> *If you have already realized more than $3,000 of capital losses over and above your realized capital gains, and you want to sell an appreciated asset that you think has gone up as far as it will go, sell that asset and use your accumulated losses to offset the gain, again watching for the holding-period issue.*

Selling Shares in Mutual Funds. See Chapter 8, Mutual Funds.

Put Options

Acquiring a put option means buying an option contract that gives you the right to sell 100 shares of stock at a set price (the "strike price") during a specific time period. Put options can be used as a means of protecting and deferring your capital gain. While deferring a sale to a subsequent year, put options protect against a decline in value.

> **TAX SAVER**
>
> *If you own appreciated securities that you are not yet ready to sell for tax reasons, you can buy put options as a way of protecting your gains against possible price declines. If the price of the stock goes above the strike price, you get the benefit of the increased price less the cost of the put, which you let expire. If the stock price declines, you may either sell your shares at the strike price or sell the put option separately. Either way, the sale and your capital gain have been deferred to next year. However, the premium you pay for the option contract must be factored into your consideration for using this planning technique.*

> **TAX ALERT**
>
> *You should remember that if the property with respect to which you purchase a put was held for 12 months or less at the time you purchase the put, your holding period will be lost until you exercise or dispose of the put.*

Selling Short against the Box

Selling short is not a hedge but rather a bet that the security price will drop. Selling short against the box means selling borrowed securities while owning substantially identical securities that you later deliver to close the short sale. That allows you to lock in a profit while delaying the recognition of a gain. Many investors with unrealized profits may want to consider a short sale against the box to postpone recognizing a gain until the beginning of the following year, provided they meet the requirements set out under "Exceptions" below.

TAXALERT

Equity Swaps and Other Transactions Designed to Reduce Risk.
Although gain or loss generally is realized for tax purposes at the time an asset is sold, exchanged, or otherwise disposed of, special rules can defer or accelerate recognition in certain circumstances.

Prior to passage of the 1997 Taxpayer Relief Act, a gain or loss on a transaction designed to reduce or eliminate risk of loss, such as a short sale against the box or an "equity swap," was not recognized until the transaction was effectively "closed."

Under the current law, you will generally be required to recognize gain (but not loss) upon entering into a constructive sale of any appreciated position in stock, a partnership interest, or certain debt instruments that has the effect of eliminating your risk of loss and upside gain potential. You will be treated as making a constructive sale of an appreciated position when you do one of the following: (1) enter into a short sale of the same or substantially identical property; (2) enter into an offsetting contract with respect to the same or substantially identical property (an equity swap, for example); or (3) enter into a futures or forward contract to deliver the same or substantially identical property. In addition, future Treasury regulations are expected to expand these rules to other transactions that have substantially the same effects as the ones described in the IRS Code.

Exceptions: There are certain exceptions to these rules. One of the most important is that short sales against the box are still permitted so long as the following requirements are met:

1. The transaction is closed within 30 days of the close of the taxable year, and
2. You hold the appreciated financial position throughout the 60-day period beginning on the date such transaction is closed, and you do not enter into certain positions that would diminish the risk of loss during that time.

TAXSAVER

A "collar" is another technique that may be useful in deferring taxes while reducing investment risk. A "zero-cost" collar involves selling a call option (giving the buyer the right to purchase the underlying property at a specified price within the option period) and using the option premium received to finance the simultaneous acquisition of a put option (giving the buyer the right to sell the underlying property at a specified price within the option period) on identical property. The put option provides some protection to the investor against a drop in value of the underlying property (i.e., the value of the option increases as the value of the underlying property decreases). However, the investor also gives up some of the upside potential of the underlying property, since he or she will be required to deliver the property (or its equivalent) to the call option holder if that option is exercised.

Wash Sales

Suppose your objective is to take a tax loss this year while preserving your investment positions. It can be done as long as you don't run afoul of the wash sale rule. A wash sale occurs when you sell stock or securities and within 30 days before or after the sale you buy, acquire in a taxable exchange, or acquire a contract or option to buy substantially the same stock or security. To the extent that the same number of stocks or securities sold are replaced in a wash sale, the loss will not be recognized for tax purposes. The disallowed loss will be added to the basis of the replacement stock or securities instead.

TAXSAVER

The easiest way to maintain your investment position in a security, recognize a loss, and avoid the wash sale rule is to buy identical securities 31 days before or after you sell your old securities at a loss. Another possibility is to reinvest in a similar security that would not be considered "substantially identical" and therefore would not violate the wash rule. For example, if you sold your investment in a mutual fund that invests in bonds, you could reinvest in another fund that owned bonds of a similar grade and yield.

Installment Sales

You can defer recognition of a gain from the current year by structuring the sale of the investments on an installment basis. In an installment sale, only part of your gain will be recognized at the time of the sale. The rest of the gain will be recognized as subsequent installments are received. Such sales need to be carefully evaluated. Stock or securities traded on established markets cannot be reported for tax purposes on an installment basis.

Like-Kind Exchanges

Generally, the tax on the gain from any real estate held for investment or business reasons can be deferred if the property is traded for similar real estate. However, if you received "boot" (that is, cash or unlike property) in addition to the like-kind property, you may have to recognize a gain up to the value of the money or unlike property received. The rules for like-kind exchanges are complicated, and you should consult with your tax advisor in order to properly structure this transaction.

OTHER OPPORTUNITIES FOR INDIVIDUALS

Qualified Small Business Stock

An individual taxpayer who holds qualified small business stock (QSBS) for more than five years can exclude from gross income 50% of any gain realized from the sale or exchange of the stock. This exclusion is limited to the greater of:

1. 10 times the taxpayer's basis in the stock; or
2. $10 million in gain from all of the taxpayer's transactions in stock of that corporation (held for more than five years).

These rules apply to stock issued after August 10, 1993.

The lower capital gains rates enacted in the 1997 Tax Act do not apply to the includible portion of the gain from the sale of QSBS. Thus, the maximum rate of regular tax on the sale of QSBS remains at 14%. In addition, an individual may roll over tax-free gain from the sale or exchange of QSBS held more than six months where the taxpayer uses the proceeds to purchase other QSBS within 60 days of the sale. Generally, the holding period of the stock purchased will include the holding period of the stock sold.

The rules for determining whether stock is "qualified small business stock" can be summarized as follows:

- The stock must be newly issued stock.
- The stock cannot be acquired in exchange for other stock.
- The issuing corporation must be a "C" corporation (i.e., not an "S" corporation that passes its income and losses directly on to the shareholders), but may not be a cooperative, Domestic International Sales Corporation (DISC), former DISC, Foreign Sales Corporation (FSC), Real Estate Investment Trust (REIT), Regulated Investment Company (RIC), Real Estate Mortgage Investment Conduit (REMIC), a corporation having a possessions tax credit election in effect, or a corporation owning a subsidiary that has a possessions tax credit election in effect.
- At least 80% of the corporation's assets must be used in the active conduct of a *qualified trade or business,* or in the start-up of a future *qualified trade or business.*
- A qualified trade or business is any business other than one involving the performance of services in the fields of health, law, engineering, architecture, accounting, actuarial science, performing arts, consulting, athletics, financial services, brokerage services, or any other trade or business where the principal asset of the business is the reputation or skill of one or more employees. A qualified trade or business also cannot involve the businesses of banking, insurance, financing, leasing, investing, or similar businesses, farming, or certain businesses involving natural resource extraction or production, and businesses operating a hotel, motel, restaurant, or similar business.
- The corporation may not have more than $50 million in gross assets (i.e., sum of cash plus the aggregate fair market value of other corporate property) at the time the qualified small business stock is issued. If the corporation meets this test at the time of issuance of the stock, a subsequent event that violates this rule will not disqualify stock that previously qualified.

For Alternative Minimum Tax (AMT) purposes, 42% of the gain (28% in the case of stock where the holding period begins after December 31, 2000) on QSBS is a "tax preference" item and must be added back to AMT income. Because of this add-back, AMT liability may limit the benefit of the exclusion. The AMT is discussed in Chapter 9, Filing Status and How to Calculate Your Tax.

Rolling Gain Over into a Specialized Small Business Investment Company

Under certain circumstances, gain on the sale of publicly traded securities will not be taxed if the proceeds from the sale are used to acquire common stock in a specialized small business investment company (SSBIC) within a 60-day period.

Special Treatment for Lump Sum Distributions

If you were at least age 50 on January 1, 1986, you may be able to elect to treat a portion of the taxable part of a lump sum distribution as a long-term capital gain taxable at a 20% rate. This treatment applies to the portion you receive relating to your participation in the qualified plan before 1974.

Donating Appreciated Assets

When making a charitable contribution, it may be tax-wise to donate appreciated marketable securities instead of cash. You will be able to avoid the capital gains tax on the property, and the charity generally sells the stock or securities, receiving cash but not paying any tax because of its tax-exempt status. If you want the stock or securities you donated in your portfolio, then take the cash you were originally planning to give to charity and repurchase the identical investment. Your investment now has a new, increased cost basis.

If you plan to make a charitable contribution of an investment asset, follow these two rules:

Rule 1

If you have appreciated property that you have held for more than a year, donate it—don't sell it and donate the cash. The following example explains why.

Example: Let's assume that you are going to donate $30,000 to your favorite charity. You have stock that you bought for $6,000 several years ago; it now has a market value of $30,000.

If you give the stock directly to the charity, you don't report any capital gain and you can deduct $30,000 as a charitable contribution deduction. Assuming you are in the 39.6% tax bracket, the charitable contribution would reduce your taxes by $11,880.

Here's what happens when you sell the stock and give the proceeds to charity. First, you have a gain of $24,000 on which you pay a 20% capital gains tax of $4,800. You would, however, be able to claim the same $30,000 charitable contribution deduction, thereby reducing your taxes by $11,880. Offsetting the taxes you pay on the gain against the taxes you save from the deduction, your net tax benefit is $7,080.

Rule 2

If you have property that has depreciated in value, sell it and give cash—don't donate the property directly. Here's why.

Example: Let's suppose that you own stock that cost $33,000 a few years ago. The stock is currently worth $30,000. If you donate it to a charity, you will get a deduction of $30,000, its fair market value. If you sell it you will have $30,000 in cash. You can give the cash to a charity and claim a charitable deduction. You will also have a capital loss on the sale of your stock of $3,000. The capital loss is also deductible.

Mutual Funds

INTRODUCTION

There are now more mutual funds than there are companies on the New York Stock Exchange. They come in all shapes and sizes but share a common purpose. All mutual funds receive money from many investors, pool the funds, and use them to purchase investments that the funds' professional investment managers select. Since the investor owns shares in the investment company—mutual funds are technically known as open-end *regulated investment companies*—he or she indirectly owns a share of its investments.

Generally, mutual funds are classified according to their investment objectives. Aggressive growth funds, for example, are characterized by high risk and high return. These funds typically seek capital appreciation and do not produce significant interest income or dividends. The objectives of balanced funds, on the other hand, are to conserve investors' initial principal, pay high current income through dividends and interest, and promote the long-term growth of both principal and income. While aggressive growth funds generally invest only in stocks, balanced funds typically invest in both bonds and stocks. There are many other kinds of mutual funds—growth and income funds, bond funds, sector funds, index funds, etc.—all with differing investing objectives and different strategies to achieve them. A general rule to keep in mind: the higher the potential reward from your investment, the greater the risk that you may not achieve the expected return.

Which mutual fund or funds you choose will depend largely upon your own investment objectives, but one factor you should definitely consider is how your mutual fund investment will be taxed. Generally, a mutual fund is a conduit for tax purposes—that is, the fund does not ordinarily pay income taxes, but its shareholders do. Gains are generally passed through to shareholders in a fund in the form of dividends and capital gains distributions. As a shareholder, you are liable for any taxes due on these distributions. Consequently, it can matter enormously how those gains are taxed.

Dividend distributions from a mutual fund, such as distribution of interest or dividends earned from the fund's investment securities, are generally considered ordinary income for tax purposes. Ordinary dividend distributions also can include any net short-term capital gains—short-term capital gains minus short-term losses—realized by the fund when it sells securities. A capital gains distribution from a fund represents net long-term capital gains realized by the fund—these are taxed at 20% or possibly 25% for a distribution from a REIT. While a fund may also realize net long-term losses from the sale of securities, it is not permitted to "pass through" these losses to shareholders. Instead, the fund must carry net capital losses forward to offset any future capital gains. Generally, all dividend and capital gains distributions from a fund are subject to federal and state income taxes. Dividends from municipal bond or municipal money market funds are one exception. These dividends are usually exempt from federal income tax and may also be exempt from state and local income taxes, depending upon where you live and your state's tax law. A second exception is dividends derived from interest earned by the fund on U.S. Government Bonds. These dividends are exempt from state but not federal tax.

This chapter explains in detail how different distributions from mutual funds are taxed, as well as the different methods by which you may calculate your gain or loss upon the sale of your shares in a mutual fund. It also discusses some of the expenses you may incur when investing in mutual funds.

DIVIDENDS

A distribution by a mutual fund of money or property to you generally will qualify as an ordinary income dividend. These dividends must be reported on your Form 1040. The mutual fund making the distribution will send you a Form 1099-DIV indicating the amount and nature (e.g., ordinary dividends, capital gains, return of capital) of dividend income you have received.

Dividends Declared One Year but not Paid Until the Next. Often a mutual fund will declare a dividend at the end of the calendar year but not pay it until January of the following year. Nevertheless, you are treated as having received the dividend in the year in which it was declared. This rule is unique to mutual funds dividends. It does not apply to regular corporate dividends, which are taxable to cash basis taxpayers in the year in which the dividends are received.

TAXSAVER

You should pay close attention to the timing of your purchase of a mutual fund. For example, if you invest in a fund near the end of the year and the fund shortly thereafter makes a year-end distribution, you will have to pay tax on the distribution even though from your point of view you are simply getting back the capital you just invested in the fund. In effect, all you've done is "bought" taxable income that the fund earned earlier in the year but had not yet paid out to shareholders. Typically, the fund's share price drops by the amount of the distribution. Your cost basis in the mutual fund however, will be the pre-distribution price you paid for the shares.

There is one consolation. Your higher basis will reduce any capital gain on a later sale. However, if you sell the fund at a loss, it will increase your capital loss. If you want to limit your tax liability and lower your basis in the shares, you should delay your purchase of fund shares until after the record date for the distribution. Usually, a fund can tell you when distributions, if any, for the year are expected. Alternatively, you can consult investment publications, which indicate distribution dates for the previous year.

Example: ABC Fund declares and distributes a $1 dividend on December 1. If you had purchased 1,000 shares at $10 per share on November 30, you will have to report $1,000 of income. If instead you bought the shares on December 2, after the record date, you will pay $9 per share and have no taxable income to report. Of course, for the shares bought on November 30, your basis would be $10 per share instead of $9.

TAXSAVER

If you are thinking of selling shares in a mutual fund, particularly near the end of the year when many funds pay dividends, you should consider redeeming your shares before any upcoming dividend payments are made by the fund. If your shares are worth more than you paid, you can take a capital gain on the redemption and avoid paying the higher tax rate on ordinary income that you would pay on an ordinary dividend. If your shares are worth less than you paid for them, you can minimize your capital losses by selling before the dividend. Remember, the net asset value per share of the fund (that is, the amount you would receive on the redemption of your shares) decreases by the amount of the dividend.

Some dividends may be treated as a tax-free return of capital. This occurs when the mutual fund does not have enough current or accumulated earnings and profits to cover the distribution. In this situation, the distribution is considered to be a "return of capital" (the amount you originally invested) and is nontaxable to the extent of the basis in your shares. (Your basis is generally the price at which you bought the shares plus or minus any adjustments.) Although the distribution is tax-free, it will reduce your basis in the mutual fund shares. To the extent that the distribution is greater than your basis in your shares, you will be treated as having a gain from the sale or exchange of the shares. This gain must be reported on Schedule D (Form 1040).

Tax-Exempt Interest Dividends

Funds that invest in municipal bonds may pay dividends that are exempt from federal taxes. In order for such dividends to qualify for tax-free status, the fund must invest at least 50% of the value of its assets in tax-exempt municipal bonds at the end of each quarter. If you invest in such a fund and receive tax-exempt income, you must report such amounts on your tax return even though you do not need to include such amounts in income. The fund will send you a statement within 60 days of the close of the year indicating whether you have received such tax-exempt interest income. These amounts will not appear on your Form 1099-DIV.

Reinvestment of Dividends

Many mutual funds offer dividend reinvestment plans in which you may use your dividends to buy more shares of stock in the mutual fund instead of receiving the dividends in cash. If you reinvest your dividends, you still must report the dividends. Whether you include the reinvested dividends in income depends on the nature of the dividend. For example, if you reinvest your tax-exempt dividends, you do not have to include them in income. For further information, see Chapter 11, Investment Planning.

TaxOrganizer

If you participate in a dividend reinvestment plan, you should keep a record of the dividends and of the shares purchased with the reinvestment. The reinvested dividends are part of your cost basis for the shares. You will need these records to figure your cost basis when you sell all or some of your shares.

Capital Gains Distributions

Mutual funds may make capital gains distributions from their net realized long-term capital gains. Even funds that invest in municipal bonds may make taxable capital gain distributions. No matter how long a time—or more to the point, how short a time—you may have owned shares in the mutual fund making the distribution, these distributions will be treated as long-term capital gains and taxed at the applicable preferential long-term capital gains rates. In addition, these long-term capital gains may be offset by unrelated capital losses you may have. Form 1099-DIV will indicate the amount of the long-term capital gain you must include in your income.

TaxAlert

As discussed in Chapter 7, Capital Gains and Losses, effective for tax years starting in 2001, the maximum capital gains rates for assets held more than five years are 8% and 18% (corresponding to the 10% and 20% rates for property held between 12 months and five years). However, Congress mandated that the 18% rate only applies to assets for which the holding period begins, or is treated as beginning, after December 31, 2000. These rates will also apply to gains earned by an individual through his or her investment in a mutual fund which meets the five-year holding period requirement for its investment (and also to investments in certain other special "pass-through" taxpayers, such as S corporations, partnerships, trusts, estates, and real estate investment trusts).

For tax years starting prior to 2001, a mutual fund can designate a capital gain dividend as a 20% gain distribution (10% for taxpayers in the 15% tax bracket). For tax years starting in 2001, a mutual fund can designate a capital gain dividend as an 8% gain distribution (for taxpayers in the 15% tax bracket if the five-year holding period has been met), or as a 20% gain distribution (10% for taxpayers in the 15% tax bracket).

For tax years starting in 2005, a mutual fund can designate a captial gain dividend as an 18% gain distribution (where the five-year holding period is met, and the gain would otherwise be taxed as a 20% gain).

In some rare circumstances, a fund may designate a capital gain dividend as an unrecaptured Section 1250 gain distribution, or a 28% gain distribution.

Before you invest in a mutual fund, you should consider the rate at which the fund turns over its assets. A fund with a high turnover rate will generate frequent gains and losses, increasing the chances that capital distributions will be short-term, rather than long-term. Short-term capital gain distributions are taxed as ordinary income dividends; long-term capital gains are eligible for the lower long-term capital gain rate.

In addition to the amounts you receive from a fund, you must report and include in your income any amount that the mutual fund credited to you from its undistributed capital gains, even though you did not actually receive such amounts. Undistributed capital gains are taxed at the corporate tax rate of 35%. The mutual fund will pay the capital gains tax, and those taxes may then be claimed by you as a credit on your return.

A mutual fund will report the amount of undistributed capital gains to you on Form 2439, not on Form 1099-DIV.

A special rule exists for capital gain distributions you receive when you sell your shares in the fund at a loss within six months from the date of original purchase. In this case, the portion of your capital loss attributable to the capital gain dividend is treated as a long-term—not a short-term—capital loss.

Potential Capital Gains Exposure. *One of the most revealing indicators of a mutual fund's future tax liability is its potential capital gains exposure. It tells the percentage of a fund's total assets that is made up of unrealized capital gains. These gains represent the growth in the securities in the fund's portfolio that will be distributed and taxed to future shareholders. Such gains are not taxable until the fund sells the appreciated securities and distributes net capital gains to shareholders. When all else is equal, a higher level of potential capital gains exposure means that owning the fund could result in a higher tax bill down the road.*

On the flip side, a fund with negative capital gains exposure gives new shareholders the potential for turbocharged returns. These funds have accumulated net capital losses prior to new shareholder ownership. Unlike net capital gains, these cannot be distributed to shareholders. Instead, the losses can be used to offset future gains realized by the fund.

As a result, the cost basis inside a fund with relative capital gains exposure exceeds the fair market value of its assets. This gives the fund the ability to shelter future gains, which can boost the net asset value of the fund without triggering a taxable event for shareholders. Thus, you can control the taxation of this type of growth while the fund eats through its losses, since no taxes are due until you sell your shares.

Foreign Tax Credit

Some mutual funds invest in foreign corporations. If a mutual fund owns securities of foreign corporations, it may have to pay foreign taxes on the income it earns from those securities. However, if the fund holds more than 50% of its total assets in foreign securities at the close of its tax year, the fund can pass through to its shareholders the foreign tax credit it receives for taxes paid at the fund level. For a discussion of the foreign tax credit and whether you should claim the credit or a tax deduction, see Chapter 9, Filing Status and How to Calculate Your Tax.

Investment Expenses

Investment expenses that you incur in the production of income generally are deductible subject to certain limitations. Investment expenses include expenses for counseling and advice, legal and accounting fees, and any investment newsletters. See Chapter 2, What You Can Deduct, for more information.

Fees

Front-End Fees. "Front-end," or purchase, fees (also known as "load charges") reduce your investment in a mutual fund, but they are still considered part of your cost basis for tax purposes.

Example: You invest $10,000 in a fund that charges a 1% load on portfolio transaction (purchase) fees. Your account statement reports a net balance of $9,900 ($10,000 minus the 1% fee). For tax purposes, however, your cost remains at $10,000.

TAXSAVER

Your basis in mutual fund shares does not include load charges (sales fees) paid after October 3, 1989, on the purchase of shares if you held the shares for 90 days or less and then reinvested the proceeds in a fund within the same fund family with a reduced load charge. Instead, the load charges be-

come part of your basis in the shares of the new fund into which you put your investment.

Before you buy a mutual fund, you should examine the sales charges and redemption fees it charges, if any. No-load funds do not have a sales charge. Mutual fund listings in newspapers generally indicate whether there is a sales charge. No-load funds have the same purchase and redemption price for fund shares. Your broker should be able to tell you which funds charge commissions.

E&Y FOCUS: Ongoing Fund Expenses

Regardless of any sales charges, all funds have ongoing expenses for administration and management that are charged as an annual percentage of the assets under management. These fees are deducted from the portfolio's investment earnings before the income is distributed to shareholders.

Management fees typically make up the majority of a fund's ongoing expenses. They represent the cost of portfolio management, which is charged by the fund's investment advisors. Managers in investment markets that require more specialized research skills—such as the small-cap and international equity markets—typically command higher fees. Also, equity funds generally charge higher management fees than do fixed-income funds.

12b-1 fees are named for the Securities and Exchange Commission rule that allows funds to charge shareholders for "distribution and marketing" expenses. These fees are often used to pay "trailing commissions," which brokers receive in addition to any front-end sales charge. In other words, the sales representatives receive an incentive to help maintain investors after the initial sale. The average 12b-1 fee among U.S. stock funds is about 0.3%, although it can run as high as 1%.

Back-End Fees. Fees may also be deducted from your fund when you redeem or sell shares. These are generally called redemption or "back-end" fees. (Certain back-end fees called "contingent deferred sales charges" or "contingent deferred sales loads" typically decline and eventually disappear over a set period of time.) If your mutual fund reports all proceeds net of redemption fees on your Form 1099-B, you do not need to adjust your tax cost. However, if your mutual fund reports gross proceeds before any redemption fees on Form 1099-B, you should increase your cost basis by the amount of the fee you paid when calculating your capital gain or loss.

Other Fees. Custodial and account maintenance fees are deductible as "investment expenses" on Schedule A of your income tax return, subject to certain limitations. See "Investment Expenses," above, and Chapter 2, What You Can Deduct: Exemptions, Adjustments, and Deductions.

SALE OF MUTUAL FUND SHARES

If you sell, exchange, or have shares redeemed (when a mutual fund reacquires its shares), you may have a capital gain or loss. You will have a short-term capital gain or loss if you held your shares for one year or less. You will have a long-term capital gain or loss if you held the shares for more than a year. The gain or loss on the sale, exchange, or redemption of mutual fund shares is the difference between the amount of the proceeds you receive and your adjusted tax basis in your shares.

TAXSAVER

Generally, you will have capital gain or loss when you exchange shares of one mutual fund for shares of another mutual fund in the same mutual fund family. So, for example, if you exchange shares in ABC Growth Fund for shares in ABC Technology Fund, you may have to recognize a capital gain or loss. Any service fee charged for the exchange generally may be added to your basis of the shares you acquired.

However, you will not have to recognize a capital gain or loss if you exchange mutual fund shares within a tax-deferred account, such as a 401(k) account, a variable annuity account, or an individual retirement account. In addition, you will not have to recognize a capital gain or loss if the shares in one mutual fund are converted into the shares of another mutual fund pursuant to a merger of the two funds, or if the redemption of your shares is treated as a dividend.

See Chapter 7, Capital Gains and Losses, for more information.

The Wash Sale Rule for Mutual Funds

The wash sale rule (see Chapter 7, Capital Gains and Losses) prevents you from selling shares of stock, taking a loss on your tax return, and buying back the substantially identical stock within the 30 days before or after the sale. The wash sale rule also applies to mutual funds. You can sell mutual fund shares at a loss and take the loss on your tax return as long as you do not repurchase shares in the same fund. You can, however, purchase the shares of a different fund with similar investment objectives and holdings.

Losses on Municipal Bond Funds

If you have held the shares of a tax-exempt fund for six months or less and you redeem the shares at a loss, you will not be able to claim the loss on your tax return to the extent you have received any tax-exempt dividends paid by the fund during the time you owned the shares.

Calculating Your Gain or Loss on Mutual Funds Sales

Determining Your Basis.   Your basis in your mutual fund shares is extremely important since it allows you to determine how much of a gain or loss you will have upon the sale of your mutual fund shares. But determining your basis can be tricky—especially because investors often acquire mutual fund shares at different dates, in various quantities, and at various places. Therefore, it is imperative that you retain all records concerning your acquisition of mutual fund shares.

Determining your original basis will vary depending upon whether you have purchased shares, received them in a reinvestment plan, inherited them, or received them as a gift:

- If you purchased shares, your basis will equal your purchase price. Any commission fees may be added to the basis of the shares you acquired.
- If you acquire shares through a reinvestment plan, your basis will equal the cost at the time of the reinvestment.
- If you inherit mutual fund shares, your basis will equal the fair market value of the shares at the date of the decedent's death or valuation date. The fair market value is the last quoted redemption price, commonly referred to as the "bid price" or "net asset value."
- If you acquire mutual fund shares through a gift, your basis in the shares may vary depending upon whether you have a gain or loss when you sell the shares. To determine your basis, you will need to know (1) the donor's basis in the shares, (2) the fair market value of the shares at the time they were given to you, and (3) whether any gift tax was paid on the shares.

  When the fair market value of the shares is less than the donor's adjusted basis, your basis in the shares (if you have gain on their sale) is the same as the donor's adjusted basis. However, if you have a loss when you sell the shares, your basis in the shares is the fair market value of the shares at the time you received the gift. If the fair market value of the shares is equal to or greater than the donor's adjusted basis, your basis is the same as the donor's adjusted basis at the time you received the gift.

  You may increase your basis by all or part of the gift tax paid, depending on the date of the gift. If you received the gift after 1976, you must increase your basis in the gift by the part of the gift tax paid that is due to the net increase in the value of the gift.

Once you have determined your original basis, you must determine your adjusted basis. Your basis must be reduced if you receive a return of a capital dividend (see "Dividends," earlier in this chapter). On the other hand, if you had to pay tax on an undistributed capital gain, your basis must be increased by the difference between your share of the undistributed capital gain you reported and the tax paid for you by the fund.

TAXORGANIZER

You should keep all confirmation statements for purchases of mutual fund shares as well as records of dividends that are automatically reinvested in your account. Your basis is increased by amounts reported to you by the fund on Form 2439 as undistributed capital gains you are required to report as income less the tax paid by the fund on the undistributed gains. Your basis is reduced by nontaxable dividends that are a return of your investment.

Identifying Which Shares Are Sold

To calculate your gain or loss, the IRS permits you to use either the cost basis of your shares or the average basis of your shares. The different methods can result in differing amounts of taxes owed. Consequently, it is important to assess which method is best for you.

If you use the cost basis of your shares, you can figure your basis by (1) the identified cost method, or (2) the first-in, first-out method (FIFO). Alternatively, if you use the average basis of your shares, you can determine your average basis using (1) the single-category method or (2) the double-category method. All of these methods are described below and the advantages and disadvantages of each method are discussed in Table 8.1 below.

TABLE 8.1   Choosing a Cost Basis Method

Cost Basis Method	Advantages/Disadvantages
Specific identification	The most flexible way to determine your gain and losses. But there are important restrictions governing its use.
FIFO	The simplest approach. But it may mean a large gain if your shares have appreciated significantly and you are redeeming only part of your account.
Average cost (single category)	The middle ground. A more modest tax burden than the FIFO method but more tedious calculations if you sell shares frequently.
Average cost (double category)	Only makes sense if (1) you have elected it in the past and are required to continue using it and (2) there is a tax benefit from maintaining separate short- and long-term average costs.

The Identified Cost Method. Using this method, you use the adjusted basis of the specific shares that you identify to be sold to calculate your gain or loss.

Example: Assume that you have six shares of Widget Fund, a mutual fund, and they have a fair market value equal to $50. You purchased two shares for $10 in 1987, two shares for $20 in 1991, and two shares for $40 in May 1999. You decide to have the fund redeem three shares of stock. Under the identified cost method, you may elect to sell the portion of your shares with the highest basis to minimize your gain—and your taxes—on the sale. Consequently, you decide to sell two shares with a $40 basis, thus recognizing a $10 short-term gain on each share. (The gain would be short-term if you sold the shares before May 2000.) You also sell one share with a $20 basis, recognizing a $30 long-term gain.

To qualify for this method you must be able to identify the shares you have sold. To do so, according to IRS regulations, you need to (1) specify to your broker or fund the specific shares that you want sold, and (2) receive a confirmation statement detailing that you asked to sell specific shares.

First-In, First-Out Method (FIFO). Generally, if you cannot adequately identify the specific shares you want sold, and you do not make an election to average your cost basis, the IRS requires the FIFO method to be used. Under the FIFO method, the shares sold are assumed to be the earliest shares purchased or acquired.

Example: Assume the same facts as in the example above. Under the FIFO method, the three shares sold would be the first three you purchased—two shares with a $10 basis and one share with a $20 basis. Assuming you sell the shares for $50 each, you will have a long-term gain of $110—a considerably greater gain than if you had used the identified cost method.

Average Basis Method. If you chose to use either the single- or double-category average basis method, you must elect to do so on your income tax return for the first taxable year in which you use the method. Once you elect to use the average basis method for some shares of a mutual fund you sell or transfer, you must use the method for all the shares of that fund that you hold. However, you can use a different cost method when you sell shares of another mutual fund in the same fund family. The average basis method cannot be applied to shares purchased from other shareholders or to shares you inherit or acquire as a gift.

Double-Category Average Basis Method. If you use this method, all of your shares of a mutual fund are divided into two categories at the time of each sale or transfer. The first category includes all shares that you have held for a year or more. The second category includes all shares that you have held for one year or less. The basis of each share in each category is equal to the adjusted basis of all shares in that category at the time of the sale or transfer divided by the aggregate number of shares in the category.

If you use the double-category method, you specify from which category the shares are to be sold or transferred. Your choice must be confirmed in writing within a reasonable time after the sale. If no written confirmation is made, it is assumed that the shares sold were from the long-term category.

After a year, shares from the short-term category are transferred to the long-term category. If none of the short-term shares have been sold, the basis of the transferred shares is their cost (not the average basis). If some of the short-term shares have been sold, the basis of the unsold transferred shares is the average basis of the shares in the short-term category at the time of the most recent sale.

Example: Assume the same facts as in the example illustrating the identified cost method. The shares in the long-term capital gain category would have an average basis of $15. The shares in the short-term capital gain category would have an average basis of $40. You specify that you want to sell three shares at $50—two from the short-term category, which would result in $20 in short-term capital gains, and one from the long-term category, which would result in $35 of long-term capital gains.

Single-Category Average Basis Method. Using this method, all shares are included in one category. The basis of each share is equal to the aggregate cost or other basis of all of the shares divided by the aggregate number of shares held.

You are restricted from using the single category method if it appears that the purpose of using this method is to convert long-term capital gains or losses to short-term capital gains or losses, or vice versa.

Example: Assume the same facts as in the identified cost method example. The average cost of the shares is $23.33. Consequently, upon the sale of three shares for $50 each, you would recognize a long-term capital gain of $80.

9

Filing Status and How to Calculate Your Tax

INTRODUCTION

This chapter explains the basics of filing status issues and how to calculate your tax. The actual calculation you will have to make is straightforward:

If your allowable standard deduction exceeds your allowable itemized deductions, your taxable income is your adjusted gross income minus your standard deduction and personal and dependency exemptions. If the sum of your allowable deductions exceeds your allowable standard deduction, you can itemize those deductions. Your taxable income will be your adjusted gross income, minus your itemized deductions and personal and dependency exemptions.

You can determine your income tax liability by using the tax tables supplied by the IRS with your tax return form booklet if your taxable income does not exceed $100,000. If your taxable income exceeds $100,000, use the tax rate schedules (reproduced in the Appendix of this book) to compute your tax.

This chapter also discusses special situations that could affect your tax liability, including investment income of children under age 14, the alternative minimum tax, and tax credits. Filing rules, estimated taxes, and withholding taxes are also explained.

WHO MUST FILE

In general, if you are a citizen or resident of the United States, you must file an income tax return by April 15 for the previous taxable year. For the taxable year 2000, income tax returns are due on Monday, April 16, 2001. You can gain additional time to file if you apply for an extension. (See discussion on page 146.) You must file a tax return if your gross income for the year is at least as much as the amounts shown in Table 9.1.

TABLE 9.1   2000 Filing Requirements

Filing Status*	Required to File Return if Gross Income Equals or Exceeds**
Single	
Under age 65	$ 7,200
Age 65 or over	$ 8,300
Head of household	
Under age 65	$ 9,250
Age 65 or over	$10,350
Married filing jointly	
Both under 65	$12,950
One 65 or over	$13,800
Both 65 or over	$14,650
Surviving spouse***	
Under 65	$10,150
65 or over	$11,000
Married filing separately	$ 2,800

*For details on determining your filing status, see discussion on page 148.
**These amounts are adjusted annually by a cost-of-living adjustment.
***You must meet the "surviving spouse" requirements; otherwise you will be treated as single or head of household. (See page 148.)
Note: The amounts in Table 9.1 do not include the additional standard deductions for blind individuals. Such individuals are entitled to an additional $850 standard deduction if married, and $1,100 if their filing status is single or head of household. These amounts are revised annually by a cost-of-living adjustment.

(See the discussion below for persons claimed by another taxpayer as a dependent.)

If married persons filing jointly do not live in the same household at the end of the taxable year, or if either of them can be claimed as a dependent by a third person, the limit for a married person filing separately usually applies.

The following persons must also file a return even if their income is less than the amounts shown above:

1. Persons claimed as dependents on another's return who have unearned income and whose total unearned and earned income exceeds $700. (See below for an exception applying to children under age 14.)
2. Persons with earnings from self-employment of $400 or more.
3. Persons receiving any advanced earned income credit payments.
4. Persons with a liability for the AMT, recapture of investment tax credit, tax due on an early withdrawal from an individual retirement account (IRA) or qualified plan, or Social Security tax on tip income.
5. Persons with wages of $108.28 or more from a church or qualified

church-controlled organization that is exempt from employer FICA contributions.

6. Persons who owe any taxes.

Generally, parents may elect (on IRS Form 8814) to include on their return the unearned income of a child who is under age 14 at the end of the tax year if that child's unearned gross income is between $700 and $7,000 and consists only of interest and dividends. If the parents make this election, the child will not be required to file a separate return. (See page 153 for a discussion of how children under 14 are taxed.)

To obtain a refund for tax that has been withheld, a return should be filed even if it is not required.

Special rules for filing requirements applicable to nonresident aliens and other individuals with special status are not discussed in this book.

How to Get an Extension of Time to File

If you need more time to file your income tax return, you can easily apply for an automatic four-month extension. All you need to do is complete an application (IRS Form 4868, *Extension to File U.S. Individual Income Tax Return*) and send it in by the original due date of your income tax return along with a good faith estimate of your tax liability. Additional extensions beyond the four-month period are granted only for good reason. Under normal circumstances, an extension of more than six months will not be granted unless you reside outside of the United States. If an extension is granted, no penalty for late payment of tax will be imposed if at least 90% of the tax liability shown on the return is paid on or before the original due date.

An automatic extension of two months is also granted to U.S. citizens and U.S. residents whose tax home is outside the United States and Puerto Rico on the date the return is due. Unlike the automatic extension for other individuals (discussed above), no application is required for this particular automatic two-month extension and there is no minimum payment required to avoid a late payment penalty.

Even though the due date for filing a return is extended, any unpaid portion of the final tax will accrue interest from the original due date to the date paid.

Interest rates for underpayments are equal to the short-term federal rate plus three percentage points. (The short-term federal rate is announced by the Treasury Department in the Federal Register.) These interest rates are adjusted quarterly and become effective during the first calendar quarter following the adjustment. Interest is compounded daily.

Which Form You Should Use

All individual taxpayers resident in the United States are required to file their returns on Form 1040, Form 1040A, or Form 1040EZ. Most taxpayers who use this book will probably find that they are required to use Form 1040.

TAXORGANIZER

Although Form 1040EZ or Form 1040A may be easier to use, you should review your tax information before deciding which form to use. You may have deductions that can be itemized, which can be claimed only if you file Form 1040. You may therefore be overpaying your taxes if you use one of the easier forms that does not allow you to claim these deductions.

TAXSAVER

Electronic Filing. *If you are expecting a refund, you should consider filing your return electronically with the IRS instead of mailing in the paper forms. Electronic filing can shrink the time for receiving your refund down to three weeks. Remember, however, that most tax return preparers and other firms authorized to make electronic filings will charge a separate fee for the service—generally about $30 to $40. If you need the refund money right away, it may make sense to pay for filing electronically.*

Every individual (other than a nonresident alien) with net earnings of $400 or more from self-employment must file a report of self-employment income and compute the self-employment tax on Schedule SE (Form 1040), even if the filing of an income tax return is not otherwise required. The self-employment tax calculation is composed of two parts. Part one, for old-age, survivors, and disability insurance (OASDI), is calculated at a rate of 6.2% applied to wages and 12.4% on net self-employment income up to $76,200 in 2000. Part two, for Medicare insurance, is assessed at a rate of 1.45% on wages and 2.9% on net self-employment income in 2000.

TAXORGANIZER

You should be aware that you are not excused from filing a return because the IRS did not send you the necessary forms. You can usually obtain the forms from your local IRS office, post office, or bank, or The Ernst & Young Tax Guide, published annually. Copies of forms may be used. Forms are also available from the Internet at the IRS site www.irs.gov among others.

TAXORGANIZER

Even if you are not required to do so, you should still file a return if:
(1) You had income tax withheld from your pay. Even if you are entitled to a refund, you cannot claim it unless a return is filed.
(2) You qualify for the refundable earned income credit.

Accounting Periods and Methods

You must determine your taxable income for a fixed period of time for each tax year. This is defined as an "accounting period." Most individual income tax returns cover a calendar year based on a 12-month accounting period from January 1 through December 31, unless permission is granted in advance by the IRS to use a different 12-month period.

In addition, you must account for your income and deductions in a consistent way that clearly reflects your taxable income. This is defined as an "accounting method." The two accounting methods most often used are the cash method and the accrual method. Individuals who do not own and operate their own business are required to use the cash method only. The cash method reports all items of income in the year in which you actually or "constructively" receive them. You have "constructively" received income when it is credited to your account or is set apart in any way that makes it available to you. You do not have to physically possess the funds. For example, interest credited to your bank account on December 31, 2000, is constructively received and taxable to you in 2000 if you could have withdrawn the funds in 2000—even if the amount is not entered in your passbook or actually withdrawn until 2001. On the other hand, you generally can deduct expenses only in the year you actually pay them.

If you are qualified to use the accrual method, you generally report income when you earn it, regardless of when you receive the money. You also generally deduct expenses as they are incurred and not when you pay them.

FILING STATUS

Your filing status will determine your filing requirements, standard deductions, eligibility to claim certain deductions and credits, and correct tax. Your filing status is determined by your status on the last day of the tax year, which for individuals is almost always December 31. So, if you were married on December 31, you are treated for tax purposes as being married for the entire tax year. Generally, the effective tax rate for single taxpayers is higher than for married taxpayers filing jointly or unmarried taxpayers filing as head of household. That is because the amount of taxable income that qualifies for the 15% tax rate is lower for single filers ($26,250) than for married taxpayers filing jointly and surviving spouses ($43,850) or heads of household ($35,150). (See tax table in Appendix on page 286.)

Single Taxpayers

Your filing status is *single* if (1) you are unmarried, or (2) you are legally separated from your spouse and you do not qualify to file as head of household or qualifying widow(er) with dependent child. (See page 286.)

Children under age 14 whose unearned income (interest, dividends, capital gains, etc.) is $700 or over are taxed under special rules. (See page 153.)

Married Taxpayers

You and your spouse may agree to file either a joint return or separate returns. A joint return may be filed by a married couple even though only one person has gross income or deductions. A joint return, however, may not be filed if (1) the individuals have different taxable years, or (2) either spouse was a nonresident alien at any time during the taxable year unless an election to file a joint return is in effect. (The catch is that a joint return requires that the worldwide income of both spouses for the entire year be included in taxable income.)

TaxSaver

If you and your spouse each have income, you may want to calculate your tax two ways: filing jointly and filing separately. You can file your returns based on the method that yields the lower tax.

TaxAlert

Separate Filing Traps. *Certain aspects of filing separately are disadvantageous:*
- *The child care and child tax credits are not available.*
- *Social Security recipients also must watch out since all Social Security benefits of separate filers are subject to the "inclusion in income rules." The net effect is that separate filers who receive Social Security will have some portion of their benefits subject to tax. In contrast, joint filers are allowed a base amount of $32,000 of income before benefits are taxable ($44,000 before the 85% inclusion rules apply).*
- *Net capital losses of joint filers can offset up to $3,000 of other income, but the limit for separate filers is $1,500. If one spouse has more than $1,500 of net capital losses, separate filing could cost you.*
- *Various educational credits are not available.*

TaxOrganizer

Substantiation. *Careful record-keeping is important to support allocations of income and deductions between spouses. Also, your ability to direct items to one spouse easily will be affected by whether you live in a common-law or community property state. In common-law states, income is traced based on earnings or ownership of property, and items to be deducted on one spouse's separate return must be paid out of that spouse's separate funds.*

Generally, income and deductions will be split 50/50 between spouses in community property states. States have different rules regarding whether income from separate property is treated as community or separate income, so it's important to check with your tax advisor in these states.

If one spouse dies, the survivor, if not remarried at year-end, may file a joint return for the year of death. A joint return is filed in the name of both spouses and includes the total income and deductions of the surviving spouse and the income and deductions up to the date of death of the other spouse. (See also Surviving Spouse, page 151.)

If a taxpayer and spouse file separate returns, the original election to file separately may normally be changed as long as an amended joint return is filed within three years of the original due date. However, if a joint return is filed, an amended separate return may not be filed for that particular taxable year after the due date, unless the executor of a deceased spouse's estate disaffirms the joint return.

TAXSAVER

When to Get Married: *If one of you has much less income than the other, consider getting married in December rather than January. You will generally be taxed less on the same income if you are married filing jointly than you would be if each of you filed single returns. If both of you have similar levels of income, choose January. Marriage partners who earn approximately the same income may pay more tax if they file a joint return or file separate married returns than they would if they could file two single returns. This is known as "the marriage tax penalty."*

When to Get Divorced: *If you both have similar levels of income, choose December since the marriage tax penalty may be avoided. If one has more income than the other and both want to save taxes, choose January.*

Individuals legally separated under a decree of divorce or separate maintenance agreement are not considered married. Although there may be a tax incentive to do so, the IRS maintains that couples who divorce immediately before year-end and remarry immediately after the start of the new year are considered married at year-end for tax purposes.

Head of Household

A separate, lower tax rate schedule can be used if you are unmarried and can qualify as a head of household. In general, an unmarried taxpayer at the close of the tax year, other than a surviving spouse or a nonresident alien, qualifies as a head of household if the individual furnished over one-half of the maintenance cost of:

1. His or her personal residence, which, except for temporary absences, is lived in during more than one-half of the taxable year by a relative who qualifies as a dependent. You do not qualify as a head of household if you can only claim a relative (other than an unmarried child, grandchild, stepchild, or adopted child; or a parent who does not live with you) as a dependent under a multiple support agreement. The residence can also be lived in by an unmarried son, daughter, grandchild, or stepchild even though not qualified for the dependency deduction, or

2. A household (even if separate) for a parent who qualifies as a dependent other than through a multiple support agreement.

In determining head-of-household status, a taxpayer whose spouse is a nonresident alien at any time during a taxable year is not considered married if an election to file jointly is not made. In addition, a married individual who otherwise qualifies for head-of-household status but for his or her marital status can file using head-of-household status if his or her spouse is not a member of the household for the last six months of the tax year.

TaxOrganizer

You should keep track of your support payments to establish your qualifications for head-of-household status.

Surviving Spouse (Qualifying Widows and Widowers)

If your spouse died in 2000, you may use married filing jointly as your filing status for 2000 if you would otherwise qualify.

If your spouse died during either of the two years immediately preceding this current tax year and you meet all the following tests, you may be able to use *surviving spouse* as your filing status if:
1. During the current year, you furnished more than one-half of the cost of maintaining your home which also constitutes the principal place of residence of your son, stepson, daughter, or stepdaughter;
2. You did not remarry before the end of the year; and
3. You were entitled to file a joint return with your spouse for the year your spouse died.

The return of a surviving spouse is accorded the same benefits as a joint return. This means that you are entitled to a lower tax rate schedule and a higher standard deduction amount if you do not itemize your deductions.

Citizens Living Abroad

If you are a U.S. citizen or resident alien (a green-card holder) living overseas, you are subject to U.S. tax on your worldwide income regardless of where such income is earned, paid, or received. However, you can elect to exclude up to $76,000 of your foreign earned income and certain foreign housing costs, and you may also claim a credit against U.S. tax for foreign income taxes you paid.

TaxAlert

The exclusion amount will increase as follows:

Year	Exclusion Amount
2001	$78,000
2002 and thereafter	$80,000

To qualify for the exclusions, you must meet one of two tests: (1) the bona fide foreign residence test or (2) the physical presence test.

The Foreign Residence Test. The bona fide foreign residence test applies to U.S. citizens only. It requires you to be a resident in a foreign country (or countries) for an uninterrupted period that includes an entire taxable year.

The Physical Presence Test. The physical presence test applies to both U.S. citizens and resident aliens. It will be met if you are physically present in a foreign country (or countries) for 330 full days during any consecutive 12-month period.

Housing Costs. You may also elect to exclude from your U.S. taxable income the excess of reasonable overseas housing expenses over a base housing amount—which is $10,171 in 2000—multiplied by a fraction: the numerator of which is the number of qualifying days of residence or physical presence and the denominator of which is the number of days in the tax year. Interest and real estate taxes are excluded from housing costs for the purpose of calculating the foreign housing exclusion. The exclusion applies only to unreimbursed employer-provided housing costs.

If you are a self-employed individual, you can deduct your foreign housing costs in computing your adjusted gross income, but the deduction is limited to the excess of foreign earned income over the foreign earned income exclusion. Any nondeductible amounts can be carried forward to the following year to the extent that you receive foreign income in the succeeding year.

Expenses, including moving expenses (which are subject to special rules), and foreign tax credits that are attributable to excluded amounts cannot be deducted or credited against your U.S. tax bill.

TAXSAVER

If you are living in a foreign country with a higher tax rate than the United States' tax rate, you may be better off forgoing the foreign earned income and housing exclusions and claiming the foreign tax credits instead. Excess foreign tax credits may be carried back to prior tax years or carried forward.

The foreign earned income and housing exclusions are elected separately. The total of the earned income exclusion and the housing cost exclusion, however, cannot exceed your total foreign earned income. The exclusion amount of up to $76,000 in 2000 is prorated on a daily basis based on the number of days in the taxable year that you meet either test. Once made, an exclusion election remains in effect for future years until revoked. If the election is revoked without the approval of the IRS, a new election may not be made until the sixth taxable year following the year of revocation.

Foreign Tax Credit

You may also elect to claim a credit for foreign income taxes paid or accrued during the tax year or you may claim the taxes paid as an itemized deduction.

As discussed above, if you elect to take either the foreign earned income exclusion or the foreign housing exclusion, or both, the amount of foreign taxes that you may receive credit for will be reduced accordingly. See page 160 for more about the foreign tax credit.

CHILDREN UNDER AGE 14

If your child was under 14 at the end of the taxable year and received more than $1,400 of unearned income, such as interest and dividends, your child's unearned income in excess of $1,400 will be taxed at your marginal tax rate.

Example: A child who does not itemize deductions has $800 of earned income and $2,100 of unearned income. The child would be taxed on $1,400 of unearned income at his or her rate. The remaining $700 would be taxed at the parents' marginal rate. The child's standard deduction is limited to $800 (based on the greater of $700 or the child's earned income, but not more than the regular standard deduction amount; see page 33).

TAXSAVER

If your child is under age 14 and you are in the top income tax bracket, income-producing property that earns up to $700 should be transferred to your child because it will escape tax completely. The next $700 is taxed at only 15%. Because any amount over $1,400 is taxed at your tax rate, you may want to tailor the child's investment strategy so that any of the child's annual unearned income over $1,400 is generated from tax-exempt or from tax-deferred instruments, such as U.S. savings bonds that will mature after the child reaches age 14.

If you are divorced, your child's tax liability is determined by using the custodial parent's tax rate. If you are a married individual filing separately, your child's tax rate is the same as the tax rate of the parent with the greater amount of taxable income.

Any child who is subject to these rules must include the parents' Social Security numbers on his or her tax return.

Including Your Child's Income on Your Return. Parents may elect (on IRS Form 8814) to include the unearned income of any of their children under age 14 on their own return instead of filing separate returns for each child. This election may be made only if (1) your child's gross income consists solely of interest and dividends totaling more than $700 and less than $7,000, (2) your child makes no estimated tax payments for the year under his or her own name and Social Security number, and (3) your child is not subject to backup withholding and he or she did not have a 1999 overpayment applied toward a 2000 estimated tax.

TaxOrganizer

If you elect to include the unearned income of any of your children under age 14 on your return, you may save paperwork, but your family could end up paying more taxes. Including your child's unearned income on your return could increase the amount of state income taxes you pay if your state's tax is based on federal income and your child would not otherwise owe state tax. Your child would also forfeit the ability to claim itemized deductions and to deduct any penalty on the early withdrawal of savings.

TaxSaver

If your children are at least age 14, you should consider taking advantage of their 15% tax bracket, which applies to the extent their taxable income is below $26,250. Here are a few ideas to consider:
- *Convert EE bonds to HH bonds, which pay interest currently, or redeem the bonds and invest in something else, like CDs, which generally produce a greater return with little additional risk.*
- *Convert growth stocks to dividend-paying stocks and mutual funds.*

Tax Rates for Individuals

The 2000 tax schedule contains five rates for individuals—15%, 28%, 31%, 36%, and 39.6%. The top tax rate on net capital gains—the excess of net long-term capital gains over net short-term capital losses—is capped at 20% but may be as low as 10%. See Chapter 7.

Alternative Minimum Tax

The tax law gives special treatment to some kinds of income and allows special deductions and credits for certain expenses. Taxpayers who benefit from these laws have to pay at least a minimum amount through a special tax. This special tax is called the "alternative minimum tax."

Individuals, trusts, and estates must pay the alternative minimum tax (AMT) if it exceeds their regular tax liability for the year. The amount subject to the AMT will be determined by adding a number of preference items to your taxable income and making various adjustments to your regular taxable income. This amount is reduced by the exemption amounts, shown in Table 9.2, and the balance is subject to the AMT rate. Your tax advisor can help you with the calculation.

TABLE 9.2 Exemption Amount

Filing Status	Base Amount	Less 25% of the Amount by Which AMTI Exceeds
Single	$33,750	$112,500
Married filing jointly, surviving spouses	45,000	150,000
Married filing separately, estates, and trusts	22,500	75,000

The AMT rate is generally 26% on alternative minimum taxable income (AMTI) of $175,000 in excess of the exemption amount, and 28% on AMTI more than $175,000 above the exemption amount. The AMT rate on long-term capital gains included in AMTI is reduced to equal the maximum rate on long-term capital gains, i.e., 20%. For married taxpayers filing separately, the 28% AMT rate applies to the extent that AMTI is more than $87,500 above the exemption amount. Furthermore, the base exemption amounts are $33,750 for single individuals and heads of household, $45,000 for married taxpayers filing jointly, and $22,500 for married taxpayers filing separately, trusts, and estates.

Tax Preference Items

Tax preference items are income and expense items that receive special treatment under the tax laws. They must be added back to the taxable income shown on your return in figuring your alternative minimum taxable income. The AMT preference items are:

1. Allowable depletion, to the extent that it exceeds the adjusted basis of the property involved.
2. The amount by which excess intangible drilling costs exceed 65% of the net income from oil, gas, and geothermal properties for the taxable year.

TAXSAVER

To avoid treating excess intangible drilling costs as a tax preference item, you may elect to capitalize and amortize these expenses over a 10-year period in your regular tax calculation.

3. Interest on specified tax-exempt private activity bonds issued after August 7, 1986, reduced by deductions that would be allowable if such income could be included in regular taxable income.
4. Accelerated depreciation on certain property bought and put into use before 1987. (Depreciation methods are described on pages 282–283.)

   (a) Allowable depreciation in excess of straight-line depreciation on real property and leased personal property that was placed in service before 1981. (Straight-line depreciation is calculated by dividing the cost of the property by its useful life.)

   (b) Accelerated cost recovery allowances in excess of the allowance that would be available on real property placed in service after 1980 and before 1987, using the straight-line method of depreciation over 15 years (18 years for most property placed in service after March 15, 1984, and 19 years for property placed in service after May 8, 1985). (*Note:* Straight-line depreciation is computed without considering salvage value); and

   (c) Accelerated cost recovery allowances in excess of the allowance that would be available on leased personal property placed in service after 1980 and before 1987, using the straight-line method, no salvage value, the half-year convention, and an extended recovery period. The half-year convention discussed on page 253 assumes the property was placed in service during the mid-point of the year for depreciation purposes.

5. The excess of the rapid amortization of pre-1987 certified pollution-control facilities over the depreciation that would be allowable.

6. 42% of the gain of qualified small business stock excluded from gross income will be treated as a tax preference item. See page 128 for a definition of a qualified small business stock.

Adjustments

Besides accounting for tax preference items, certain adjustments (increases or decreases) must be made to taxable income to arrive at alternative minimum taxable income. In general the adjustments are:

1. An alternative depreciation deduction (using less accelerated methods and longer depreciable lives) is substituted for the regular tax depreciation deduction for real and personal property and certified pollution-control facilities placed in service after 1986. Recomputations are done in the aggregate—that is, the amount of the adjustment is not determined on a property-by-property basis. *Note:* The adjustment does not apply if you have elected to apply the alternative depreciation system (ADS) for regular tax purposes. (See page 253 for details.) *Note:* For property placed in service after 1998, use the same recovery period you use to figure your depreciation for regular tax purposes to figure any AMT adjustment.

2. Mining exploration and development costs must be amortized over 10 years using the straight-line method.

3. The percentage-of-completion method of accounting must be used for long-term contracts entered into on or after March 1, 1986. Certain small construction contracts entered into on or after June 21, 1988, must use new simplified procedures for cost allocations in the percentage-of-completion calculation.

4. An alternative tax net operating loss deduction replaces the regular net operating loss deduction.
5. The installment method of accounting is disallowed for certain installment sales occurring after March 1, 1986.
6. The treatment of itemized deductions is modified as follows:
   - Medical expenses are deductible only to the extent that they exceed 10% of the taxpayer's adjusted gross income.
   - State, local, and foreign real property and income taxes and state and local personal property taxes are deductible for alternative minimum tax (AMT) purposes only if they are deductible for regular tax purposes in computing adjusted gross income.
   Note: These are taxes related to business, rental property, and farming that are deducted on Schedules C, E, or F.
   - Investment interest is deductible to the extent of net investment income that is adjusted for amounts relating to tax-exempt interest earned on certain private activity bonds.
   - Home mortgage interest is allowed as a deduction for AMT purposes, but the definition of such interest is narrower than that of "qualified residence interest" for regular tax purposes. Refinanced home mortgage interest that is applicable to any mortgage in excess of the outstanding mortgage before refinancing is not deductible for AMT purposes.
   - No deduction is allowed for miscellaneous itemized deductions that are subject to the 2% of adjusted gross income limit for the regular tax computation.
7. No deduction is allowed for personal exemptions and the standard deduction.
8. Circulation expenditures and research/experimental costs must be amortized over 3- and 10-year periods, respectively.
9. Deductions for passive farm losses are denied except to the extent that the taxpayer is insolvent or the activity is disposed of during the year.
10. Rules limiting passive loss deductions also apply to the AMT, except that (a) otherwise disallowed losses are reduced by the amount by which the taxpayer is insolvent, and (b) all AMT adjustments and preferences are taken into consideration in computing income and/or losses from passive activities.
11. For beneficiaries of estates and trusts, the difference between a distribution included in income for regular tax and the AMT income shown on Schedule K-1 must be taken into account.
12. For property disposed of during the year, the gain or loss is refigured to take into consideration the impact that AMT adjustments, such as depreciation, have on the taxpayer's basis in the property.
13. For partners in partnerships and shareholders in S corporations, the income or loss is refigured to take into account AMT adjustments.
14. If exercising an incentive stock option (ISO), the taxpayer needs to adjust for the difference between the option price and the fair market value at the time the option is exercised if the stock received is vested. In calculating the AMT gain or loss on the subsequent sale of the ISO

stock, the AMT basis in the stock is the sum of the option price paid and the AMT adjustment included in alternative minimum taxable income when the stock became vested. If the stock is disposed of in the year of exercise, there is no adjustment.

You will pay the alternative minimum tax only if it is higher than your regular tax. You may, however, offset your AMT liability by using any foreign tax credit, as computed under the AMT rules, that you are allowed to claim. Other personal nonrefundable credits can also reduce the total of your AMT and regular tax liability. These nonrefundable credits include the credit for child and dependent care expenses, the credit for the elderly or disabled, the education credits, the child tax credit, the adoption credit, the mortgage interest credit, and the District of Columbia first-time home-buyer credit.

AMT Credit. The law provides a credit against the regular tax for all or a portion of the AMT you paid in previous years. The credit is equal to the AMT attributable to deferral, rather than exclusion, items. Deferral items, such as accelerated depreciation and ISOs, are those that have the effect of reducing your regular taxable income relative to alternative minimum taxable income in early years but the situation reverses over time. When you pay AMT as a result of deferral adjustments or preferences, the law gives you a credit that can be used to reduce your regular tax liability in the future, but only to the extent your regular tax exceeds the AMT. This credit helps you avoid double taxation on the same income. Exclusion items, such as certain tax-exempt interest income, reduce your regular taxable income permanently. Since these items never reverse in the future, no AMT credit is provided for exclusion items. The AMT credit is carried forward indefinitely from the year of payment and cannot be carried back.

TAXSAVER

If you know you will be subject to exclusion-item-generated AMT in a given year, you should consider accelerating income into that year to be taxed at 26% or 28% rather than a possibly higher regular tax rate in the future. Likewise, consider deferring deductions, especially those that are not deductible for AMT purposes and will give you no benefit. For example, state income taxes are not deductible for AMT purposes. Therefore, you should not prepay your state income taxes in an AMT year. Many people ordinarily do prepay those taxes before year-end in order to claim that deduction for the current tax year. Another approach would be to elect to depreciate assets using the straight-line method of depreciation for regular tax purposes rather than an accelerated method.

CREDITS THAT REDUCE YOUR TAX

The credits discussed below may be used to offset your current income tax liability. For this purpose, income tax does not include certain other taxes, such as the alternative minimum tax and the additional taxes resulting from a premature distribution from certain retirement plans or an annuity contract.

Earned Income Credit

The earned income tax credit (EITC) is a refundable credit available to lower-income workers. For more information, see *The Ernst & Young Tax Guide 2001.*

Credit for Dependent Care Expenses

If you have dependent care expenses and your adjusted gross income is $10,000 or less, an income tax credit is available equal to 30% of certain employment-related expenses incurred for such care. The amount of the credit will decrease by 1% (but not below 20%) for each $2,000 (or part thereof) of your adjusted gross income in excess of $10,000. The maximum amount of employment-related expenses that can be taken into account for the credit is $2,400 for one qualifying individual and $4,800 for two or more qualifying individuals.

A qualifying individual is a dependent under the age of 13 for whom you are entitled to claim a dependency deduction, or a dependent or spouse who is physically or mentally incapable of caring for himself or herself.

For married taxpayers, expenses are limited to the lesser of the two earned incomes. However, the credit is available to married couples who file jointly when one spouse is physically or mentally incapable of caring for himself or herself or is a full-time student at an educational institution for five months during the year. Certain payments to relatives and to children over 19 who are not claimed as dependents will be considered qualified expenses. Married taxpayers must file a joint return in order to claim the credit.

Employment-related expenses are ordinarily expenses for household services and for the care of a qualifying individual that are incurred to enable you to be gainfully employed. Eligible expenses must be reduced by the amount excluded from your income for employer-provided dependent care assistance, including benefits received from cafeteria plans to which you have contributed. (See page 31.)

Credit for the Elderly and the Permanently and Totally Disabled

If you or your spouse is 65 years old or older, you may be entitled to a credit of as much as $1,125 against your tax. Furthermore, taxpayers under 65 years of age who are permanently and totally disabled may also be eligible for the credit. You are permanently and totally disabled if you cannot engage in any substantial gainful activity because of your physical or mental condition. A physician must certify that the condition has lasted or can be expected to last continuously for 12 months or more, or that the condition can be expected to result in death. Disabled veterans may file a VA Form 21-0172, "Certification of Permanent Total Disability," instead of the physician's statement.

In general, married persons who do not live apart must file a joint return to claim the credit. If both you and your spouse are 65 or older, you may qualify for the credit if your adjusted gross income is less than $25,000 and you received less than $7,500 of nontaxable Social Security or other nontaxable pensions. If you file as a single individual, you do not qualify for the tax credit if you are 65 years old or over and (1) you receive nontaxable Social Security or other nontaxable pensions of $5,000 or more, (2) your adjusted gross income is $17,500 or more, or (3) your tax is zero. Generally, the credit is not available to a nonresident alien.

Foreign Tax Credit

An individual may elect to claim a credit instead of a deduction for foreign income taxes. The foreign tax credit that may offset your U.S. tax liability is limited to the ratio of foreign-source taxable income to worldwide taxable income multiplied by the U.S. tax. To the extent that you use the foreign earned income exclusion (page 151), the foreign tax available for credit must be scaled down. To be able to use the credit in an earlier year, you must make a binding election to take the credit for foreign taxes on the accrual method.

Excess credits may be carried back two years and forward five years. The foreign tax credit must be recomputed to determine the foreign tax credit you are allowed to use against any alternative minimum tax liability.

TaxSaver

Because $1 of tax credit reduces your tax liability by $1, whereas $1 of deduction will only reduce your federal tax liability by at most 39.6¢, it is generally a good idea to elect to take a credit for foreign taxes paid rather than a deduction.

TaxAlert

Since 1998, individuals with de minimis foreign taxes are exempt from the limitation and can take the credit without bothering with this tedious calculation. The de minimis amount is defined as $600 or less for joint filers ($300 or less for anyone else). You cannot use this exception if you have a credit carryover.

Credit for Adoption Expenses

Certain taxpayers who adopt a child are entitled to claim a maximum nonrefundable credit of $5,000 per child, for qualified adoption expenses.

If you adopt a special needs child you would get an additional $1,000 credit. Qualified adoption expenses include adoption fees, court costs, attorney's fees, and other expenses that are directly related to a legal adoption of an eligible child.

The credit is phased out ratably for parents with adjusted gross income, as specially defined in the law for this purpose, above $75,000 and is fully phased out at $115,000.

Other Credits

Investment Tax Credit. The regular investment tax credit is generally no longer available for property placed in service after 1985, with certain exceptions.

Expenditures to rehabilitate certified historic structures and other qualified buildings that are to be used for nonresidential purposes are still eligible for the investment tax credit. For qualified buildings placed in service after 1986, the credit is equal to 10% of qualified expenditures for nonresidential buildings first placed in service prior to 1936 and 20% for certified historic structures. The 20% credit is available for both residential and nonresidential buildings. The regular investment tax credit and the business energy credit do not apply to any portion of the basis in the property that qualifies for the rehabilitation credit.

Transitional rules apply to property placed in service before 1994 and qualifying under additional transition rules.

General Business Credit. The investment credit is combined with the alcohol fuel credit (page 267), and the research credit (page 267) into one general business credit. This credit can be claimed against 100% of the first $25,000 of tax liability net of all other nonrefundable credits and 75% of the remaining tax liability. Excess credits can be carried back for three years or carried forward for a 15-year period. Excess credit carryovers generally are used on an earliest-year-first basis, followed by current-year credits and credit carrybacks.

If property on which the investment credit was previously taken is disposed of before the end of the period used in initially determining the credit, the credit must be recomputed, and the unearned portion may have to be recaptured as additional tax in the year of disposal. For ACRS property (see page 251), a portion (33% for three-year property, 20% for other property) of the credit amount is earned for each full year subsequent to being placed in service. If the property disposed of was subject to the limitation applied to used property, you may reselect used property on which no investment credit was taken in the year of acquisition to take the place of the property disposed.

Credit for Excise Taxes Paid on the Use of Gasoline and Special Fuels. A credit or refund is available for the federal excise tax paid on gasoline for nonhighway business use, qualified bus and taxicab use, and certain aviation use. A boat must be used as a commercial fishing vessel for the fuel use to qualify for the credit. A credit or refund is also available for special fuels used for certain nontaxable purposes or resold during the tax year. The credit claimed must be included in income if the cost of the product was deducted as a business expense according to your method of accounting.

Child Tax Credit. A tax credit is available for each qualifying child under the age of 17 in the amount of $500 for the year 2000 and thereafter. A qualifying child is an individual for whom you claim a dependency exemption and who is your son, daughter, stepchild, or eligible foster child. Grandparents can claim a child credit for grandchildren if the grandchildren can be claimed as dependents on the grandparents' tax return.

A phaseout of the credit is predicated on your adjusted gross income and on the number of qualifying children. The maximum child credit available ($500 times the number of qualifying children) is reduced by $50 for each $1,000 by which your adjusted gross income (AGI) exceeds the threshold amounts.

The following chart illustrates how taxpayers with one child, three children, and five children would fare under the credit phaseout.

Maximum amount of credit available			When AGI reaches:		
Number of qualifying children			Single/ Head of household	Married filing jointly	Married filing separately
1	3	5			
$500	$1,500	$2,500	$ 75,000	$110,000	$ 55,000
0	$1,000	$2,000	$ 85,000	$120,000	$ 65,000
0	$ 500	$1,500	$ 95,000	$130,000	$ 75,000
0	0	$1,000	$110,000	$140,000	$ 85,000
0	0	$ 500	$120,000	$150,000	$ 95,000
0	0	0	$130,000 and above	$160,000 and above	$105,000 and above

For large families (with three or more qualifying children) the credit would be partially refundable and limited to your tax liability plus the employee share of FICA taxes minus the earned income credit. Generally, if your child tax credit exceeds the regular tax liability, you must determine if the tax liability plus the employee share of FICA taxes paid exceeds the earned income credit. If so, the amount by which the child credit exceeds the amount calculated above is refundable to you. The refundable portion of this credit is not available for advance payment.

TAXALERT

Generally, you may not deduct education and training expenses unless they are required by your employer or improve your job skills. However, you can elect either a nonrefundable Hope scholarship tax credit or a Lifetime Learning credit for eligible education expenses.

These two credits, as well as the tax-free withdrawals from Education IRAs (see page 94), are mutually exclusive. For each eligible student in each tax year, the taxpayer must elect either of the tax credits or the exclusion from gross income for withdrawals from Education IRAs.

The credits are phased out for single taxpayers with modified AGI of $40,000–$50,000 and for couples filing jointly with modified AGI between $80,000–$100,000. After the year 2001, the income phaseout ranges will be indexed for inflation. The credits are not available to married taxpayers filing separately.

For both the Hope Scholarship credit and the Lifetime Learning credit, "qualified tuition" does not include any other amounts excludable from gross income or amounts deductible as an expense.

You should be aware that the child tax credit and the various educational credits can lower your regular tax liability so much that you may be subject to the AMT.

THE HOPE SCHOLARSHIP CREDIT

The Hope Scholarship tax credit is equal to 100% of the first $1,000 of eligible expenses, and 50% of the next $1,000 of expenses, for the first two years of postsecondary education. For tax years beginning after 2001, the $1,500 maximum Hope credit amount will be indexed for inflation.

Such expenses include qualified tuition and related expenses, but not room, board, or books. The qualified tuition and related expenses must be incurred on behalf of you, your spouse, or a dependent.

Limitations on the Hope Credit

1. The Hope credit can be claimed only for *two tax years*. Thus it is possible that you may not be able to actually claim the credit for the entire first two years of education.
   Example: Rosemary begins college in September 2000. She will take only a little more than a half-time class load her first semester. Her fall 2000 tuition fees are $750. She attends full-time during 2001 and 2002 to finish her first two years of college. Tuition is $3,000 per year. Although Rosemary went to school during 2000–2002, she can claim a Hope scholarship tax credit for only two of those years. The maximum tax credit she can claim for 2000 is $750 and the maximum she could claim for 2001 is $1,500. However, if she delays beginning school until 2001 she can claim the Hope tax credit of $1,500 for 2001 and 2002.
2. The individual must be at least a half-time student for at least one academic period that begins during the year.
3. The Hope credit is permitted only for the first two years of postsecondary education.

4. The credit is disallowed if the student is convicted of a felony drug offense.

The Hope credit is effective for expenses paid after December 31, 1997, for academic periods beginning after that date.

THE LIFETIME LEARNING CREDIT

The Lifetime Learning credit is equal to 20% of qualified tuition and fees incurred during the tax year on behalf of you, your spouse, or any dependents. For expenses paid after June 30, 1998, and before January 1, 2003, up to $5,000 of qualified tuition and fees per taxpayer return will be eligible for the 20% Lifetime Learning credit (i.e., the maximum credit per taxpayer return will be $1,000). For expenses paid after December 31, 2002, up to $10,000 of qualified tuition and fees per taxpayer return will be eligible for the 20% Lifetime Learning credit (i.e., the maximum credit per taxpayer return will be $2,000).

You may claim the Lifetime Learning credit for an unlimited number of tax years, but the maximum amount of the Lifetime Learning credit that can be claimed on a taxpayer's return per year is capped at the maximums described above.

Qualified tuition and fees for the Lifetime Learning credit include amounts incurred for undergraduate or graduate-level (and professional degree) courses. The credit is available for the tuition and fees of a student who attends classes on at least a half-time basis as part of a degree or certificate program. It also is available for any course of instruction at an eligible educational institution (whether the student is enrolled on a full-time, half-time, or less than half-time basis) to acquire or improve the student's job skills.

Example 1: Rosemary, in the above example describing the Hope scholarship tax credit, could claim a Lifetime Learning tax credit of $150 (20% times $750) for 2000.

Example 2: Sam and Debbie earn a total of $75,000 and have three dependent children attending postsecondary schools in 2000:

	Annual Tuition
Lauren—graduate school	$1,500
Mark—fourth year college	2,000
Tom—first year community college	1,000

Sam and Debbie can claim a $1,000 Hope scholarship credit for Tom (100% of first $1,000 of tuition expenses) as well as the Lifetime Learning tax credit for Mark and Lauren. The family has eligible education expenses of $3,500 and can claim a tax credit of $700 (20% times $3,500). Tom's expenses are not eligible for the Lifetime Learning tax credit because the family is claiming the Hope tax credit for those expenses. Thus, the family can claim $1,700 in education tax credits for 2000.

Example 3: Assume the same facts as in Example 2 and assume further that Debbie attends law school at night at an annual tuition cost of $10,000. Only a maximum of $5,000 of tuition expenses per return are eligible for the Lifetime Learning tax credit. The entire family's maximum Lifetime Learning tax credit is $1,000. Total tax credits that can be claimed for 2000 are $2,000.

The Lifetime Learning credit is effective for expenses paid after June 30, 1998, for education furnished in academic periods beginning after such date.

ESTIMATED TAX PAYMENTS AND WITHHOLDING

The IRS requires that you pay your anticipated tax liability as it accrues through withholding and/or the payment of estimated taxes in quarterly installments.

You are automatically exempt from estimated tax payments if you fall into one of two categories:
1. Your tax for the current year, after credit for withheld taxes, Social Security tax refunds, and backup withholding is less than $1,000, or
2. You had no tax liability for the preceding tax year and were a U.S. citizen throughout such year. This rule does not apply if the preceding tax year consisted of less than 12 months or if a return was not filed for the preceding year.

Withholding Tax from Your Wages. Income tax is generally withheld from your wages and salaries based on the amount you earned and the withholding information you have supplied your employer on Form W-4, *Employee's Withholding Allowance Certificate.* If you have significant income from other sources such as self-employment, alimony, interest, dividends, and rent, or the amount of tax withheld from your wages and salaries is not enough, you may have to make estimated tax payments.

Estimated Tax Payments. Estimated tax may be paid in full when you determine you are liable for such tax or in equal installments. Estimated tax payments for a calendar-year taxpayer are due on April 15, June 15, and September 15, and January 15 of the following year. If a filing or payment due date falls on a Saturday, Sunday, or legal holiday, the next working day is substituted. You can make your estimated payments either through crediting an overpayment from your prior year's return to the current year or by sending in your payment with a payment voucher, Form 1040-ES.

If conditions requiring estimated tax payments do not arise until after March 31, a calendar-year taxpayer must make payments on the due dates shown in Table 9.3.

TABLE 9.3 Estimated Tax Payment Deadlines

Date Requirement Met	Date Payments Due*
After March 31 and before June 1	June 15 and September 15, 2000 and January 16, 2001
After May 31 and before September 1	September 15, 2000 and January 16, 2001
After August 31	January 16, 2001

Corresponding dates apply to fiscal-year taxpayers for payments and returns.

The amount of estimated tax you pay may be amended on or before any subsequent installment date.

A complete return may be filed by January 31, with payment of the balance of tax due for the calendar year, in lieu of a January 15 payment of estimated tax.

TAX*SAVER*

It is generally not a good idea to file your tax return by January 31 if you owe tax with the return. You will be better off keeping any additional tax you owe in an interest-generating bank account for two-and-a-half months rather than paying your tax bill early.

The IRS does not issue reminder statements for installments due on estimated taxes. It is your responsibility to remit each installment on a timely basis. (See below for information on waiver of the underpayment penalty for certain taxpayers.)

Any unpaid tax is generally due by the original due date of the tax return, which is April 16, 2001, for a calendar-year 2000 taxpayer. If you have overpaid your tax, you may elect to have the overpayment refunded or applied against next year's tax liability.

TAX*SAVER*

If it appears during the year that you will have underpaid your current year's taxes because previous estimated payments and/or withholding prove insufficient in meeting your actual tax liability, you can correct the situation by instructing your employer to withhold greater amounts from your wages for the rest of the year. Payments that are withheld are considered paid evenly throughout the year.

Underpayment Penalties. You may be penalized for not paying enough tax for a particular installment period. The amount subject to the penalty is the amount by which the required installment, defined as the lesser of items 1 or 2 below, exceeds the amount paid for the quarterly period:
1. 90% of the tax shown on the return (after certain adjustments), allocated evenly to each of the quarterly periods; or

2. 100% of the prior year's tax, allocated evenly to each of the quarterly periods (provided the prior year comprised 12 months and a return was filed for such year); if your 1999 adjusted gross income exceeds $150,000, you must pay 108.6% of the 1999 tax liability to avoid underpayment penalties for 2000; if your 2000 adjusted gross income exceeds $150,000, you must pay 110% of the 2000 liability to avoid underpayment penalties for 2001.

   Example: Ms. Green's adjusted gross income in 1999 was $175,000, while her 1999 tax liability was $40,000. Her 2000 income tax liability is $55,000. Ms. Green will avoid an underpayment penalty in 2000 if the total amount of tax withheld and estimated tax payments exceeds 108.6% of her 1999 tax liability, or $43,440. To avoid a penalty in 2001, she would have to pay in $60,500 (110% of $55,000) since her adjusted gross income also exceeded $150,000 in 2000.

The underpayment penalty may also be avoided by using a special rule based on your annualized income. Under the special rule, no penalty is imposed for a quarter if the cumulative amount paid by the installment date equals or exceeds 90% of the cumulative estimated tax as computed on annualized income.

In general, the annualized method allows you to calculate your quarterly payment based on taxable income received up to the end of the latest quarter, annualized to a 12-month period. You can usually benefit from the annualized method if you do not receive your taxable income evenly throughout the year (for example, if you are the owner of a ski shop that receives most of its revenue during the winter months).

The use of the methods for determining the underpaid amount, described above, may vary from quarter to quarter to provide the minimum underpayment amount by quarter. Remember, however, that if you pay the annualized income installment, you must add the difference between the amount you pay and the required installment to the required installment for the next period if the annualized income method is not used for the next period.

The tax computed for purposes of determining the quarterly payments required to avoid the underpayment penalty includes the self-employment tax and all other taxes (including the alternative minimum tax), minus any allowable credits.

If the amount paid for a quarterly period is greater than the amount required to avoid penalty, the excess is applied first against underpayments in prior quarters, and then against subsequent underpayments. Any penalty is assessed from the installment due date to the date paid or the original due date of the return, whichever is earlier. The rate of the penalty is the same as the rate of interest for underpayments of tax. However, the penalty is not compounded daily, whereas the interest is.

Special requirements and exceptions are provided for farmers, fishermen, and nonresident aliens.

TAXALERT

The underpayment of estimated tax penalty is not imposed where the total tax liability for the year, reduced by any withheld tax and estimated tax payments, is less than $1,000.

EMPLOYMENT TAXES ON SERVICES BY DOMESTIC EMPLOYEES

If you have a domestic helper who qualifies as your employee, you and your employee may be subject to Social Security and Medicare taxes as well as federal and state unemployment taxes.

This may affect your 2000 Individual Income Tax Return (Form 1040), so it deserves your careful attention. This chart will give you the general rules for calendar year 2000. The application of this flowchart assumes that the household worker is properly classified as an "employee" rather than an "independent contractor" for payroll tax purposes. Although it has been called the "nanny-tax," you should know that it also applies to cooks, sitters, chauffeurs, yard workers, and so forth, who are employees.

Did you:	If yes, then:
A. Pay to any household employee, age 18 or older, cash wages aggregating *$1,200* or more in 2000? (Exclude wages paid to taxpayer's parents, spouse, or children under age 21.)	Employer and employee shares of Social Security and Medicare taxes are payable on the cash wages of each employee who received $1,200 or more in 2000.
B. Agree to withhold federal income tax on wages of any household employee in 2000?	Amounts withheld must be remitted to the IRS.
C. Pay total cash wages of $1,000 or more in any calendar quarter of 2000 to household employees? (Exclude wages paid to taxpayer's parents, spouse, or children under age 21.)	Federal Unemployment Tax Act (FUTA) tax is payable on the first $7,000 paid to each employee in 2000.

and . . .
■ Amounts due are to be shown on Schedule H of Form 1040, which must be filed with your 2000 return.
■ You must have (or apply for) an employer identification number.
■ If either Question A or B is answered *yes* for a given employee, Form W-2 must be provided to that employee by 1/31/01 and transmitted with Form W-3 to the Social Security Administration by 2/28/01.

For more information, see the *Ernst & Young Tax Guide 2001*.

PENALTIES

The penalty imposed for late filing is 5% of the unpaid amount for each month or part of a month that it remains unpaid up to a maximum of 25% of the unpaid tax. If you fail to file for more than 60 days, the penalty may not be less than the smaller of either $100 or 100% of the tax required to be shown on the return. If the return is filed on time but is not accompanied by payment of the balance due as shown on the return, the penalty is one half of 1% of the balance due for each month or part of a month of delinquency (up to a maximum of 25% of the unpaid tax). The penalties apply unless the taxpayer can show reasonable cause for the delay. Additional penalties are also imposed on underpayments of tax due to negligence or fraud, and on substantial understatements of tax liability.

10

Year-End Planning for Individuals

INTRODUCTION

This chapter takes a look at the future direction of the tax law and suggests some strategies that you might adopt to better cope with change.

Generally, when tax rates are stable, you would be wise to defer as much income as possible from one year to a later year and to accelerate deductions so that you can postpone the payment of the tax. This strategy allows you the use of more money for a longer period of time. However, you need to take care to have enough cash on hand to pay the tax when it is due. On the other hand, if you expect to be in a higher tax bracket next year than you are this year, you might consider accelerating income into the current year and deferring deductions.

In theory, the strategy is simple: realize income when your tax rate is low and pay expenses when it is high. Marriage, divorce, promotions, retirement, illness, death, or sales of major assets can cause your taxable income to change from one year to another. All of these life-cycle events require special tax planning. The following discussion highlights several strategies that can help you save money on your taxes for 2000 and beyond.

The first step in your year-end planning will be for you to estimate your 2000 and 2001 taxable income. The worksheets provided on pages 184–185 will help you do this.

Shifting Income

There is a 24.6% spread between the highest (39.6%) and lowest (15%) marginal tax rates. Tax savings can potentially be realized by shifting income among family members, especially to children. Higher-income parents should consider transferring assets that generate ordinary income, such as dividends and interest, to children age 14 or older in order to take advantage of their lower tax bracket. For example, shifting $10,000 of investment income from a parent in the 39.6% tax bracket to a child over 14 who is in the 15% bracket (which currently applies to taxable income up to $26,250) can save the family $2,460 in taxes per year. Even greater tax savings may be achieved by spreading ordinary income among all of the taxpayer's children to take advantage of each child's lower tax bracket. Finally, since children under age 14 pay only $105 ($700 × 15%; see Chapter 9) in tax on the first $1,400 of unearned income they receive (unearned income above $1,400 is taxed at their parents' highest marginal tax bracket—the so-called kiddie tax), shifting income-producing property that earns up to $1,400 to a child under age 14 can save the family as much as $449.40 in taxes each year [$1,400 × 39.6% (parents' rate) − $105 (tax paid by the child)].

Accelerating deductions to the current year would be potentially beneficial if the deductions will not be lost or substantially diminished by the 3% of adjusted gross income limit on certain itemized deductions or other limitations on deducting itemized deductions. The 3% limit is explained on page 56.

Limits on Certain Itemized Deductions

Given the limits on certain itemized deductions and exemptions for certain high-income taxpayers (explained in Chapter 2), your best planning move, if possible, would be to exercise some control over the amount of your adjusted gross income. If you can keep your income below the level at which deductions become subject to certain limitations in one year, you would be able to deduct the full amount of personal exemptions and deductions. Obviously, you would want to take as many deductions as possible in such a year.

The Alternative Minimum Tax Rate

As discussed in Chapter 9, the alternative minimum tax (AMT) is a tax system imposed on the regular tax system to prevent taxpayers from taking too great an advantage of special tax breaks such as accelerated depreciation, interest on certain tax-exempt bonds, and so on. Taxpayers who do not use these tax preferences to lower their regular income tax will not be subject to the AMT. Taxpayers who do avail themselves of tax preferences may still escape the AMT because their alternative minimum taxable income is reduced by exemptions:

Filing Status	Exemption Amount	Exemption Phased Out by 25% of Amount in Excess of	Exemption Fully Phased Out at
Married filing jointly	$45,000	$150,000	$330,000
Single/Head of household	33,750	112,500	247,500
Married filing separately	22,500	75,000	165,000

High-income taxpayers who avail themselves of tax preferences may be subject to the tax if they do not plan carefully.

Taxpayers subject to the AMT will pay tax at the following rates:

Rate	*Married Filing Separately*	*All Other Filers*
26%	Up to $87,500 over exemption amount	Up to $175,000 over exemption amount
28%	Greater than $87,500 over exemption amount	Greater than $175,000 over exemption amount

Taxpayers subject to the alternative minimum tax may find that accelerating income and deferring deductions may be the most effective planning approach. For further discussion of the AMT, see Chapter 9.

TaxAlert

You should be aware that the child tax credit and the various educational credits can lower your regular tax liability so much that you may be subject to the AMT.

Filing Status

In general, the effective tax rates on total family income for married taxpayers filing jointly and heads of households are lower than for a taxpayer who files individually (see Filing Status in Chapter 9 and the tax tables in the Appendix for more information.) Thus, if you are eligible to file a joint return for the year, you probably should. For a married person filing jointly for 2000, the 15% tax bracket applies to income ranging from $0 to $43,850. For an individual filing for 2000, the 15% tax bracket applies for taxable income ranging from $0 to $26,250. Not only can you save on your taxes, but for most people, it's simpler to file a joint return. Since a husband and wife are treated as one taxpayer, you won't have to sort out which deductions are his and which are hers.

Effects of Filing Status

There are circumstances where single individuals will find that their combined tax is higher after they marry. This is commonly known as the "marriage penalty."

Example 1: Bob Jones and Mary Smith each have taxable income of $60,000. As single individuals, they are each in the 28% bracket. But if they marry they will have a joint income of $120,000 and part of their income will be in the 31% bracket.

TaxSaver

If your filing status will change before the end of the year, you should decide whether to defer income and accelerate deductions or the opposite, de-

pending on whether or not you will be subject to the marriage penalty. You also should consider whether you would be better off filing separate returns.

Example 2: Two people are married and one spouse has medical expenses of $10,000; the other has none. Both have adjusted gross income of $50,000. They are allowed a medical deduction for amounts in excess of 7.5% of AGI. If they file a joint return, the medical deduction would be $2,500 ($10,000 − [7.5% × $100,000]). If they file separate returns, all other things being equal, the medical deduction would be $6,250 ($10,000 − [7.5% × $50,000]).

TAXSAVER

You should figure your tax both jointly and separately to see which produces the best result.

Your filing status may also affect the limitations on itemized deductions. All taxpayers, whether filing as individuals, heads of household, or jointly, have their itemized deductions reduced by an amount that is equal to 3% of the excess of their adjusted gross income over $128,950 ($64,475 for married persons filing separately). Certain expenses and losses, such as medical expenses, casualty and theft losses, and investment interest expense, are not subject to this limitation but may be subject to other limitations. A working couple with a combined AGI over $148,950 will have their deductions reduced by $600 (3% of $20,000). However, two single individuals each with AGI of $73,300 are both beneath the $128,950 limitation.

When to File as a Head of Household. If you are unmarried at the end of the year, you might save money by filing as a head of household instead of filing a single return. To qualify, in addition to being unmarried, you must maintain a household that was the principal home for the year of a child, grandchild, or other relative who qualifies as your dependent.

If you are still married but have lived apart from your spouse for at least six months of the year, and you have custody of your child, you may be able to file as head of household instead of married filing separately. You will benefit from lower tax rates and you also may be able to claim the standard deduction even if your spouse itemizes deductions. If your income is high enough that some of your exemptions may be phased out, you should consider letting your spouse claim dependents.

If Your Spouse Died during the Year. If your spouse died during the year, leaving you with one or more dependent children, you may continue to file jointly for the two years following your spouse's death and take advantage of the more favorable married-filing-jointly rates. You may claim an exemption for your deceased spouse in the year of death, but not in subsequent years.

INCOME

Compensation

High tax rates enhance the benefits of deferred compensation plans and other tax-deferral arrangements, if you anticipate being in a lower tax bracket when the income is eventually received. For example, 401(k) plans, individual retirement accounts, Keogh plans, other retirement plans, and life insurance policies that build up cash benefits over a period of years should most certainly be considered if you are in this situation.

Bonuses.   Bonuses generally are income to you when you receive them, not when earned. But they are also deductible by your employer when paid. If you want to defer income, you may be able to arrange with your employer before the amount of the bonus is determined that you will not be paid your bonus until next year. Your employer may balk. Yes, he or she gets to keep the bonus money longer, thereby helping cash flow, but having the money in company coffers also increases the company's taxable income. So, if you want to defer your bonus payment, remember to ask early in the year. You can't wait until your employer is passing out the checks and say "I'd like mine next year."

Deferred Compensation.   Another way to defer income from one year to the next is to use a deferred compensation plan. These plans are designed for executives who can afford to defer a portion of their income until a future date. Under these plans the executive makes an election to defer some portion of his or her income until a stated time and is taxed on the deferred income only when it is received.

Deferrals can be made from regular salary or from bonuses. To be effective, however, an election to defer income must generally be made before that income is earned. Further, the executive and the employer must enter into a *written* deferral agreement. Be aware, however, that the IRS may be suspicious of short-term deferrals, say, from December 2000 to January 2001. One problem with deferred compensation plans is that they must be subject to the claims of general creditors and may be subject to the whims of future management.

TaxSaver

An acceptable way to fund deferred compensation—generally over a relatively long period—is to use a "rabbi trust." A rabbi trust is generally an irrevocable trust established by the employer to pay deferred compensation to the employee. Although the trust's assets must remain subject to claims of the employer's creditors, the trust arrangement protects the individual from the whims of the employer and from a change in control of the company. The employee is not protected if the employer becomes insolvent or goes into bankruptcy.

Even more secure than a "rabbi trust" is a "secular trust." Funds held in a secular trust are not accessible by an employer's creditors. However, the price for the added security is that you must pay tax currently on any amounts contributed to the trust. In turn, the company is allowed a current tax deduction when funds are transferred to the trust.

401(k) Plans. If your employer has a 401(k) plan, you can elect to defer into the plan a certain amount of your salary on a pretax basis. These amounts are withheld from your salary and are not reported as taxable income until withdrawn from the plan. Before the end of the tax year, it is usually a good idea to make sure you have made as large a contribution to your 401(k) plan as possible. As of 2000, you can elect to defer up to 25% of your wages up to a maximum of $10,500. Also see the discussion of 401(k) plans in Chapter 5, IRAs, 401(k) Plans, and Other Retirement Plans.

Taxation of Social Security Benefits

The law taxes up to 85% of Social Security benefits received by higher income recipients. The added tax burden means that certain Social Security recipients would benefit from shifting some of their investments from income-producing assets to investments that favor capital appreciation. Or, you may stagger the recognition of income so that you create alternating years of high and low income. Under the right circumstances, you may be able to reduce the amount of Social Security benefits taxed in the *low-income* years without increasing the amount of benefits that otherwise would have been taxed in the *high-income* years.

Interest Income

Taxable Interest. One way to defer interest income from now until next year is to purchase short-term (one year or less) certificates of deposit before the end of the year. Not just any CD will do: it must be the type on which interest is not made available, without substantial penalty, before the 2001 maturity date. The advantage is that you can postpone the accrual of interest income in 2000.

Treasury bills offer a similar opportunity. T-bills do not pay interest but are sold at a discount and mature at their face value. The difference represents interest. It is not taxable to you until the T-bill matures if you hold it until that time. By buying a T-bill that matures next year, you can defer reporting interest from the date of purchase until the following year.

Example: Suppose you have $50,000 in a savings account that credits you with interest on the last day of each month. If, on November 1, 2000, you purchase a six-month CD or a three-month T-bill, you will be able to defer the November and December interest until next year.

Tax-Exempt Interest. Tax-exempt bonds and bond funds should appeal to high tax bracket taxpayers, especially those in the 39.6% top marginal tax bracket. As tax rates rise, taxable securities must provide higher yields in order to match the yield offered by tax-exempt bonds of similar quality and time to maturity.

Example: If you are in the 31% tax bracket, a taxable bond yielding 8.69% is comparable to a municipal bond with a 6.0% tax-exempt yield. However, if you are in the 39.6% bracket, you would need almost a 10% yield on a taxable bond to match the municipal bond's 6.0% return. In addition, bear in mind that some states have income tax rates over 10%. Consequently, your combined federal and state marginal tax rate—factoring in the phase-out of deductions and exemptions for higher income taxpayers and other "back door" tax increases—can exceed 50%. An investor living in such a high tax state would need a 12% taxable bond to achieve the same after-tax return as a 6% municipal bond.

Here's a chart showing the equivalent taxable investment yields for tax-exempt yields ranging from 5%–10% at various individual tax rates.

Your Tax Bracket	*Tax-Exempt Equivalent Yields*					
	5%	6%	7%	8%	9%	10%
15%	5.88	7.06	8.24	9.41	10.58	11.76
28%	6.94	8.33	9.72	11.11	12.50	13.88
31%	7.25	8.70	10.14	11.59	13.04	14.49
36%	7.81	9.38	10.94	12.50	14.06	15.60
39.6%	8.28	9.93	11.59	13.25	14.90	16.55

For example, if you are in the 36% bracket, a 7% yield on a tax-exempt investment provides you with an after-tax return equivalent to a taxable investment yielding 10.94%.

Alimony

Alimony is treated as income to the recipient and a deduction for the payor. The tax law allows a great deal of discretion to both the payor and payee of the alimony about how to set up payments that will provide the maximum tax benefit to both parties. Therefore, there are a variety of year-end planning opportunities to consider.

Example: Individuals finalizing a divorce or separation agreement in the final months of 2000 can negotiate a disproportionately large deductible payment for 2000 as long as it does not exceed the average of the total payments for 2001 and 2002 plus $15,000.

This is a very complex area of the law. Therefore, you should consult with your tax advisor, and it is also important to keep your records in good order. See Chapter 2 for more details.

Business Expenses

Business Travel. The IRS allows employers to reimburse employees for business automobile travel on a per-mile basis. In 2000 expenses for mileage were calculated at 32.5 cents per mile. However, actual expenses will frequently exceed the allowable reimbursement. In many cases you will be entitled to a larger deduction for automobile expenses if you use your actual automobile expense figures rather than the IRS per-mile allowance.

Unreimbursed Business Expenses. Many self-employed taxpayers don't realize that they are entitled to deduct the cost of unreimbursed business expenses that could include business gifts of up to $25 per person. These unreimbursed business expenses should be treated as trade or business expenses, not as miscellaneous itemized deductions subject to the 2% of adjusted gross income floor. An employed executive who buys an attaché case and is not reimbursed would treat the expense deduction as a miscellaneous itemized deduction, subject to the 2% floor. However, if a self-employed individual makes a similar purchase, it is a trade or business expense, fully deductible on Schedule C. For more information, see Chapter 3, Travel and Entertainment Expenses.

Vacation Homes

Review your personal use before the year ends to avoid the loss of your deduction for interest and taxes (see Chapter 4).

Capital Assets

Stock. You may wish to consider deferring the recognition of capital gains from 2000 to 2001. Several strategies can be used to defer the gain on the sale of stock until the following year (see the discussion of capital gains and losses in Chapter 7).

Passive Activity Losses. You can recognize suspended losses from a "passive activity" when you dispose of your entire interest in it. Year-end may be a particularly opportune time to recognize such losses. These passive activity losses can offset active or passive activity income or portfolio income. "Passive activities" are discussed on page 11. You should consult your tax advisor before recognizing passive activity losses.

E&Y FOCUS: Mutual Fund Strategies

As the year-end approaches, many funds will be realizing substantial amounts of their gains, which will flow through to you as capital gain distributions. You can ask your funds' distributors to estimate the expected distributions and their timing. This information is critical if you are trying to produce a net loss that will offset up to $3,000 of ordinary income.

Also, if you are contemplating a mutual fund purchase now, try to avoid "buying the distribution"—i.e., buying shares just before the fund's record date for the year-end distribution. Before you act, find out if the fund has significant realized gains. If it does, consider waiting until after the record date before making your purchase.

TaxSaver

Specifying shares of stock, mutual funds, and other investments is another tax-smart investment strategy. For instance, let's say you first purchased shares in a fund for $30, and over the years the share price rose to $50 as you continued to purchase additional shares. Now the price has dropped to $40 and you decide to sell a portion of your investment. Overall, you still have the potential to realize a large gain.

However, if you have adequate records, you can identify and sell the shares you paid $50 for, and sell them to realize a $10 loss that will offset any other gains you realized this year. See page 125 for additional details.

Business Property

Selling property at a loss this year can keep your adjusted gross income down. This not only reduces your taxable income but can also—if your adjusted gross income is above a certain level—actually increase the amount of your exemptions and itemized deductions.

The sale of certain business property qualifies for special tax treatment. If you sell it at a loss, the loss is an ordinary income loss. If you sell it at a gain, the gain is treated as long-term capital gain. It's one of the few win-win situations left in the tax law—sole proprietors should pay special attention.

Giving Business Property to Charity. If you are a self-employed individual and are thinking about giving business property to charity, make sure that you won't be better off from a tax standpoint selling the property and making an outright contribution to the charity from your personal funds.

ADJUSTMENTS AND DEDUCTIONS

These days, reducing your adjusted gross income (AGI) can be as important as reducing your taxable income. Your personal exemptions are phased out if your AGI is above a certain amount. Furthermore, your itemized deductions are limited if your AGI exceeds $128,950 ($64,475 if married filing separately).

Adjustments

You may be able to reduce your adjusted gross income through various adjustments:

- Your IRA deduction and your spouse's deduction, if applicable;
- One-half of self-employment tax;
- Health insurance for self-employed individuals;
- Keogh and Simplified Employee Pension (SEP); and
- Alimony.

All of these items, except alimony (see page 25), are discussed below.

Self-Employment Tax and Health Insurance for Self-Employed Individuals

If you pay self-employment tax, half of it is deductible.

Self-employed individuals and employee-owners of 2% or more of the stock in an S corporation may deduct (as an adjustment to gross income) 60% of the premiums paid for health insurance coverage of the individual and his or her spouse and dependents for 2000 and 2001; 70% for 2002; and 100% for 2003 and beyond.

IRAs, Keoghs, and SEPs

IRAs. Contributions can be made up to the due date of your tax return, not including any extensions, and still be deductible on your previous year's tax return. Thus, you have until April 16, 2001 to make an IRA contribution and claim it on your 2000 return. By contributing pre-tax dollars to an IRA, you can accumulate savings while reducing your taxable income. For a further discussion of IRAs, see Chapter 5.

TaxSaver

Although you can make a contribution to an IRA at any time up to the unextended filing date of the return in which the deduction is claimed, the earlier you make the contribution the greater the ultimate benefit. Here is an example:

Taxpayers A, B, and C contribute the maximum amount possible to their IRAs. Only the contribution pattern differs. A makes annual contributions of $2,000 beginning on January 2; B contributes $166.66 January 31 and the end of each month thereafter; and C makes an initial contribution on April 15 of the following year. This table shows the effect over time of their contribution patterns assuming a constant 8% rate of return.

For example, assuming 10 years of contributions (i.e., $20,000), the balance of the account for taxpayer A would be $33,794 whereas taxpayer C would have $30,498.

Taxpayer	Number of Years of Contribution		
	10 years	*20 years*	*30 years*
A contributes 1/2	$33,794	$106,754	$264,267
B contributes monthly	32,422	102,420	253,539
C contributes the next 4/15	30,498	96,342	238,494

Keogh Plans. Individuals with self-employment income may establish a retirement plan known as a Keogh plan, to which they may make tax deductible contributions. (For details, see Chapter 2.) Although a plan must be established by year-end, unlike an IRA, you have until the due date of your return, including extensions, to make the maximum allowable contributions. A Keogh plan is a qualified retirement plan. Participation in a Keogh plan limits IRA deductions. Consequently, before establishing one you should consult your tax advisor. A rule of thumb is that a start-up business should produce at least $15,000 in self-employment income before a Keogh plan becomes as cost effective as an IRA.

SEPs. A Simplified Employee Pension (SEP), like an IRA, can be established after the end of the taxable year for which the deduction is being claimed. The plan must be established prior to the due date of the *employer's* tax return including any extensions. For further details about SEPs, see Chapter 5.

ITEMIZED DEDUCTIONS

To receive the maximum tax benefit when itemizing your deductions, you should generally try to bunch your deductible payments in years in which they exceed the amount of your standard deduction and also exceed the floors based on adjusted gross income for medical expenses and miscellaneous deductions.

Your first decision is to choose between itemizing deductions or taking the standard deduction amount ($7,350 in 2000 for married taxpayers filing jointly and qualifying widow(ers); $4,400 in 2000 for single filers; $6,450 for heads of households; and $3,675 for married persons filing separately). You should choose whichever alternative yields the higher deduction. (See Chapter 2 for a further discussion of itemized deductions and the standard deduction.) If it is likely that you will opt to itemize your deductions, you'd be well advised before the end of the tax year to review them and see if there are ways you can slide some into whatever tax year might yield a more favorable result. Casualty and theft losses cannot be planned. It's also usually difficult to plan deductible moving expenses related to your job. So, for practical purposes, you should focus your review on the following four types of expenditures:

- Medical and dental expenses in excess of 7.5% of your adjusted gross income
- Certain state and local taxes
- Interest expenses
- Contributions to charity

Each of these types of expenses is discussed below.

Medical and Dental Expenses

Your medical expenses, including certain health insurance premiums, are deductible only to the extent that they exceed 7.5% of your adjusted gross income (AGI) (10% if you are subject to the alternative minimum tax, AMT). While you do not have control over medical emergencies, you do have control over elective medical procedures. These should be bunched in years when your AGI is lower. That way your medical expenses are more likely to exceed the 7.5% floor. You may be even better off if you participate in your employer's cafeteria plan (see page 31, "Cafeteria Plans," for further explanation).

Taxes You Paid

State and local income and property taxes generally are itemized deductions. For the most part you will have paid your state income taxes, and in some instances your local income taxes, through withholding. However, before year-end you may wish to pay those taxes that you would normally pay early next year because your liability was not fully satisfied through withholding. Also, taxpayers with large state and local tax liabilities may be subject to the AMT, since these taxes are not deductible for AMT purposes.

Interest You Paid

Qualified Home Mortgage Interest. Typically, homeowners make monthly mortgage payments throughout the year. The mortgage interest on those payments generally is deductible subject to the rules and limits explained in Chapter 2.

Personal or Consumer Interest. Although personal or consumer interest is not deductible, interest on a home equity loan is deductible. Therefore, one way to increase your interest deduction is to consolidate your personal and consumer loans into a home equity loan. Many banks are now structuring what used to be personal and auto loans as home equity loans. (There is a further discussion of home equity loans in Chapter 4.)

Contributions to Charity

Most taxpayers make many of their charitable contributions at the end of the tax year. The reason is simple: you can have use of the money for the entire year and, at the same time, you can take the tax deduction for that year. If you made your contribution in January, you would be entitled to the same tax deduction but would not have use of the money for the rest of the year. Charitable contributions are available only if you itemize your deductions. You'll find a comprehensive discussion of charitable contributions in Chapter 6.

TaxSaver

A few points to consider, especially at year-end:
1. *If cash is not readily available, you can use a credit card to charge donations to charity. They will be deductible in 2000 even though you don't pay the charge until 2001.*
2. *If you are going to give publicly traded stock to a charity, check with your stock broker to ensure that you have readily transferable title to the property that you want to donate to charity.*
3. *A contribution of qualified appreciated long-term capital gain stock to a private foundation will qualify for a full fair market value deduction.*

Deferred Giving. There are ways to make deferred contributions to a charity and also claim a deduction: (1) A charitable "remainder" trust lets a donor retain an interest in the property's current income stream and to claim a current charitable deduction for the present value of the remainder interest given to charity. (2) A charitable "lead" trust pays income to a charity for a term of years (the lead), at the end of which the principal of the trust reverts to the grantor or other noncharitable beneficiary. This technique can result in a current deduction equal to the present value of the income the trust will pay to the charity. You would include income on your return as the trust earns it. If the trust is funded with tax-free bonds, the interest you receive in future years is treated as tax free. If you want to establish a charitable remainder or lead trust, you should do so before year-end and with the assistance of a professional advisor. Also, see Chapter 6 for details.

Miscellaneous Deductions

Generally, only the amount of miscellaneous deductions that, considered as a group, exceed 2% of your adjusted gross income is deductible. Therefore, you should bunch these expenses as much as possible so that the total will exceed the 2% floor. If it appears that you will not exceed the floor this year, defer these expenses until next year if you can. Alternatively, accelerate expenses to this year if that will enable you to exceed the 2% floor.

TaxSaver

Married persons who customarily file jointly should consider filing separately to maximize miscellaneous deductions. Note, however, that miscellaneous itemized deductions are not allowed for the calculation of the alternative minimum tax.

Exemptions

Review the amount of support you have provided so far this year to your dependents, children, and parents, to ensure that you meet the support test that allows you to claim an exemption for them as dependents. Also, be aware of the rules that phase out the tax benefits of exemptions if your adjusted gross income exceeds certain levels. See Chapter 2.

Paying Your Taxes

An important aspect of tax planning, particularly year-end tax planning, is how and when you pay your tax liability. This affects your cash flow and may result in real savings for you.

You should review not only your expected tax liability but also when that tax is paid. Significant overpayments are essentially interest-free loans to the government, but underpayments may result in a nondeductible penalty. See page 166.

TaxSaver

If you have not paid enough up to this point, consider increasing your federal and state withholdings from salary or wages for the remainder of the year. Taxes withheld are considered paid evenly throughout the year. You can also increase or start withholding on pension and Social Security payments. Therefore, increased withholdings at the end of the year could eliminate an underpayment in the beginning of the year. In addition, itemized deductions would increase as a result of the additional state taxes withheld. However, taxpayers claiming large state tax deductions may subject themselves to the AMT.

If you project a significant overpayment, reduce your tax payments for the balance of 2000 by at least the amount of your overpayment. This step should be done only when estimates are considered fairly accurate. Reducing current payments below your tax bill for the year will cause a larger amount to be due with your return. That balance due, unlike the return itself, generally cannot be extended beyond the original due date of the return (i.e., April 16, 2001, for 2000 calendar-year taxpayers).

Worksheet to Estimate 2000 and 2001 Federal Income Tax*

Gross income	1999 (actual)	2000	2001
Wages and salaries	$_____	$_____	$_____
Interest income	_____	_____	_____
Dividends	_____	_____	_____
Income or loss from trade or business	_____	_____	_____
Net capital gains or losses	_____	_____	_____
Rents and royalties	_____	_____	_____
Income or loss from partnerships, trusts, estates, and S corporations[1]	_____	_____	_____
Pensions and annuities	_____	_____	_____
Taxable Social Security benefits	_____	_____	_____
Other	_____	_____	_____
Less: Deductions for adjusted gross income (AGI)			
Alimony paid	(_____)	(_____)	(_____)
Payments to an IRA or Keogh plan[2]	(_____)	(_____)	(_____)
Other	(_____)	(_____)	(_____)
Equals: AGI	$_____	$_____	$_____

Itemized deductions

Medical and dental (in excess of 7.5% of AGI)	$_____	$_____	$_____
State and local income taxes, property taxes[3]	_____	_____	_____
Qualified residential interest	_____	_____	_____
Investment interest expense[4]	_____	_____	_____
Charitable contributions	_____	_____	_____
Casualty and theft loss (in excess of 10% of AGI)	_____	_____	_____
Moving expenses	_____	_____	_____
Other: Tax preparation fees, investment fees, and employee business expenses[5]	_____	_____	_____
Total itemized deductions	_____	_____	_____
Less: 3% of AGI adjustment[6]	(_____)	(_____)	(_____)
Adjusted itemized deductions	_____	_____	_____
Standard deduction	_____	_____	_____
AGI less the higher of adjusted itemized deduction or the standard deduction[7]	_____	_____	_____

Less: Number of exemptions ×
  $2,800 (2000)[8]   (_____) (_____) (_____)
Equals: Taxable income   _____ _____ _____
Regular tax (from tax rate schedule,
  see page 286)[9]   _____ _____ _____

*Does not include the alternative minimum tax (AMT) computation (see the discussion of the AMT on page 154).

1. *Except for rental losses allowed up to certain AGI limits, passive activity losses in excess of passive activity income from each activity are disallowed.*
2. *If you or your spouse are a participant in an employer-maintained retirement plan, your IRA deduction may be limited.*
3. *If you have unusually large deductions for state and local taxes and/or substantial tax preference items, see page 154; you may be subject to the alternative minimum tax.*
4. *Investment interest expense deductions are limited to the amount of the taxpayer's net investment income.*
5. *Most miscellaneous itemized deductions are deductible only to the extent they exceed 2% of AGI. Employee business expenses in excess of reimbursement are miscellaneous itemized deductions.*
6. *See page 56 if your AGI is in excess of $128,950 ($64,475 if married filing separately).*
7. *See page 33 for more about 2000 standard deductions and page 34 for personal exemptions. To estimate your 2001 income, use 2000 amounts.*
8. *In 2001, the exemption amount will be adjusted for inflation. At this printing, the amount is not known. To estimate your income, assume it will be the 2000 amount of $2,800. These should be adjusted for the phaseout of exemptions as described on page 34.*
9. *If you have net capital gains, the maximum rate is 20%; see Chapter 7.*

II

How to Improve Your Financial Future

Everyone hopes for or dreams about a bright financial future. Yet, not enough Americans are doing much to secure it. Consider, for example, that, although Americans are richer per capita than individuals in most other countries, they save or invest a smaller percentage of their income than do the Japanese, Swiss, Portuguese, Turks, Greeks, Italians, and Norwegians, to mention just a few. Now there are more and more reasons for Americans to be concerned. Many corporate pension plans are not as generous as they once were, and while many Americans are working well past age 65, they are living longer, too.

Taxes are not the only consideration in planning your financial future, but they are an important one. Savvy investors can defer taxes so that they have more of their money building their nest egg. At some point, depending on your age and need for income, you may want to consider investments that are tax-free. Now—not later—is when you need to plan how you are going to afford to retire. And, as unwelcome a task as it may be, you need to consider planning your estate and how you want to provide for your heirs. In some important respects, you can enhance the quality of your life by giving serious consideration to how you want your assets handled after your death.

11

Investment Planning

Introduction

The best way to achieve your financial goals and objectives is to plan. The planning process needs to take into account your personal investment biases and your tolerance for risk. Generally, the more risk you are willing to take, the higher the potential returns. But, are you comfortable trading stocks and bonds? Or would you feel better putting your money in fixed-income government securities? You also have to set realistic goals for the rate of return you expect to earn on your portfolio. The purpose of this chapter is *not* to suggest where you should and should not invest. That task is something you, and perhaps your investment advisor, have to tackle.

But tax-saving strategies enable you to keep more of your investment profits and improve your financial future. This chapter will provide you with brief descriptions of various popular investment products, their tax consequences, and tax strategies you should be aware of when establishing your financial plans and investment portfolio. Table 11.1 briefly describes various types of investments and the tax treatments of the income generated from them.

Where to Start. Investment planning can't take place in a vacuum. In coming up with your investment strategy, you need to take into account your current net worth and current and future cash needs.

Getting Started

Before tackling the strategies and planning approaches discussed in this book, it will help if you focus on your individual financial position. Take a few moments completing these worksheets to get an understanding of not only your net worth but where your money comes from and where it goes.

Table 11.1   Tax Attributes of Various Investments

Security	Description	Tax Attributes
Cash, CDs, and Savings Accounts	Money in bank, government insured up to certain limits.	Annual interest taxed.
Treasury Bills	Short-term (up to 1 year) debt obligation of U.S. Treasury.	Interest earned taxed at maturity or earlier if bills are sold. Interest exempt from state and local taxes.
Treasury Notes	Medium-term (2-year to 10-year maturity) debt obligation of U.S. Treasury.	Annual interest taxed. Interest exempt from state and local taxes.
Treasury Bonds	Long-term (more than 10 years' maturity) debt obligation of U.S. Treasury.	Annual interest taxed. Interest exempt from state and local taxes.
Inflation-Indexed Treasuries	10-year maturity debt obligation of U.S. Treasury. Principal is adjusted annually on the basis of changes in the consumer price index.	Annual interest taxed. Increase in principal taxed currently. Interest exempt from state and local taxes.
Ginnie Mae—GNMA	A security representing a share in a pool of mortgages in which the timely payment of interest and principal is guaranteed by the Government National Mortgage Association.	Annual interest is subject to federal, state, and local tax. The principal, which can be paid off sooner or later than expected, is not taxable.
U.S. Savings Bonds	Debt obligation of U.S. Treasury. Pays interest rates depending on your purchase date.	Interest exempt from state and local taxes. Federal tax is deferred on Series E and EE bonds. Can be exempt from federal tax if bonds are used to fund higher education, but income limits and other restrictions apply.

Table 11.1 Tax Attributes of Various Investments (*continued*)

Security	Description	Tax Attributes
Municipal Bonds	Debt obligations of states, cities, or towns or their agencies.	Interest exempt from federal tax and in state where issued. Interest on certain private activity bonds can be subject to AMT.
Corporate Bonds	Debt obligations of corporations.	Annual interest taxed. Special rules for bond premium and discount: the amount paid above or below a bond's face value.
Zero Coupon Bonds	Fixed rate debt obligations of U.S. Government, state, or corporation. No annual interest paid. All earned interest paid at maturity.	U.S. Government and corporate interest taxable each year as though it had been paid. State obligation interest is tax exempt.
Stock, Common and Preferred	Security denoting units of equity ownership in a corporation.	Dividends, when paid, generally taxable. Appreciation, if any, taxed when stock sold, generally at a favorable tax rate. Losses are deductible but subject to limitations.
Mutual Fund Shares	Shares in a company that invests money from many investors to buy stocks, or bonds, or both, in many corporations. Some funds invest in government bonds only.	The fund's earnings paid to shareholders are treated as dividends or capital gains. Dividends may be taxable or exempt depending upon their source.

Your Net Worth

AS OF _____

ASSETS
Cash Equivalents
   Checking/Savings Accounts $_____
   Money Market Accounts   _____
   Money Market Fund Accounts   _____
   Certificates of Deposit   _____
   U.S. Treasury Bills   _____
   Cash Value of Life Insurance   _____
     Total $_____
Investments
   Stock Options (appreciation) $_____
   Mutual Fund Investments   _____
   Partnership Interests   _____
   Other Investments   _____
     Total $_____
Retirement Funds
   Pension (Present Lump Sum Value) $_____
   IRAs/Keogh Accounts   _____
   Employee Savings Plans, e.g., 401(k)   _____
     Total $_____
Personal Assets
   Residence(s) $_____
   Collectibles/Art/Antiques   _____
   Automobiles   _____
   Home Furnishings   _____
   Furs and Jewelry   _____
   Other Assets   _____
     Total $_____
TOTAL ASSETS $_____

LIABILITIES
   Charge Account Balances $_____
   Personal Loans   _____
   Investment Loans (margin, real estate,
     etc.)   _____
   Home Mortgages/Home Equity Loans   _____
   Life Insurance Policy Loans   _____
   Projected Income Tax Liability   _____
   Other Liabilities   _____
TOTAL LIABILITIES $(_____)

NET WORTH $========

Your Cash Flow

	Annual Amount
SOURCES OF CASH	
Salary and Bonuses (net of deductions)	$_____
Self-Employment Income	_____
Dividends	_____
Interest	_____
Net Rents and Royalties	_____
Social Security	_____
Pension	_____
Distributions from Trusts/Partnerships	_____
Other Income	_____
Total Cash Available	$_____
USES OF CASH	
Home Mortgage (or apartment rent)	$_____
Utility Payments	_____
Home Maintenance	_____
Property Taxes	_____
Car Payments	_____
Car/Commuting Expenses (including parking, subway, gas)	_____
Credit Card/Loan Payments	_____
Insurance Premiums (life, health, car, home, etc.)	_____
Income Taxes	_____
Employment Taxes	_____
Clothing	_____
Child Care	_____
Food	_____
Medical Expenses	_____
Education	_____
Vacations	_____
Entertainment	_____
Alimony	_____
Charitable Contributions	_____
Gifts	_____
Personal Items	_____
Other Payments	_____
Total Expenses	$(_____)
Net Cash Inflow/(Outflow)	$=======

You also need to think about saving money—and investing it prudently—for your retirement. You should also give some thought to estate planning. Will your estate be liquid enough to pay debts and estate administration expenses due after you die, or will assets have to be sold to cover these expenses? (See Chapter 13 for more information about estate planning.)

And, of course, there are taxes. An investment strategy, an estate plan, or almost any other financial plan can't be developed properly without giving thought and consideration to tax consequences.

But we urge that you keep two important principles in mind:

1. You should adopt a systematic and disciplined saving program.
2. You should diversify your investment portfolio among different types of assets—cash and cash equivalents, fixed-income securities, equities, and real estate.

Diversification can ease the effects that market fluctuations can have on your portfolio. It does not eliminate risk or guarantee that you will meet your financial goals, but it is the most prudent way to reduce risk. Also, when purchasing specific stocks or mutual funds, you should consider "dollar cost averaging," i.e., the systematic purchase of a specific dollar amount at regular intervals regardless of the price level of the stock or the market in general. Dollar cost averaging is based on the assumption that the market rises in the long term and fluctuates in the short term. As a result of using this technique, you will purchase more shares when the market value of the investment has declined and fewer shares when the value has increased, resulting in a lower average cost per share than you might otherwise obtain. In addition, dollar cost averaging offers a regular and disciplined approach to investing in equities.

Capital Gains and Losses

The top tax rate on ordinary income in 2000 is 39.6% for taxpayers with taxable income over $288,350 ($144,175 for married persons filing separately), while the maximum tax rate on net long-term capital gain is 20%. Gains on property will be treated as long term only if the property is held for more than 12 months. (For more information on how to figure a capital gain or loss, see Chapter 7.)

Because ordinary income and capital gains are included in your adjusted gross income for purposes of figuring the limitation on itemized deductions and the phaseout of personal exemptions, the effective rates on ordinary income and capital gains actually exceed 39.6% or 20%, respectively.

TAXPLANNER

The 19.6 percentage-point differential between the top tax rate and the maximum long-term capital gain rate encourages high-income taxpayers to favor investments that offer capital appreciation, which are taxed at the lower capital gain rate when the investment is sold, over investments that generate current income and dividends, which can be taxed at a rate as high as 39.6%.

TAX*SAVER*

There are a number of planning techniques you can use to save or defer taxes if you sell securities or other capital assets. The advantage you have is that you generally control the timing of a transaction so you can recognize the capital gain or loss in the year of your choice. A cautionary note: your decision to buy or sell should be based on sound economic and investment criteria and not solely on the tax effect of the transaction. Here's a list of some techniques you can use that can influence how and when you pay taxes:

Sell the Shares You Bought for the Highest Price First. If you bought shares in a single company at different times, you may want to identify the specific shares you sell. This will enable you to sell the shares with the highest cost first and may produce, depending on the sales price, a loss or a lower capital gain. If you don't specify what shares you are selling, it will be assumed that the first in were the first out. See Chapter 8 (Mutual Funds) for a complete discussion of the identified cost method.

Sell Now, Buy Back Later. If your objective is to generate a tax loss this year while preserving your investment position, you can sell the securities and repurchase them later. However, you cannot deduct any losses you sustain on the sale if you or your spouse repurchases (or enters into a contract or option to repurchase) substantially identical securities within 30 days before or after the sale. Such a repurchase would violate the wash sale rules, which are explained on page 127.

Purchasing Put Options. You can use a put to lock in your gain without paying tax in the current year. The use of put options is explained on page 126.

Selling Short against the Box. This is another way to defer capital gains tax until the following year and at the same time lock in your gain. See page 126 for further details.

Installment Sales. You can postpone the gain on the sale of assets such as real estate or stock of a closely held business—but not the stock of a publicly traded company—by using the installment sale method. As a seller, you may be able to report your gain only as you receive payments. For information on how to qualify a sale and report your gain under the installment sale method, see page 128. Installment sales can also be an effective year-end planning tool.

Charitable Remainder Trust. The use of a charitable remainder trust may provide (1) for the deferral or elimination of tax on capital gains, (2) a current income stream, and (3) a future gift to charity. Establishing such trusts requires careful analysis, involves additional costs, and should be done only after consulting with an experienced tax and financial planning consultant. See Chapter 6, Charitable Contributions, for further details.

Selling Your Home. If you sell your home, up to $250,000 ($500,000 if married and filing a joint return) of gain can be excluded from gross income, provided you owned and lived in the home for at least two of the previous five years. See page 74 for details.

TaxSaver

You can use capital losses to offset your capital gains, thus lowering your taxes. If you have capital losses greater than your capital gains in any year, you may use the net losses to offset up to $3,000 of ordinary income. For a further explanation, see Chapter 7.

Annuities

Annuities are arrangements in which an investor pays one or more premiums to an insurance company in exchange for the promise of distributions at some future date.

Annuities fall into two categories: fixed and variable. With a fixed annuity, the investor pays the premium to the insurance company and the company credits a specified rate of interest on the cash value of the annuity. That rate is generally guaranteed for a term of one or more years. With a variable annuity, the premium is allocated by the investor among stock funds, bond funds, and money market funds. Premiums for an annuity can be paid annually or all at one time. The premium amount can be fixed or can vary, depending on the terms.

At some point, the investor can withdraw the funds from the annuity. A variety of payment terms is available, including payments over the investor's lifetime or the joint lives of the investor and another person. The amount of the payments will depend upon a number of factors, including the amount of premiums paid and the earnings over the years.

Interest or gains earned from a tax-deferred annuity are not taxed until withdrawn. When distributed, they are taxed at ordinary income rates. In addition, the tax law provides that certain distributions that are not in the form of regular period payments, made before age 59½, are subject to a penalty of 10% of the taxable portion of the distribution.

E&Y FOCUS: Should You Buy an Annuity?

While taxes are of obvious concern to an investor considering a deferred annuity, the costs associated with using deferred annuities as tax-advantaged investments should also be considered.

Typically, the insurance company will allow the investor to withdraw, without charge, a certain percentage (e.g., 10%) of the cumulative premium paid or the actual value of the account each year. Amounts withdrawn in excess of stipulated percentages will be assessed a surrender charge. These charges vary among companies and products, but generally are between 5% and 10% of the amount withdrawn and generally decline over a period of 5 to 10 years. Variable annuities may also be subject to additional annual charges that can total 0.5% to 2.25% of the value of the account. These charges lower the annual yield of your annuity.

An investor should also consider whether deferring tax is a worthwhile objective. Since the earnings and gains of the annuity will be taxed as ordinary income when distributed, the deferral might not be advantageous if ordinary income tax rates are higher at the time of withdrawal. Also, capital gains that might have been taxed at preferential capital gains rates are taxed when distributed at ordinary rates. On the other hand, the deferral will have allowed the money in the annuity to compound tax-free until withdrawal.

Here are some points to consider when selecting an annuity:

1. Since you could be "doing business" with the insurer for decades, it pays to buy from strong, quality insurers. However, you should note that variable annuities are *not* part of insurer's general account.

2. An investor who purchases a fixed annuity should examine whether the current interest rate is competitive and for how long a period the rate is guaranteed. You should ask for data on how the company determines the interest after the end of the period for which the rate is guaranteed.

3. An investor who buys a variable annuity should look at the breadth of investment choices within the annuity and the track record of *all* the funds.

4. For both fixed and variable annuities, consider the applicable surrender charges for withdrawals. Also, be sure you understand what the fees, expenses, and charges are and how they work.

Dividend Income

Most, but not all, dividends you receive are taxable, and that can make a world of difference when contemplating your investment options—and your taxes.

Ordinary dividends are taxable income and must be reported on your Form 1040. See page 7 for details. The corporation making the distribution will inform you about whether the dividends are taxable or not.

Nontaxable corporate distributions include the following:

- Stock received in a stock split.
- Mutual fund dividends that represent tax-exempt interest (these may be subject to the AMT and/or state and local taxes).
- Return of capital.
- Dividends on insurance policies (unless they exceed net premiums).
- Dividends on veterans' insurance.
- Stock dividends or stock rights. If you receive a nontaxable distribution of stock or stock rights—in effect, a certificate entitling you to buy additional stock—your adjusted basis of the old stock must generally be apportioned between the old and the new stock, based on their proportionate market values. Tax is not paid until the stock is sold. See page 7.

Exceptions: If a corporation offers you a choice between a cash dividend or a stock dividend, can you choose between a taxable and nontaxable dividend? Unfortunately not. The previously nontaxable stock dividend will now be considered taxable income because you could receive taxable cash in its place. Therefore, is it better to take cash? Not necessarily. If you believe in the company's potential, you might choose the stock dividend with the hope that the price of the shares will rise. You must include in your taxable income the market value of the additional shares on the date the dividend is paid. The new shares will have their own basis, equal to the market value you include in your taxable income. Other instances in which stock dividends may be taxable include the following:

1. When preferred stock is issued to some shareholders and common stock to others;
2. When the dividends are on preferred stock;
3. When convertible preferred stock is issued and the same result in (4) occurs;
4. When there is an unequal distribution in which some shareholders receive cash and you receive a stock dividend that increases your percentage of ownership in the corporation; and
5. When there is an increase in a shareholder's proportionate interest in the company even if no shares are physically issued.

E&Y FOCUS: Should You Participate in a Dividend Reinvestment Plan?

Many companies now offer dividend reinvestment plans, which let you use your dividend to buy more shares of stock rather than receive cash, and with some companies you may purchase additional shares directly from the company. This can be an effective approach to saving money and buying additional shares at regular intervals without a brokerage commission. Of course, how good an idea this is depends on how the stock performs. It's not a way, however, to save or defer taxes.

You have to include your reinvested dividend in income. If the company allows you to buy stock at less than its fair market value under a reinvestment plan, you must report the difference between the fair market value of the stock and the amount you invest as taxable income. The fair market value of the stock is its price on the date the dividend is paid.

Individual Retirement Accounts (IRAs)

IRAs represent an attractive investment vehicle, because earnings and appreciation on the funds you invest in a traditional IRA accumulate "tax-free" until you begin withdrawals. Additionally, with a Roth IRA, withdrawals may be entirely tax-free (see page 92). Second, your contributions to a non-Roth IRA may also qualify for a deduction from your gross income. Pages 88–95 describe IRAs in general.

Interest Income

Investors are always looking for interest income at attractive yields. Interest you receive from U.S. Government obligations, bank accounts, corporate bonds, or loans you made to others, to name a few sources, is taxable at ordinary income tax rates. However, interest received from obligations of a state, U.S. territory or possession, or one of its political subdivisions is excluded from gross income for federal income tax purposes; consequently, the interest paid is generally lower. The savvy investor should focus on the after-tax yield of an investment.

TAXSAVER

Tax-free bonds, including tax-free zero coupon bonds, are one of the few remaining tax shelters available. But you should proceed with caution. Since the mid-1980s, municipal bond prices have been extremely volatile. Before purchasing a portfolio of municipal bonds, you may want to consult closely with an investment advisor. Also remember that the interest from certain municipal bonds is subject to the alternative minimum tax.

Series EE Bonds. Though subject to federal income tax, Series EE bonds offer an attractive "tax-sheltered investment." If you do not elect to pay taxes on interest each year, the interest on the bonds can be deferred and taxed when the bonds are either redeemed or reach final maturity, thereby allowing you to select the most desirable taxable year to recognize the income. If EE bonds are used for educational purposes, the interest, for many taxpayers, is not just deferred, it is tax-free. For more details, see page 7.

TAXSAVER

Certain high-income taxpayers do not qualify for the tax break on Series EE bonds used for educational purposes. If this is the case, you might consider buying the bonds in your child's name. When the child reaches age 14, he or she may cash them in and will be taxed at his or her rate, rather than yours, which presumably is higher.

Investment Expenses

There are specific limits on what constitutes an investment expense and how much you can deduct. See page 53.

Investment Interest Expense

Investment interest expense is interest paid on indebtedness allocable to property held for investment. See page 44 for further details.

Rental Property

Rental income includes any payment you receive for the use of property. You may deduct expenditures that you incur in renting the property. Special rules apply to vacation homes that you rent out. See Rental Income and Expenses, page 10.

Tax Shelters

The 1986 Tax Reform Act eliminated most tax shelters, largely prohibiting investors from claiming what are now called "passive losses"—a loss from a business in which you do not materially participate (see page 11).

Municipal Bonds. Municipal bonds are among the last, true tax shelters left. Interest income from "munis" can be tax-free—at the federal, state, and city level. A taxable investment would have to pay nearly 8% in order to throw off as much after-tax income as a municipal bond yielding 5.75% if, say, your marginal tax rate is 28%. For high-income taxpayers, municipal bonds are even more appealing. For example, residents of high-tax states like California or New York may find that the combination of federal, state, and local levies can push their overall marginal tax rate as high as 50%. That means that a taxable investment would have to produce an 11.5% return to equal the return of a 5.75% municipal bond exempt from municipal, state, and federal taxes.

Still, municipal bonds are not without risks. As noted in the TaxSaver on page 199, bond prices have fluctuated sharply over the last few years. Sharp drops in bond prices have occurred in response to reductions in the credit rating of a city or county. And now there is a new danger on the horizon. Just as home mortgages can be refinanced when interest rates fall, most long-term municipal bonds can be redeemed at the discretion of the issuer. January 1 and July 1 are the usual call dates.

Other Shelters to Consider. "Working interests" in oil and gas partnerships still enjoy some tax breaks. While Congress has cracked down on real estate limited partnerships, investors in low-income housing and active landlords may still be entitled to claim some tax benefits. See discussion regarding business credits in Chapter 15 and active real estate participation in Chapter 1.

All tax shelters need to be evaluated carefully. Generally, you should make an investment when it satisfies your investment criteria, not because of the potential tax breaks you might receive.

T*AX*S*AVER*

Nine Tax-Saving Opportunities. *Many people haven't explored legitimate ways to shelter income—either by deferring taxes or earning tax-free income. Here's a list of questions you might ask yourself to see if there are any tax-saving opportunities you may have overlooked:*

- *Am I maximizing my contribution to my 401(k) account?*
- *Do I have a Keogh plan or a Simplified Employee Pension in which I can make a contribution based on my self-employment income?*
- *Would my company set up a deferred compensation plan for me?*
- *Have I considered whether having more tax-exempt municipal bond interest is appropriate for my situation?*
- *Am I managing my investment income in a way that allows me to deduct all the interest I pay on my margin account?*
- *Should I make contributions to a deductible IRA, Roth IRA, or other nondeductible IRA?*
- *Will shifting income to a child who's in a lower tax bracket help reduce the family tax bill?*
- *Have I looked into how trusts could fit into my estate plan?*
- *Have I considered a home equity loan with deductible interest to replace nondeductible interest on car loans and credit cards?*

12

Retirement Planning

As this book was being prepared in September 2000, Congress was still considering legislation that could affect individuals' tax planning for the coming year. We strongly encourage you to consult with your tax advisor for the most updated information.

INTRODUCTION

Most middle-aged individuals worry about accumulating sufficient funds to ensure a secure retirement. Nevertheless, retirement planning is probably one of the most neglected aspects of personal financial planning. This chapter offers ideas to help you develop your retirement strategies and objectives.

To formulate a sound retirement plan, you need to answer two questions: how much will I need? and where will it come from? Your retirement planning timetable depends on your personal circumstances and goals. But you'd be wise to follow a few general guidelines. First, it's never too soon to plan for your retirement, and second, it's never too late. Late-in-life planning doesn't mean that you won't be able to retire on your timetable. Rather, it's simply more difficult to accumulate the necessary funds. The earlier you begin, the easier it will be to meet your goals.

PLANNING FOR RETIREMENT EXPENDITURES

As with any aspect of personal financial planning, the starting point is identifying your objectives. When considering how much money you will need to meet your retirement objectives, three factors predominate:

1. **Your Current Standard of Living and the Amount of Cash Flow Needed to Maintain This Standard.** A cash flow analysis for the current year should be prepared. This involves determining your annual cash receipts from all sources, including compensation and income from investments, and comparing that total to your annual expenditures including housing, food, transportation, and entertainment. From this analysis, you can develop a projection for your first year of retirement of how much income you will need on an annual basis. If possible, factor in the costs based on where you think you would like to live when you retire. There can be substantial differences between the cost of living in different parts of the country—Manhattan versus

parts of Arizona, for example. (See Chapter 4 for a discussion about domicile.)

2. **Medical Expenses and Insurance.** Because the medical expenses associated with a serious illness can destroy the best-made retirement plan, medical insurance coverage must be carefully evaluated.

3. **The Level of Discretionary Expenditures You Want (or Need).** A review of the discretionary expenditures you plan to make for items such as a new or second home or to assist children or grandchildren with educational costs will help determine how much in additional funds you will have to set aside to meet your objectives.

RETIREMENT CASH FLOW AND INFLATION

When planning for retirement expenditures, one especially important consideration is the effect of inflation. Because you probably don't plan to work during retirement—though more and more retirees do—your income will in large part be fixed. Inflation robs you of buying power and can erode the best retirement plan.

As a general rule, you should invest some of your money in assets that have historically been good inflation hedges, such as common stocks and quality real estate. The income streams from stocks and real estate tend to increase with inflation. Corporate earnings and rents rise. Note, however, that these types of investments increase your exposure to the risks of the market. If you invest in fixed income securities it is important not to invest all of your assets in securities of a single maturity. By purchasing fixed income investments of varying maturities, both short-term and long-term, you retain flexibility to deal with changing interest rates that usually rise as inflation rises.

SOURCES OF RETIREMENT INCOME

The three main sources of retirement income are company retirement plans, your own retirement savings, and Social Security. For many individuals, the absence of any one of these can cripple a secure retirement.

Company Retirement Plans

The most important aspect of any company retirement plan is understanding the benefits provided by the plan and the payment options available.

There are generally two basic choices on how traditional retirement plan benefits will be paid:

Joint and Survivor Annuities. In most instances, benefits will be paid in the form of an annuity, meaning that you (and your spouse, if you're married) will receive monthly payments for as long as you live. Most frequently, companies offer a joint and survivor annuity under which annual payments are made for the joint lives of the employee and spouse. If the employee dies before his or her spouse, a reduced amount (as elected by the spouse but usually equal to one-half of the initial payment amount) is paid for the remainder of the survivor's life.

Lump Sum Payments. Some company plans may offer a "lump sum" option, meaning that the entire retirement amount allocated to an employee is paid in a single sum. All pension plans and most other retirement plans require that *both* spouses waive the right to a joint and survivor annuity in order for a lump sum distribution to be made.

Tax Treatment of Annuities and Lump Sum Payments. In general, the entire amount of an annuity received each month will be taxable as ordinary income. If you contributed on an after-tax basis to your annuity retirement program, a special rule allows you to recover tax-free the amount of your contribution, spread out over a period that is based upon your age at the time annuity payments begin.

While annuity payments are generally taxed as ordinary income, qualified lump sum distributions may be entitled to special tax treatment. (See discussion under "Pensions or Annuities," page 17 in Chapter 1.)

TaxSaver

Which Plan to Choose. *If your employer's qualified retirement plans offer the choice, should you select annuity payments or a lump sum?*

Your choice depends on various factors, including the amount of the distribution, your marginal tax bracket during retirement, the pretax yield that can be earned on investments, your expected distribution period, and the degree of control you want over your investments.

Since annuities generally provide for monthly payments over the lifetime of a retired employee and his or her spouse, recipients can expect a steady stream of payments each and every month no matter how long they live. A lump sum fund, however, could be prematurely exhausted if one or both spouses were to outlive his or her life expectancy.

On the other hand, if you choose annuity payments and you or your spouse dies prematurely, any unpaid portion of your account balance could be forfeited. With a lump sum distribution, the retiree gets possession of the full amount of his or her account balance up front. Whatever is left over at the retiree's death is available to pass on to heirs.

Some retirees welcome the discipline imposed by receiving a monthly annuity check. It forces you to stick to a monthly budget, which may be similar to how you were used to managing money during your working years. Receiving a large lump sum up front may present too much of a temptation to overspend or may make it difficult to manage a budget.

However, being locked into monthly annuity payments prevents you from pulling out extra funds if needed for an emergency or taking advantage of an investment opportunity. Lump sum recipients have full access to their account assets, as needed. Moreover, unless annuity payments are indexed or variable, inflation will steadily erode your purchasing power. Lump sum proceeds, on the other hand, can be invested in assets that provide a hedge against inflation.

Recipients of a lump sum distribution have complete flexibility to invest and manage their account assets as they choose. Of course, they also face the risk that poor investment results may leave them with insufficient retirement income. If you select an annuity, the promise of a predictable level of monthly payments relieves you of any investment burden.

To figure out the best payment scheme for you, you need to consider both the income tax ramifications of each type of distribution and your personal objectives for the use of the funds. If you are comfortable about directly managing your retirement funds, the investment flexibility and tax-planning opportunities available with a lump sum distribution normally are better suited to your personal financial objectives.

IRAs, Keogh Plans, and Simplified Employee Pensions (SEPs)

An important source of retirement savings can be an IRA, a Keogh plan, or a Simplified Employee Pension (SEP). An individual retirement arrangement (IRA) is a personal retirement savings plan where the earnings and appreciation on funds you invest compound "tax-free" until you begin withdrawals. A Roth IRA allows you to avoid tax on earnings and appreciation *entirely* if distributions meet certain requirements. If you are self-employed and own your own business, you may have a retirement plan commonly known as a Keogh plan. SEPs are usually set up by employers to make contributions toward their own (if self-employed) and their employees' retirement. All of these plans, as well as tax strategies related to each of them, are discussed in Chapter 5. Table 12.1 demonstrates the benefits of a consistent savings strategy.

Retirement Investment Strategy

There are many other ways to save for retirement; in some cases an investment can meet both your current lifestyle objectives and your retire-

TABLE 12.1   Compounding Table for Depositing $300/month

After-Tax Return	Year 5	Year 10	Year 15	Year 20	Year 25
4%	$19,890	$44,175	$ 73,827	$110,032	$154,239
5%	20,402	46,585	80,187	123,310	178,653
6%	20,931	49,164	87,246	138,612	207,898
7%	21,478	51,925	95,089	156,278	243,022
8%	22,043	54,884	103,811	176,706	285,308
9%	22,627	58,054	113,522	200,366	336,337

ment objectives. For example, buying a vacation home *might* be appropriate both as a purchase you can enjoy currently and as an investment consistent with your retirement goals. You needn't be concerned about simply putting money away if your investment strategies are consistent with your long-range retirement goals. Nearly any investment can be used toward funding your retirement. However, as you near retirement, changes in your investment strategies may be appropriate.

Investment Risk.   The amount of investment risk assumed should probably be reduced—especially if you have already built up a retirement fund that meets your objectives. Should risky investments fail while retirement is decades away, you'll have time to recover. But if investments sour at, say, age 62, you may not have enough time to recoup the losses.

Liquid Assets.   Your need for liquidity should be matched to your investments. A carefully planned strategy of converting illiquid assets (which served you well during your "earning years") into more liquid assets that you can consume during retirement years should be pursued. The idea is to avoid forced sales of illiquid assets at inopportune times causing, among other things, unplanned tax liabilities.

Cash Flow.   If you need current cash flow for living expenses, you should generally choose steady income over potential appreciation.

Diversification.   Diversification—that is, not putting all your eggs in one basket—enables you to reduce the impact that an underperforming or failed investment could have over your entire portfolio. Diversification entails spreading your investment dollars across different asset categories, like stocks, bonds, and real estate, and among different investments within each category. Determining how much and in what assets and asset categories to invest depends upon your attitude toward risk and your financial objectives. However, even as you approach retirement and begin to shift your portfolio toward more conservative and liquid assets, it is important to keep your investments diversified.

Social Security

Social Security is an essential ingredient of personal retirement plans.

Figuring Your Benefit.   The calculation of your probable monthly benefit is complicated. To save time and headaches, you can request an estimate of your tentative benefits by filing Form SSA-7004-PC, "Request for Earnings and Benefit Estimate Statement." The form is simple to complete and the information could be invaluable to your personal planning. Copies of the form can be obtained from your local Social Security office, by calling (800) 772-1213, or by visiting http://www.ssa.gov on the Web.

The maximum monthly benefit for a 65-year-old worker retiring in 2000 is $1,433. For each year short of the current normal retirement age of 65 that you retire, the maximum entitlement is reduced. The earliest age at which you're eligible to receive retirement checks is 62, with a 20% reduction in benefits. For those born after 1937, the normal retirement age is scheduled to increase gradually to age 67. Retirement benefits will still be available to these workers at age 62, but will be further reduced.

How to Lose Benefits. You can be penalized if you take Social Security benefits and continue to work. A recent change in the law, however, has eliminated the penalty for many recipients. In 1999, retirees between ages 65 and 69 lost $1 in benefits for every $3 earned above $15,500. Recipients under 65 forfeited $1 of benefits for each $2 earned over $9,120. This rule, however, was limited to *earned* income. So, for example, dividends and interest income didn't jeopardize benefits, no matter what their amount.

The Senior Citizen's Freedom to Work Act of 2000 now eliminates the retirement earnings test beginning with the month in which a retiree attains full retirement age—currently age 65. Recipients under age 65, however, will still forfeit benefits to the extent they have excess earnings.

Your spouse can receive either one-half your monthly benefit (scaled back if benefits begin before age 65) or his or her own individual entitlement based on personal earnings, if higher. As long as you were married for at least 10 years, your former spouse remains entitled to a benefit equal to half your monthly benefit even after a divorce.

Working beyond Age 65. Regardless of your age, if you work, your wages or self-employment income are subject to Social Security and Medicare taxes. On the other hand, there's a reward for working past normal retirement age. For each month you postpone collecting your Social Security benefits beyond age 65 (and before age 70), your retirement benefit is increased by what's called a "delayed retirement credit." The table below shows the monthly and maximum yearly delayed retirement credit for individuals who will reach age 65 by 2003.

Delayed Retirement Credit

Turn age 65 in	Monthly Credit	Maximum Yearly Credit*
2000 or 2001	1/2 of 1%	6.0%
2002 or 2003	13/24 of 1%	6.5%
2004 or 2005	7/12 of 1%	7.0%

*The maximum yearly credit increases by ½ of 1% every other year up to a ceiling of 8% for those turning age 65 in 2008 or beyond.

Income Tax on Benefits. Up to 85% of your Social Security benefits may be subject to federal (and perhaps state) income taxes. Whether 85%, 50%, or none of your Social Security benefits are subject to tax depends on how much of your "provisional income" exceeds certain thresholds. "Provisional income" for this purpose generally is made up of your federal adjusted gross income plus tax-exempt interest and one-half of your Social Security benefits. (For a detailed explanation see page 15.)

Early vs. Late Retirement.   Generally, you'll come out ahead by withdrawing your Social Security benefits early—e.g., at age 62—rather than waiting to age 65, even though the monthly benefit may be 20% less. That's because you'll have received three additional years of benefits. Mathematically, it would take about 12 years—until age 77—for the higher benefits available based on retirement at age 65 to catch up. And this is calculated before taking into account earnings on the investment of the benefits during the intervening years. However, if you are going to continue to work after age 62, there is the possibility of your losing some of your benefits.

Taxes on Wages and Self-Employment Income.   The Social Security program and the Medicare program are financed by a payroll tax on both the employee and the employer and by a self-employment tax. See the Appendices for tax-rate information.

13

Estate and Gift Planning

INTRODUCTION

Although it is not possible to take it with you, with careful thought and astute planning it is possible to provide your heirs, loved ones, and friends with a significant portion of your wealth. This chapter discusses the estate tax, the gift tax, and the generation-skipping transfer tax. The chapter also contains some ideas and techniques in estate planning that may aid you in making your plans for the future.

Frequent tax law changes continue to have a significant impact on estate planning. This makes it more difficult to protect your assets from the ravages of time unless you plan effectively. As a result of these changes, and because your goals and expectations constantly change as you go through life, you should periodically review your estate and gift tax plan. A review will help you: (1) discover how your objectives may have changed; (2) assess whether your plan can still achieve your objectives; and (3) determine how recent legislative changes may affect existing plans and whether you can accomplish your goals more advantageously.

This chapter is intended as an introduction to estate planning. You should seek professional advice especially if your financial or family situation is complicated; if you own interests in closely held corporations or other illiquid assets; or if your spouse is not a U.S. citizen.

GETTING STARTED

A periodic review of your personal financial plan makes sense. Filing an annual income tax return forces most taxpayers to look over their situation. Yet many—perhaps most—individuals allow years to go by without adequately considering possible changes in property holdings or key provisions in wills and trusts. To be on the safe side, you should periodically examine the following six basic tax and financial considerations:
1. Have there been any changes in the tax laws or rulings that might adversely affect your present estate plan?

2. Does your estate have sufficient cash or other liquid assets to take care of debts, taxes, funeral expenses, and estate administration expenses?
3. Have there been any changes in your family's circumstances—births, adoptions, deaths, marriages, illness or disability, special schooling needs, etc.—that might call for revisions in your estate plan?
4. Should you initiate a plan to give away some of your assets as gifts to your children, to other family members, or to charitable institutions? If you have already been giving gifts, should you continue to do so? Which assets are most appropriate for such a gift program?
5. Is the current form of ownership of your family assets appropriate for saving taxes and expenses and providing you the flexibility you need to deal with unexpected situations?
6. Have you designated a beneficiary for, and decided on the form of payment of, distributions from qualified employee benefit programs?

Do You Need a Will?

A will is a legal document that specifies who receives what at your death and who will manage your estate. Even if you die without a will, you already have an estate plan of sorts. Generally, assets you own jointly with another person—a bank account, stock, personal residence, or business interest, or where you have designated a particular beneficiary, as under an insurance policy—will be passed on to the joint tenant or designated beneficiary. But, assets you own in your name alone will be passed on in accordance with your state's laws.

If you die without a will—*intestate* is the legal term—state laws determine how your estate is divided up among your surviving spouse, children, and parents—and what happens when there is no surviving spouse. Only rarely, however, will state law conform with your wishes. Often, the biggest problem is not the distribution of the property but rather the guardianship of minor children. If both parents die without a will that directs who will be guardian of a minor child, the court and the state social welfare department will make the decision. So, even if you do not have enough assets to have to pay federal estate tax, it's a good idea to draw up a will.

ESTATE TAX FUNDAMENTALS

Who Has to Pay Federal Estate Tax?

The law provides two major exemptions from federal estate tax:
1. There is no federal tax on the first $675,000 of assets. This amount is scheduled to increase gradually to $1,000,000 by 2006.
2. There is an unlimited marital deduction for assets passing to a spouse who is a U.S. citizen. Any amount given or left at death to a surviving spouse, whether given outright or in certain types of trusts, is exempt

from federal estate tax. For more information, see the discussion later in this chapter.

These exemptions certainly make planning easier for most Americans, but they shouldn't lull you into thinking that estate planning is unnecessary. For starters, you may be worth more than you think. Many middle-class families now own homes that are worth several times what they cost. Moreover, stock prices have increased in value considerably in recent years. The high rates of inflation that were common in the 1970s may return. Even if your assets currently do not exceed $675,000 (or the future increased exemption amount), at the time of your death they might.

How to Value Your Estate

Assets Subject to Estate Tax. Federal estate tax is a levy on the transfer of property at death. Your gross estate will include the value of all property to the extent of your interest in it at the time of death. Following are types of property included in your gross estate by law:

Tangible Personal Property, Real Estate, and Other Assets. This category includes property you own that is transmitted at death according to provisions of a will or state intestacy laws. Such property is commonly referred to as the probate estate. Examples: real estate, stocks, bonds, furniture, personal effects, jewelry, works of art, an interest in a partnership, an interest in a sole proprietorship, a bank account, and a promissory note or other evidence of indebtedness you hold.

Jointly Owned Property. In general, one-half of the value of property owned by a husband and wife jointly will be included in the estate of the first spouse to die. The unlimited marital deduction prevents the transfer of the property from the deceased to the surviving spouse from being subject to federal estate tax. Upon the survivor's death, however, the entire property will be subject to tax (assuming it is still held at the time of death).

If two people who are not married own property jointly, the entire value of the property is included in the gross estate of the first to die, unless the estate can prove that all or part of the payment for acquiring the property was actually furnished by the other joint owner. If you and another joint owner acquired property by gift or inheritance, only your fractional share of the property is included.

Life Insurance. Your gross estate will include life insurance proceeds that are received (1) by or for the benefit of your estate or (2) by other beneficiaries if you own all or part of the policies at the time of your death. "Ownership" includes the power to change the beneficiary of the policy, the right to cancel the policy and receive the cash value, the right to borrow against the policy, and the right to assign the policy, among other things.

TaxSaver

You can transfer ownership of a life insurance policy to your children or to a trust for your family's benefit and reap significant tax advantages. To be effective in keeping the proceeds out of your estate, the gift must be made more than three years before death. The three-year waiting period can be avoided for a newly purchased policy if proper steps are taken to have someone else (e.g., a trustee of an irrevocable trust) apply for the policy and own the policy from its inception. These types of irrevocable life insurance trusts can be structured so that you contribute money each year to the trust for paying premiums. Frequently, your payments can qualify for the annual gift tax exclusion (explained on page 218). Setting up such a trust can be an effective way to get insurance proceeds to your heirs without incurring gift or estate tax.

Employee Benefits. The value of payments from qualified pension plans and other retirement plans payable to surviving beneficiaries or the estate of an employee (or the owner, in the case of a Keogh/HR 10 plan) generally is included in your gross estate.

Certain Gifts and Gift Tax Paid within Three Years of Death. Gifts of property made during your lifetime are generally not included in your gross estate, but must be figured in the estate tax calculation if they exceed the $10,000 annual gift tax exclusion (discussed later). However, life insurance proceeds are included in your estate if the policies or ownership of the policies were given away within three years of your death. Also included is any gift tax you have paid within three years of your death. Lifetime gifts that a decedent retains some interest in (e.g., a life income interest) or control over (e.g., voting rights in closely held stock given as a gift) will be included in the decedent's gross estate.

Allowable Deductions and Exclusions. Deductions are allowed for funeral and administration expenses of the estate, and debts, unpaid mortgages, and other indebtedness on property included in the gross estate. Also allowed are such special deductions as the marital deduction and the charitable deduction. (See later sections for more details on these special deductions.)

Funeral and Administration Expenses. Deductible funeral expenses include burial costs, costs for a burial lot, costs for future care of a gravesite, etc. Deductible administration costs include executor's commissions, attorney's fees, accounting fees, appraisal fees, and court costs.

Family-Owned Business Deduction. An estate can deduct a portion of the value of a qualifying business interest if the interest comprises a substantial portion of the assets of the estate and satisfies family ownership and material participation tests. The maximum deductible amount is the excess of $1.3 million over the allowable unified credit equivalent in the year of the decedent's death.

Other Deductible Estate Expenses. To be deductible, debts must be enforceable personal obligations of the decedent, such as outstanding mortgages or personal bank loans, auto loans, credit card balances, utility bills, etc. The deductible amount also includes any interest accrued on such debt at the date of death. Transfers made under a marital property settlement because of a divorce may be treated as estate expenses. Taxes are also deductible debts if they are accrued and unpaid at date of death. Deductible taxes include accrued property taxes, gift taxes unpaid at death, and income taxes.

Valuing Estate Property. Property is included in an estate at its "fair market value," which is the price at which property would change hands between a willing buyer and a willing seller. Property that trades on an established market may be valued easily. For example, publicly traded stocks and bonds are valued based on the average of the high and low selling price on the date of death (or, if elected, the date six months after death). However, interests in closely held businesses or partnerships must generally be appraised, taking into account the business's assets, earning capacity, and other factors. An accountant can assist you in appraising business interests for estate or gift tax valuation purposes.

Your gross estate is valued as of the date of your death or six months later (also known as the alternative valuation date), whichever your personal representative elects. An election to value the estate six months after date of death will generally apply to all assets in the estate, but is available only if the election results in a decrease in your gross estate and estate tax liability. The amount remaining after subtracting any allowable deductions is your taxable estate. The federal estate tax is computed on this amount. Gifts made after 1976 are also factored in and can increase the marginal tax bracket of the estate.

Basis to Beneficiaries

Property acquired from a decedent generally gets a new basis. In most cases, the new basis is the fair market value at date of death or alternative valuation date, whichever is used for estate tax purposes.

How Your Estate Is Taxed

Tax Rates. The federal estate tax is progressive, ranging from a marginal rate of 18% to 55%. The 55% top rate applies to estates larger than $3 million. (See the table of rates in the Appendix.) As noted previously, the first $675,000 (for 2000 and 2001) of gifts and transfers at death are exempt from estate tax because of the unified credit (see below). A surcharge of 5% is imposed on taxable estates larger than $10 million to phase out the benefit of the graduated rates.

Credits. Your estate can claim certain credits before figuring the amount of federal estate tax owed. The credits include:

Unified Estate and Gift Tax Credit. Each individual is entitled to a so-called unified credit. For 2000 and 2001, the credit is $220,550, which is the amount of tax generated by a transfer of $675,000. In other words, no federal estate or gift taxes will be assessed on the first $675,000 of an individual's combined taxable gifts and transfers at death. To the extent that the credit has been used to offset gifts the decedent made during his or her lifetime, the credit against the estate tax is reduced.

The amount of the credit increases each year as follows:

Year	Unified Credit Equivalent
2002–2003	700,000
2004	850,000
2005	950,000
2006 →	1,000,000

If the amount you give away during your lifetime and in your estate exceeds $10 million, an additional 5% tax is imposed to effectively phase out the benefit of the progressive estate tax rates. For example, in 2000 the phaseout will cause a taxable estate of $17,184,000 or more to pay tax at a rate of 55% on every dollar, against which the unified credit would then be allowed.

TAXSAVER

While you should have your will reviewed on a regular basis, it is especially important to be sure it is drafted to take advantage of the unified credit available under the law in existence at the time of your death—and is not limited to $675,000 or less.

State Death Tax Credit. A credit is allowed for estate and/or inheritance taxes paid to any state or the District of Columbia. The tax must actually be paid on property included in the gross estate. The credit is limited to an amount computed under a graduated rate table based on the amount of the taxable estate, reduced by $60,000. (See the table in the Appendix.)

Foreign Death Tax Credit. A credit is allowed against the federal estate tax for any death taxes actually paid to a foreign country, Puerto Rico, or the Virgin Islands on property that is also subject to the federal estate tax. The credit is limited to the U.S. tax attributable to the property taxed by the foreign country.

Credit for Tax on Prior Transfers. Under certain circumstances a credit is allowed against the federal estate tax for part or all of any estate tax paid on property transferred to the present decedent.

State Tax Considerations. All states impose some kind of inheritance or estate tax. In many states, the estate tax is simply the amount of the federal credit for state death taxes. Consequently, in these states, if there is no federal tax, due to the unified credit, there is also no state tax. However, some states have estate or inheritance taxes that are not tied to the federal credit. Furthermore, some states do not allow an unlimited marital deduction, as the federal government does. In these states, state death tax considerations may influence how your estate plan should be structured.

The Marital Deduction. One of the most significant tax-saving provisions of the law is the marital deduction. As its name implies, it is a special deduction available only to married persons, where the transferee spouse is a U.S. citizen. An estate is allowed an unlimited deduction for the value of property transferred to the spouse of the deceased. Thus, in effect, the marital deduction permits a couple to postpone paying any estate tax until the surviving spouse dies.

TaxSaver

Most married individuals will want to take advantage of both the unified credit and the unlimited marital deduction to reduce the federal estate tax to zero in the estate of the first spouse to die. (See the following examples about several ways this can be done.)

TaxSaver

By placing property in a special trust, you can arrange for your spouse to receive a lifetime income interest in certain property. After your spouse dies, the property will be passed on to whomever you have stipulated in the trust document.

The marital deduction is unavailable for property transferred by gift or at death to a surviving spouse who is not a U.S. citizen at the time the transfer is made. Instead, the law provides that tax-free gifts to a non–U.S. citizen spouse can only total $103,000 per year. There is, however, no lifetime limit to the total value of gifts you can give tax-free to a spouse who is not a U.S. citizen.

TaxSaver

Your will can be drafted so that your property is placed in a special type of trust that benefits a spouse who is not a U.S. citizen. The trust enables estate tax on the property to be postponed until the property is distributed out of the trust or the surviving spouse dies. This type of trust is called a Qualified Domestic Trust. It permits property to qualify for the marital deduction if certain requirements—which provide that the property will eventually be subject to estate tax—are met.

Examples: Here are three examples for computing the gross estate, the taxable estate, and the estate tax due for three different size estates of married individuals who are assumed to have died in 2000, each of whom was the first of the two spouses to die.

At his death, Tom had $3,000 in savings and checking accounts, 100 shares of marketable securities worth $70 each, and a residence worth $175,000. Tom's personal property consisted largely of a collection of rare coins valued at $80,000. The rest of his property included his car, clothing, and other personal effects. In addition, Tom accumulated $105,000 in his employer's deferred bonus and 401(k) plans, and his estate was the beneficiary of a whole-life insurance policy and an employer-maintained group term policy.

Harriet's and Dick's gross estates were larger than Tom's. And there were other differences, as well. Harriet was the sole proprietor of a consulting business valued at $450,000 at the time of her death. Dick was a law firm partner whose interest in the firm was valued at $525,000 when he died. Dick also owned a beach house, which his father had willed to him outright.

Step 1: Computing the gross estate.

| | *Computing the gross estate of* | | |
	Tom	Harriet	Dick
Assets			
Cash	$ 3,000	$ 15,000	$ 60,000
Marketable securities	7,000	20,000	50,000
Business equity	0	450,000	525,000
Residence	175,000	235,000	185,000
Vacation residence	0	0	90,000
Personal property	95,000	25,000	40,000
Deferred compensation	105,000	50,000	75,000
Ordinary life insurance	10,000	80,000	570,000
Group-term insurance	50,000	50,000	75,000
Gross estate	$445,000	$925,000	$1,670,000

Step 2: Computing your taxable estate.

The executor of your estate will subtract from the total value of your gross estate all those deductions allowable under the tax law, including the marital deduction.

Tom's will provided that his wife was to receive his total estate after payment of debts, thereby reducing the taxable value of the estate to zero. Tom could do this because of the unlimited marital deduction (discussed above).

In Harriet's case, the size of her estate's marital deduction was the product of some planning. The deduction was designed to dovetail with the unified credit available in the year of her death in order to eliminate any estate tax liability.

Dick's estate planned to use less than the full amount of the marital deduction that could have been used. He and his wife, Elaine, decided that with his bequest and her separate assets, she would not require ownership of all of Dick's estate. Thus, because of their children's needs, a decision was made to give more than $675,000 of his assets to them, even though taxes would be paid by his estate. The plan could have been structured to pay no taxes at the time of Dick's death if he were to leave only $675,000 to the children with the rest going to Elaine. The children could have then received the additional assets from Elaine as gifts or from her estate, and depending on the size of her estate, the amount of taxes she would pay may be more or less than in their original plan.

	Tom	*Harriet*	*Dick*
Gross estate	$445,000	$925,000	$1,670,000
Deductions			
Funeral expenses	3,000	4,000	6,000
Estate administration expenses	2,000	15,000	44,000
Debts	2,000	1,000	2,000
Mortgages	38,000	28,000	48,000
Marital deduction	400,000	200,000	550,000
Charitable deductions	0	2,000	20,000
Total deductions	$445,000	$250,000	$ 670,000
Taxable estate	$ 0	$675,000	$1,000,000

Step 3: Computing the federal estate tax.

Computing federal estate tax is straightforward. A "tentative" tax is computed using the tax rate tables. Then, the unified credit ($220,550 maximum for 2000) and any allowable credit for state death taxes paid are applied as direct, dollar-for-dollar offsets against the tentative tax specified in the federal estate tax tables for your taxable estate. Estates over $10 million must add back the 5% surtax discussed previously.

	Tom	*Harriet*	*Dick*
Gross estate	$445,000	$925,000	$1,670,000
Deductions	445,000	250,000	670,000
Taxable estate	0	675,000	1,000,000
Tentative tax	0	220,550	345,800
Unified credit	0	220,550	220,550
State tax credit	0	0	33,200
Estate tax	$ 0	$ 0	$ 92,050

The Fundamentals of the Gift Tax

You might think that the government would make it easy to give money away to noncharitable recipients. In some respects it does. You can give up to $10,000 annually ($20,000 if you file a joint return and your spouse consents) to as many individuals as you want without paying any gift tax.

(Although the 1997 Tax Act provides that this amount will be indexed for inflation, the first increase—to $11,000—is not likely to occur until around 2002.) But, above that amount, gift tax is imposed (see pages 214 and 289 regarding the unified credit). The reason is that without such a tax people could escape death taxes—assuming they were willing to give away a large portion of their property before death.

Any gift you give above the annual amount that is exempt from tax is, in effect, included in your estate when you die. The value of the gift is not the value at the date of your death but the value at the time you gave the gift. In addition, there are some special rules. A gift of life insurance, for example, made within three years of your death will be included in your gross estate at its full face value. Any gift tax you pay on gifts made within three years of your death is also added to the value of your taxable estate. Nevertheless, giving gifts can substantially reduce your overall gift and estate transfer taxes as well as fulfill other desires. But gift-giving does require careful planning—and the commitment to make the gifts before it is too late.

Basis to the Recipient of a Gift

In general, the basis of appreciated property acquired by gift is the donor's basis for tax purposes. If a gift tax return was filed, the recipient—or donee—should examine it for information regarding the donor's basis, the holding period, and the amount of depreciation. The basis of gifts received after 1976 is increased by the amount of the federal gift tax attributable to the difference between the donor's basis and the gift's fair market value, if higher as of the date of gift.

How to Give Tax-Free Gifts

The Gift Tax Annual Exclusion. As noted above, you may give up to $10,000 each year to as many individuals as you want without incurring any gift tax (the $10,000 exclusion is indexed for inflation). And, if your spouse joins in making the gift (by signing a consent on a gift tax return), you may give $20,000 to each person annually without paying any tax. But this annual gift tax exclusion applies only to gifts of "present interests"—items that can be used, possessed, and enjoyed presently. Examples of a gift of a present interest include gifts of money, holiday presents, and so forth.

Gifts of "future interests" do not qualify for the annual exclusion. Gifts of future interests include remainder interests, reversions, or any other interest that won't give the recipient the right to possess, enjoy, or profit from the gift until some future date or time. An exception: gifts in trust to minors are subject to special rules that may allow an otherwise future interest to qualify for the annual exclusion.

Gifts to Pay Medical or Educational Expenses. In addition to the annual exclusion, an unlimited gift tax exclusion is available to pay someone's medical or educational expenses. The beneficiary does not have to be your dependent or even related to you, although payment of a grandchild's expenses is perhaps the most common use of the exclusion. Also, contributions to a qualified state tuition program (QSTP) will be eligible for the regular $10,000 exclusion.

TaxSaver

In order for a gift to be exempt from taxes, you must make the payment directly to the medical or educational institution providing the service. The beneficiary of the gift should not actually receive the payment. In addition, educational expenses include only tuition. Room and board, books, and other fees will not qualify for the unlimited exclusion, although they can, of course, qualify for the annual gift tax exclusion.

TaxSaver

You can reduce your taxable estate substantially through a planned annual program of $10,000 (or $20,000 if you are married) gifts. All gifts within the exclusion limits are exempt from federal estate taxes. In addition, outright gifts that qualify for the annual exclusion are also protected from generation-skipping transfer taxes (see page 224). Obviously, you cannot hope to significantly reduce the tax your estate will pay by making gifts in a single year. But, the estate tax savings can be substantial if you embark upon a carefully planned gift-giving program that extends for a number of years before your death.

TaxSaver

Under the 1997 Tax Act, a donor who makes contributions to a QSTP in excess of the $10,000 annual exclusion amount may elect to take the contributions into account ratably over the five-year period starting with the year of the contributions. If the donor dies before the end of the five-year period, the portion of the contribution allocable to the period after the donor's date of death is included in the donor's gross estate.

TaxSaver

Another major tax advantage of making a gift is that future appreciation in the gift's value and after-tax income earned on the property are not included in your estate.
   __Example:__ Suppose you give stocks worth $50,000 to your children now. If you die in 10 years and the stock is worth $130,000, the $80,000 of appreciation will not be included in your estate. Nor will you (or your estate) include any dividends paid on the stock after the gift.

Gift Tax Charitable Contribution Deduction. An unlimited gift tax deduction is available for gifts to certain charitable organizations.

The Gift Tax Marital Deduction. The gift tax marital deduction allows you to transfer unlimited amounts of property during your lifetime to your spouse without gift tax. Property can be transferred outright or in trust. Also, a gift of a lifetime income interest in property to your spouse can qualify for the marital deduction, if it is structured properly. You should consult with your tax advisor.

> ### TaxSaver
>
> *The gift tax marital deduction can help you lower the taxes on your estate. Consider: in order for one spouse to make full use of his or her unified credit, it may be desirable to make gifts to that spouse so that he or she will have an estate at least equal to the unified credit equivalent—$675,000 in 2000 and 2001. Since the gift tax marital deduction allows you to make unlimited tax-free transfers to your spouse, you can build up his or her assets without worrying that your gifts will be taxable.*

Some words of caution: the unlimited marital deduction is not allowed for gifts to a spouse who is not a U.S. citizen, although tax-free transfers of up to $103,000 are permitted each year. (See section on the marital deduction under "Estate Tax Fundamentals" earlier in this chapter.) Furthermore, the amount of the gift tax marital deduction for a particular state may differ from the federal amount. It is therefore vital to get professional advice before making any significant gifts.

Example: Giving Gifts without Paying Gift Tax. This example illustrates how you can set up a substantial gift program and avoid paying any gift tax. Note, however, that part of the unified credit is being used. (The unified credit is discussed earlier in this chapter.)

During the course of one year, James made outright gifts of $100,000 to his wife, Helen, and $40,000 to each of his three children, for a total of $220,000.

James incurred no gift tax on Helen's gift because of the unlimited marital deduction. James and Helen were entitled to a total of $60,000 in annual exclusions (based on $20,000 for each child) because they elected to treat one-half of those gifts as made by Helen. That still leaves, however, a taxable gift of $60,000 to the three children. By applying a portion of their unified credits, James and Helen can entirely eliminate paying gift tax. Assuming that this was their first gift using their unified credits, they will have reduced the remaining assets in their estates that will be considered tax-free from $675,000 to $645,000 respectively.

E&Y FOCUS: How Paying Gift Tax Can Reduce Your Overall Taxes

Most of us have a natural aversion to paying taxes, and gift taxes are no exception. However, if you have a sizable estate that is well in excess of what you need to live on, it might be worthwhile to consider whether paying gift taxes *now* can save on estate taxes *later*. The end result is that more of your assets bypass the IRS and reach your heirs.

Example: Here's a simple example to show how paying gift tax can put more money in your heirs' hands. Assume Chris and Mimi have each survived their spouses and now have $2.5 million of liquid assets. Chris holds on to the full $2.5 million until death, while Mimi makes a gift of $1 million to her children (in addition to annual gifts that are excluded from tax). Assuming neither had previously made taxable gifts and Mimi lives for three years after the gift, this is how their taxes would compare:

Chris:	Taxable estate			$2,500,000
	Tentative federal estate tax		$1,025,800	
	Less: Unified credit in 2003		(229,800)	
	Net federal estate tax			796,000
	Net estate to heirs (a)			$1,704,000
Mimi:	Pregift estate			$2,500,000
	Taxable gift in 2000		$1,000,000	
	Tentative gift tax	$345,800		
	Less: Unified credit in 2000	(220,550)		
	Gift tax paid		125,250	
	Estate reduction			1,125,250
	Taxable estate			1,374,750
	Tentative estate tax		618,628	
	Less: Remaining unified credit in 2003		(9,250)	
	Net federal estate tax			609,378
	Net estate to heirs			765,372
	Plus gift			1,000,000
	Total to heirs (b)			$1,765,372
	Gift advantage (b) − (a)			$ 61,372

By making the gift and paying gift taxes, the gift tax of $125,250 was removed from Mimi's estate. This resulted in $61,372 more of Mimi's estate actually getting to Mimi's children. That doesn't even take into account the benefit of keeping the postgift appreciation and after-tax income on the $1 million out of Mimi's taxable estate. One important catch is that the gift must be made more than three years before death, or the gift taxes will be considered part of your estate. In addition, you will lose the "time value" of money on any gift tax paid between the time of the gift and your date of death. Further, if the gifted property is appreciated, the donee will have to pay capital gains tax upon its sale, whereas that tax is not payable on inherited property. This disadvantage will not be as costly with the reduction in capital gains rates to 20% (or 10% for gains in the 15% bracket). Finally, you must be comfortable with the nontax consequences of making a large gift that will deplete your estate.

Giving Gifts to Minors

Before a parent or grandparent gives a gift to a minor child, certain legal and practical matters need to be considered. Because a child typically cannot manage his or her own affairs and because parents usually do not want to give young children unfettered control over gift property, some special arrangements need to be made. The tax law, too, poses some challenges since only gifts of "present interest"—property for the beneficiary's immediate enjoyment—qualify for the $10,000 annual gift tax exclusion. Furthermore, state laws frequently discourage outright gifts to minors. Many states commonly prohibit or discourage the registration of securities in the name of a minor and impose supervisory restrictions upon the sale of a minor's property. Consequently, gifts to minors can take different forms and have different tax consequences.

Outright Gifts. The $10,000 annual gift tax exclusion is available for these gifts unless the property being given as a gift is a "future interest." Income from the property is taxed to the minor, and the property is included in the minor's estate if he or she should die. However, because of the "kiddie tax," which requires that a child's unearned income be taxed at the parent's rate until the child reaches age 14, your child may actually be taxed at your rates on any income he or she receives from the property.

Guardianship. A guardianship is an arrangement where property is under a guardian's legal control subject to formal (and possibly burdensome) accounting to a court. The gift, income, and estate tax consequences are the same as for outright gifts. Thus, such gifts also qualify for the $10,000 gift tax exclusion.

Custodial Arrangements. To overcome the legal disability minors have in owning property outright, all 50 states, the District of Columbia, and the Virgin Islands have adopted the Uniform Gifts (or Transfers) to Minors Act. Under this act, a custodian may hold both cash and securities for a minor until he or she reaches adulthood. Securities may be registered in the name of any bank, trust company, or adult as custodian for the minor. Custodial gifts to minors are considered completed gifts for gift tax purposes, and such gifts are eligible for the annual gift tax exclusion. The income from the gift property during the custodial period is taxable to the minor (subject to kiddie tax provisions). However, if you use the income for your minor child's maintenance and support, it is taxable to you because you are the person legally obligated to support the minor.

TAXS**AVER**

Generally, you should not act as custodian of your own gifts to your minor child. If you do and if you die before your child becomes an adult, the value of the custodial account maintained for your child's benefit will be included in your estate. Instead, your spouse may be the custodian. If you and your spouse both make gifts to your minor child, in essence splitting your gifts to take advantage of the annual gift tax exclusion, you should consider making a third party the custodian for the child.

Present Interest Trust. Special rules enacted by Congress provide a method of making gifts to minors that qualify for the annual exclusion. A gift to a qualifying trust established for an individual under the age of 21 will be considered a gift of a present interest and qualify for the $10,000 annual gift tax exclusion. The trust instrument must provide that the gift property and its income:

- May be expended for the benefit of the beneficiary before reaching age 21, and
- To the extent not so expended, will pass to the beneficiary upon becoming age 21.

If the child dies before reaching age 21, the funds must be payable to the child's estate or as the child may designate under a general power of appointment. This rule applies to trusts for children under the age of 21, even if a state law has reduced the age of majority to age 19 or 18.

Crummey Trust. This is a type of trust to which you can transfer property and have the gift qualify for the annual gift tax exclusion. The distinguishing characteristic of a Crummey trust (which takes its name from a court case) is that it gives the beneficiary the annual right to demand distributions from the trust equal to the lesser of the amount of the contributions to the trust during the year or some specified amount (e.g., $5,000 or 5% of the trust's value). The beneficiary (or legal guardian) must be notified of the power to withdraw the body of the trust, although the power is permitted to lapse or terminate after a short period of time, such as 30 days. If the beneficiary fails to make a demand during the window period, after being notified that a contribution was made, the right lapses for that year's contributions. To the extent the beneficiary (or guardian) has the right to demand distribution of the year's contribution, that contribution is considered a "present interest" and, therefore, qualifies for the annual gift tax exclusion.

In all other respects, the Crummey trust is very flexible. The trustee can be required to accumulate income until the child reaches a specified age above age 21. The trustee also can be restricted to using trust assets and income for specific purposes (e.g., college expenses). The trust is useful as a vehicle for permanently removing assets from the parents' gross estates.

Totten Trust. An "In Trust For" or so-called Totten Trust is created when a donor deposits his or her own money into a bank account for the benefit of a minor and names himself or herself as trustee. Under the laws of certain states, this is an informal and revocable arrangement. Upon the donor-trustee's death, the funds avoid probate and pass directly to the minor. However, the trust is not considered a separate entity for tax purposes because the donor retains complete control over any property in the trust. Accordingly, the donor will be taxed on the income as if the trust were not in existence. Also, assets in the trust account will be included in the donor's estate.

Coping with the Generation-Skipping Tax

An additional tax may apply to gifts or bequests that skip a generation. For example, a gift of property directly from a grandparent to a grandchild (which effectively "skips" the intervening generation) would be subject to the generation-skipping transfer tax.

The reason for the tax is simple. It's designed to impose the equivalent of the gift or estate tax that would have been paid if the intervening generation had received the gift or bequest. So for a direct gift from a grandparent to a grandchild, the generation-skipping transfer tax represents the amount of tax that would have been paid if the property had first been transferred to the child, who then died leaving the property to the grandchild.

The Generation-Skipping Transfer Tax Is Stiff. This tax is imposed at the maximum estate and gift tax rate of 55%. It is payable in addition to any estate or gift tax otherwise payable as a result of the transfer. Fortunately, most individuals will escape paying it. First, $10,000 ($20,000 if made with the consent of a spouse) outright gifts from a grandparent to grandchildren that qualify for the annual exclusion are exempt from this tax. Furthermore, each individual is entitled to an aggregate $1,030,000 exemption (indexed for inflation) from the tax for lifetime gifts and transfers at death. Since a married couple can "gift-split," they can make up to $2,060,000 in generation-skipping transfers without incurring the tax. In addition, any subsequent appreciation on the transferred property after it is given will escape generation-skipping transfer tax.

> **TaxSaver**
>
> *A wealthy individual can maximize his or her opportunity to avoid the imposition of the generation-skipping tax on transfers to grandchildren and later generations by allocating the $1,030,000 exemption for gifts during his or her lifetime.*
>
> *If your living descendants are already well provided for, you may want to consider establishing a "dynasty trust." As its name implies, the trust can benefit future descendants by sheltering assets from estate, gift, and generation-skipping transfer taxes for several generations.*

How to Use Trusts

A trust is possibly the most useful personal financial planning tool available—aside from a written plan itself. A trust is an arrangement under which one person or institution holds legal title to real or personal property for the benefit of another person or persons, usually under the terms of a written document setting forth the rights and responsibilities of all parties. Its primary virtue is that it can hold property for the benefit of other persons, now or in the future, and often avoid some taxes that otherwise would have to be paid.

Irrevocable Trusts. An irrevocable trust may not be changed or revoked after its creation. It is usually created to remove property and its future income and appreciation from the estate of the creator of the trust. A present interest trust and a Crummey trust, both of which have just been discussed, are irrevocable trusts. You might also use an irrevocable trust if you want to make a gift to someone but want to prevent the assets from being spent too quickly. An irrevocable trust also can be used to protect assets you give from your beneficiary's creditors.

However, property placed in an irrevocable trust will not be removed from your estate if you retain certain interests or powers in the trust—such as an interest that entitles you to receive the income from the trust for the rest of your life or the power to determine which beneficiaries will receive distributions. In addition, any transfer to an irrevocable trust will be subject to gift tax to the extent you relinquish control over the property. If someone else will receive the current income from the trust, or if it is a present income trust, the $10,000 annual gift tax exclusion can shield at least part of the property transfer to the trust from gift tax.

Besides saving you estate tax, irrevocable trusts created for your children can cut your income taxes. The amount of income tax savings depends on how much other income your children already receive and whether the "kiddie tax" applies to them. Also, there are very strict rules that limit the amount of control you or your spouse may keep over the trust in order for you not to include the trust's income on your tax return. The income from the trust will be taxed to you if the trust is used to pay for an item that you are legally obligated to provide as support for the beneficiary.

Revocable Trusts. A revocable trust (also known as a "living trust") is created during your lifetime, and you may amend or revoke it at any time. The trust instrument stipulates how the assets held by the trust are to be managed during your lifetime. This type of trust can also act very much like a will; the trust instrument can include instructions about how the assets in the trust should be distributed after your death.

What distinguishes a revocable trust from other kinds of trust arrangements is that you keep the power to reclaim the trust assets or contribute additional property to the trust at any time and for any reason. Thus, in effect, if you set up a revocable trust you really have not committed your self to anything—at least until you die and the trust becomes irrevocable. For all practical purposes, you continue to own the trust property; the trust merely gets legal title. Since you keep complete control over the trust and its assets, the property held in it will be included in your gross estate for estate tax purposes. Also, all income and deductions attributable to the property in the trust will be included on your income tax return. On the other hand, you will not be liable for any gift tax when you contribute assets to the trust. This is the case even though the trust names the beneficiaries who will inherit the property upon your death. However, a gift will occur if you give up your power to revoke or amend the trust; or if income or principal is actually paid to someone else.

Essentially, there are no tax advantages gained by establishing a revocable trust. But there can be some real financial and administrative advantages, including:

Avoiding Probate and Ancillary Administration.   Revocable trust assets pass to the beneficiaries you name in the trust document and are not controlled by your will. This cuts out the costs and delays arising from the probate process, but first check the laws in your state. Many states have streamlined the probate process and reduced the associated costs. Also, unlike probate, with a revocable trust the identity and instructions for distributing estate property are not part of the public record. Further, if you own real property in a state other than your state of domicile, a revocable trust will avoid the ancillary probate administration in that state that would otherwise be required.

Avoiding Legal Guardianship.   If you become incapacitated, the assets kept in your living trust would be managed by a trustee you named in the trust document. Otherwise, the determination of whether and to what extent you are disabled or incompetent and who is going to handle your affairs could be left to public, and potentially costly, guardianship proceedings. A durable power of attorney can also be an effective tool for prearranging the management of your affairs in the event you become incapacitated.

Relief from Financial Responsibility.   If desired, an independent trustee can be used immediately to relieve you of the details of managing your property and investments, record-keeping chores, and the preparation and filing of income tax returns.

Living trusts have some drawbacks and are not suited for everyone:

- Expect to pay legal fees and other expenses, such as recording fees, to set up the trust and transfer property to it. You will also owe recurring trustee and administrative charges if you use a corporate trustee rather than managing the trust yourself.

- You will not necessarily save on other legal, accounting, and executor's aid to handle your estate. Whether your assets are held in a living or pass through probate, the same sort of work will generally be needed to value your assets, prepare federal and state tax returns, settle creditors' claims, and resolve disputes among beneficiaries.

TaxSaver

Two reminders: (1) If you establish a living trust, be sure that any property covered by the trust is legally titled in the trustee's name. This is a straight-forward, but often overlooked, point. (2) After setting up a living trust, you must remember to conduct your personal business affairs through the trust. This is not difficult but can be a burden. Property held outside the trust at your death will be subject to probate—except for life insurance proceeds (payable to a beneficiary other than your estate) and property held jointly with right of survivorship, which by law would avoid probate.

How to Raise Cash to Pay Estate Taxes

In many instances, the estate of an owner of a closely held business—or for that matter, any estate—may not have sufficient cash to pay all the estate's obligations, including estate taxes. Without sufficient liquidity, the estate may be forced to sell a portion of the business to raise the necessary cash. But there are special rules for the estates of owners of closely held businesses. The techniques described below can help alleviate liquidity problems.

Stock Redemptions to Pay Death Taxes

A special tax provision (Section 303 of the Internal Revenue Code) allows certain redemptions or partial redemptions of closely held stock to be treated as a sale or exchange, not as a dividend. (Dividends would normally be treated as ordinary income and be taxed at a potentially higher rate.) Since the estate's basis in the decedent's stock will be the stock's fair market value at the date of death, only postdeath appreciation will be taxed upon the redemption and only up to the maximum long-term capital gains tax rate of 20%. To qualify for what is called a Section 303 redemption, the value of all the stock of the corporation included in the decedent's gross estate must exceed 35% of the decedent's adjusted gross estate. The adjusted gross estate is the gross estate less the allowable deductions for funeral and administration expenses, debts, the family-owned business deduction, and certain losses (but before any charitable deduction or marital deduction). A qualifying redemption under Section 303 is limited in amount to the sum of the following items:

- Federal and state death taxes,
- Funeral expenses, and
- Estate administration expenses.

TaxSaver

An estate does not actually have to be illiquid in order to qualify for this special redemption. The estate may redeem stock up to the maximum amount referred to above, even if the estate otherwise has sufficient liquid assets to take care of its expenses and taxes. It is often desirable to redeem stock under this special provision because it can otherwise be difficult for the decedent's heirs to withdraw funds from the corporation without paying tax at ordinary income rates.

INSTALLMENT PAYMENT OF ESTATE TAX

The estate taxes attributable to a decedent's closely held business can be paid over a 14-year period if certain conditions are met. This 14-year payout offers a very favorable interest rate plus a 5-year deferral on the first installment of estate taxes. The deferral provision only applies to an "interest in a closely held business." To qualify, the value of the closely held business must exceed 35% of the adjusted gross estate. The amount of estate tax that qualifies for a deferred payout is limited to the portion of the total tax that is attributable to the decedent's business interest. Thus, if the decedent's qualifying stock constitutes 62% of the adjusted gross estate, then 62% of the total estate tax liability may be deferred.

Even though none of the tax attributable to the closely held business interest is paid for five years, the interest on the tax for the first four years must be paid annually. Starting in the fifth year, the estate tax due plus interest may be paid in up to 10 yearly installments.

The interest rate charged on the deferred estate tax attributable to the first $1 million in value of the closely held business interest is 2%. An interest rate equal to 45% of the rate applicable to tax underpayments applies to the deferred estate tax in excess of that amount.

E&Y FOCUS: Estate Planning—Steps to Take Now

Here's a handy checklist of estate planning measures you need to consider:

- Review with your spouse your current financial situation and your entire personal financial plan (including plans for your retirement as well as plans for the years after one of you has died).
- If any adult member of your family does not have a will, or if any wills have not been reviewed within the last three years, contact your attorney. This is especially important because of the frequency of tax law changes.
- Compile a list documenting where all your important financial and legal papers are located. Inform all appropriate persons of your list. If you have not already done so, be sure your spouse or whomever you designate as your personal representative knows your attorney, accountant, trust officer, broker, insurance advisor, and other appropriate individuals.

- Compile information on the cost and approximate purchase date of all your assets, including your residence.
- To reduce federal estate taxes, consider assigning ownership rights of your group term life insurance to children, a trust, or other appropriate recipient.
- Review whom you have designated as a beneficiary for your employee retirement or Keogh plan and other employee benefits.
- Review how your assets will be passed on to your beneficiaries.
- Make sure that you have provided for the legal guardianship and personal custody of your minor children.
- Review your will or any trust you have set up with your attorney. In particular, you and your spouse should check the provisions in your wills that pertain to what would happen to your estates if both of you died at the same time. Have you, for example, properly divided your assets to take maximum advantage of the marital deduction and the unified estate and gift tax credit (discussed on pages 214 and 289)?
- If you and your spouse do not have durable powers of attorney, health care proxies, or living wills, consider having them drawn up soon. If the answer to any of the following questions is yes, you may need professional assistance to help you determine whether there are tax problems on the horizon. Remember: a "yes" answer is a warning flag, but not necessarily a signal that there is a problem.

Are you:

- Making significant cash gifts to members of your family that are likely to continue indefinitely?
- Planning to make gifts to grandchildren within the next few years? In your will?
- Anticipating a significant inheritance? Is your spouse?

Do you:

- Hold assets jointly with your spouse, other than your residence and a working banking account?
- Have a simple will that leaves all property you own at the date of your death outright to your spouse?
- Own any real property in a state other than the state of your residence?
- Have a child or other relative with a serious medical problem that may require special consideration in your will or trust instrument?
- Have substantially more or less property than your spouse?

Have you:

- Moved your residence to a different state since you last executed your will?
- Named your estate as the beneficiary of your life insurance or your retirement plan benefits?

CONCERNS REGARDING COMMUNITY PROPERTY

Community property is most often property acquired by spouses while they are married and domiciled in a community property state. But not *all* property acquired during the marriage is community property. If one spouse individually receives a gift or inheritance, it is not community property but rather is "separate property" owned solely by the recipient. Property acquired or otherwise owned by each spouse prior to marriage is also considered separate property.

Community property and marital property are treated differently from noncommunity property when someone dies. In a noncommunity property state, the basis of the decedent's property is increased or decreased for tax purposes to fair market value as of the date generally of the decedent's death. However, when one spouse in a community property state dies, the basis of *both* spouses' interest in all community property is stepped up or down, that is, increased or decreased to the fair market value at date of death.

III

Tax Strategies for Businesses

One of the most important decisions you make in starting a new business is choosing how to organize your new concern—as a sole proprietorship, a general, limited, or limited liability partnership, a limited liability company (LLC), an S corporation, or a regular corporation (otherwise known as a C corporation). There are, of course, advantages and disadvantages to each, and the nature of your business to a considerable extent will determine the choice you make. Yet, you would be well advised to be familiar with each of the different options because the consequences of your choice will be far-reaching.

From a business perspective, ownership structure and liability protection are often the key considerations in making the choice. From a tax perspective, an important consideration is whether business profits are to be taxed at the business entity level or at the owner level. A sole proprietorship is not a separate legal entity from its owner; thus, the owner is not protected from liabilities and other claims arising from the business. Partnerships, LLCs, S corporations, and C corporations are separate legal entities, affording varying levels of liability protection.

For tax purposes, a business is treated as:

1. A sole proprietorship with the income reported directly on the owner's return;

2. A partnership, with the income reported directly on the partners' returns;

3. An S corporation, whose income is reported directly by its shareholders; or

4. A C corporation, which is a separate taxpaying entity. The shareholders of a C corporation also pay tax on the corporation's earnings when they are distributed.

The rules relating to the classification of a business into one of the four categories above are discussed in the following chapter. Also in this chapter is discussion of how businesses are taxed. We've also included tax savings strategies that could benefit your business.

14

Choosing the Right Entity for Your Business

INTRODUCTION

A business may generally be conducted as a sole proprietorship, a general or limited partnership, a limited liability company (LLC), or a corporation. From a business perspective, ownership structure and liability protection are often the key considerations in choosing the type of entity for doing business. From a tax perspective, an important consideration is whether business profits are taxed at the business entity level or at the owner level. This chapter offers some suggestions on how to choose the right structure for your business and what the tax consequences of that decision are likely to be.

CHOOSING THE PROPER BUSINESS ENTITY

Business Considerations

In deciding the form in which you will do business, taxes are an important consideration *but* by no means the only one. In subsequent paragraphs, we will discuss the various types of entities you can use in operating a business. Following are some items you need to consider in making that decision:

1. Are there any state laws governing your choice of a particular business entity?
2. Do you need to protect your personal assets from the potential liabilities of the business?
3. Will you need to obtain capital from outside sources to expand your business?

4. Do you intend to transfer ownership interests in the business to your children, grandchildren, or other relatives and/or would you like employees to have an equity interest in the business?

The answers to these questions can affect your choice of business entity.

State Law Considerations. A state may require a business, such as a bank or an insurance company, to be incorporated. In this case, your choice of entity may be limited to corporate form. A business that is required to operate in corporate form will be taxed as a corporation. However, as discussed below, a qualifying corporation may elect to be treated as an S corporation. A state may also preclude certain professionals from limiting their personal liability, which may affect the form in which such professionals may conduct business.

Liability Protection. Individuals conducting a business often are concerned about avoiding potential personal liability for business obligations. States generally require individuals to form and conduct the business in an entity separate and distinct from its owners in order to get liability protection.

Need for Outside Capital. If you anticipate needing capital from outside sources, this should be considered in your decision as to choice of entity. For example, a common source of financing for start-up businesses is venture capital. If you choose to operate as an S corporation, an investment by a venture capital firm may result in the termination of your company's S election, causing it to be taxed as a regular corporation. In this case, you may be better off initially operating as a partnership or an LLC. On the other hand, if you anticipate going public to raise capital, the corporate form may be preferable. However, as discussed below, there may be tax disadvantages to operating as a corporation. An important factor to consider is that generally you can change the tax status of your business to a corporation on a tax-free basis; however, changing the tax status of a corporation generally results in gain recognition, if the value of the business has appreciated.

Transfer of Ownership. The ease in selling or transferring an interest in a business entity is another consideration in selecting a type of business entity. For example, if you want to provide your employees with an equity interest in the business, operating in corporate form may be the best choice. This is because traditional equity-based compensation plans (such as incentive stock option plans) are generally more easily implemented for corporations.

Tax Considerations

For tax purposes, a business is treated as:
1. A sole proprietorship with the income reported directly on the owner's return;

2. A partnership, with the income reported directly on the partners' returns;

3. An S corporation, whose income is reported directly by its shareholders; or

4. A C corporation, which is a separate taxpaying entity. The shareholders of a C corporation also pay tax on the corporation's earnings when they are distributed.

A business's legal form may not be determinative for tax purposes because the tax entity classification rules, called "check-the-box," allow certain taxpayers to choose to be treated as a different entity for tax purposes than they are for state law purposes.

Under the check-the-box rules, incorporated business entities and certain types of businesses, like insurance companies, will always be treated as corporations for tax purposes. A partnership or LLC with more than one member is generally taxed as a partnership; however, such entities may elect to be taxed as a corporation. A single member LLC is generally disregarded. Thus, for example, a single member LLC owned by an individual is treated as a sole proprietorship, and a single member LLC owned by a corporation is treated as a division or a branch. A single member LLC may also elect to be taxed as a corporation. While the check-the-box regulations provide flexibility for partnerships and LLCs, a sole proprietorship is always treated as such.

The legal and tax considerations associated with the various types of businesses are discussed below.

TYPES OF BUSINESSES

Sole Proprietorship (Including Certain Single Member LLCs)

A sole proprietorship is simple to form and does not require a separate transfer of assets. It is not a separate legal entity from its owner. Accordingly, a sole proprietor has unlimited personal liability for the debts of the business. In other words, a sole proprietor's liability is not limited to business assets; the proprietor's individual assets are also at risk.

A sole proprietorship is not treated as a separate taxable entity for federal income tax purposes. The income generated by the sole proprietorship is simply included on its owner's individual income tax return along with other items of income and deduction. Thus, the income of a sole proprietorship is taxed once, at its owner's individual income tax rate.

Gross profit or loss for the year from the sole proprietorship is reported on Form 1040, Schedule C (or Schedule C-EZ if certain tests are met), and it becomes part of a sole proprietor's adjusted gross income. In addition to owing income tax on such income, the sole proprietor will usually be liable for self-employment tax. The sole proprietor will usually have to make quarterly estimated tax payments as well (page 264). A net loss from the business can generally be deducted by the owner in computing adjusted gross income.

Profit (or loss) is computed as income less allowable deductions. Income includes cash, property, and services received by the business from all sources unless specifically excluded under the tax code. Allowable deductions include all ordinary and necessary expenses incurred in connection with the business. For sole proprietorships in the business of selling goods or inventory, the primary expense may be the cost of goods sold. The cost of goods sold represents the cost of materials, labor, and overhead included in the inventory sold during the year. Other expenses that are deductible on Schedule C include salaries and wages paid to employees (but not the owner), interest on loans used in the business, rent, depreciation, bad debts, travel and entertainment, insurance, and real estate taxes. (See the discussion on pages 262–263.)

A sole proprietor's business is easy to terminate. The business assets can be used by the sole proprietor for personal use or in other businesses. Alternatively, a sole proprietor may sell the assets. Because a sole proprietorship is not a separate entity, a sale of the business will be treated as if each asset of the business had been sold separately. The gain or loss on such a sale is the total of the gains or losses as separately computed for each individual asset and is taken into account on the sole proprietor's individual income tax return. For more information on computing the gain or loss from the sale of business assets, see page 178.

An LLC that is owned by one individual generally is taxed as a sole proprietorship (however, an election may be made to tax a single member LLC as a corporation). This arrangement may be advantageous from a business perspective because, although the tax consequences are the same for a sole proprietorship and a single member LLC taxed as a sole proprietorship, an LLC affords its owner liability protection not available to a business legally conducted as a sole proprietorship.

Partnership (Including LLCs treated as Partnerships)

In contrast to a sole proprietorship, a partnership is an entity that is separate and apart from its individual partners. Partnership interests may be held by *general* partners or *limited* partners (LLC interests are held by "members"). The general partners in a partnership are jointly liable for the debts of the business. In addition, general partners are jointly and individually liable for wrongful acts committed by a general partner in the course of the partnership's trade or business. Like a sole proprietor, the personal assets of a general partner are subject to the claims of the partnership's creditors (although any partner required to pay a partnership liability may assert a right to be indemnified by the other partners). A limited partner, however, usually is subject to the claims of the business's creditors only to the extent of his or her capital contribution to the partnership or to the extent he or she is obligated to contribute in the future under the partnership agreement; this is also the case for an LLC member. If you are a limited partner rather than a general partner, you do not materially participate in the management of the partnership. A limited partnership (i.e., a partnership with limited partners) must have at least one general partner whose assets are subject to the claims of the business's creditors. An LLC, on the other hand, need not have a member whose assets are subject to the claims of creditors.

Partnerships generally are formed based on a written partnership agreement under applicable state partnership law, although oral agreements or the conduct and relationship of the parties may be sufficient for an entity to be treated as a partnership for federal income tax purposes. Generally, it is preferable to have a written partnership agreement in place that satisfies the requirements under a state's partnership law.

Many states have authorized the registration of a limited liability partnership (an LLP) as a form of partnership. In an LLP, the personal assets of a partner are not subject to partnership liabilities for the conduct of other partners. LLPs may be treated like partnerships for federal income tax purposes.

An LLC is formed under the applicable state's limited liability company statute.

A partnership is not a taxable entity (unless it elects to be taxed as a corporation); however, it must compute its income each year and file a partnership return (Form 1065) on or before the 15th day of the 4th month after the end of the partnership's tax year. Most decisions affecting the determination of partnership income are made by the partnership and are binding upon the partners.

An LLC with more than one member is generally taxed as a partnership (unless it elects to be taxed as a corporation).

As a partner, or as a member in the case of an LLC treated as a partnership, you are individually liable for tax on your share of partnership income, which is determined under the partnership agreement, even if such income is not distributed to you. You report your share of income or loss for the partnership year that ends with or within your own taxable year. This income includes guaranteed payments of interest and salary paid to you as a partner in the partnership, that are deducted in determining the partnership's income. These payments are usually considered ordinary income to you.

Because you are required to include partnership items on your personal income tax return, any item that may impact your tax liability, if separately stated, must be reported separately by the partnership. The items listed below are examples of such items:

- Net income or losses from rental real estate activities;
- Net income or losses from other rental activities;
- Portfolio income or losses, including interest, dividends, and royalties;
- Gains and losses from the disposition of property used in a trade or business and certain involuntary conversions;

- Charitable contributions;
- Foreign income taxes;
- Other items as required, such as: contributions made on behalf of the partners to a qualified pension or profit-sharing plan, and items subject to a special allocation under the partnership agreement that generally differ from the partnership allocation of profit and loss;
- Any item that would result in a different tax liability to a partner if not taken into account separately (e.g., investment interest expense or percentage depletion);
- Allowable tax credits; and
- Deductions relating to the election to expense certain depreciable business assets.

In addition, as a partner, you are required to account separately for your share of partnership items of income and deductions that are considered tax preference items for alternative minimum tax purposes. (See page 155.)

Generally, all partnerships must conform their tax years to that of their principal partners unless the partnership can establish, to the satisfaction of the IRS, a business purpose for having a different tax year. (Prior to 1986, partnerships had considerable leeway in selecting tax years.)

Deductions you claim for losses from the partnership may be limited by the at-risk rules and passive activity loss provisions. (See the discussion in Chapter 1.)

A partner may terminate his or her interest in a partnership by selling the partnership interest to another partner or to a third party. Alternatively, a partner may retire from the partnership and receive liquidating distributions. How the payments are characterized will determine how they are taxed. You should consult your tax advisor.

Regular or C Corporation

A C corporation is recognized as a legal and tax entity separate from its owners. Stockholders generally are sheltered from any liabilities of the corporation. (*Note:* In closely held corporations, lenders often require stockholders to guarantee the payment of the corporation's debt, thus reducing the potential benefit of limited liability—one of the benefits of forming a corporation.) Ownership in a C corporation may be divided into any number of shares of various classes of stock with different voting and dividends rights. A corporation also can issue debt or equity securities other than stock. Convertible bonds, stock rights, stock warrants, and stock options provide investors with alternative forms of investment.

You generally may incorporate, on a tax-free basis, an existing sole proprietorship or partnership (some important exceptions apply), or even a new business. In addition, most property may be transferred to an existing corporation in exchange for the corporation's stock without recognizing any gain in the transferred property if, after the exchange, the existing corporation is controlled by those transferring the property.

A C corporation is taxed on its taxable income whether or not the income is distributed to the stockholders. Earnings distributed to stockholders generally are taxable as ordinary dividends to the extent of the corporation's earnings and profits. As a result, corporate earnings generally are subject to "double tax"—first at the corporate level, and again when distributed to stockholders.

TAXSAVER

Paying higher salaries to stockholders of C corporations, if such remuneration is reasonable, can avoid the double taxation of the business income.

E&Y FOCUS: Executive Compensation

Closely held corporations contemplating an initial public offering (IPO) should consider the impact an IPO may have on executive compensation. A publicly held corporation is not allowed a deduction for compensation in excess of $1 million paid or accrued for the tax year to certain employees. The employees covered by this rule are the chief executive officer of the corporation (or an individual acting in that capacity) and the four highest compensated officers (other than the C.E.O.) whose compensation is required to be disclosed to shareholders under Securities and Exchange Commission (SEC) rules. Although a phase-in period applies to new public companies, planning ahead can eliminate problems in the future. For example, certain kinds of compensation, such as performance-based compensation, are excluded from the $1 million cap.

As a result, publicly held corporations faced with the $1 million cap on deductible compensation should consider restructuring their compensation packages for covered employees to ensure that as much compensation as possible is deductible; for example, structuring it as performance-based compensation. In addition, incentive stock options, which do not generate a deduction for employers (where certain holding period requirements are met), may become increasingly attractive for employers that are running up against the $1 million cap for covered employees. The lower capital gains tax rate may also make incentive stock options an attractive way to compensate employees.

To the extent that a corporation pays interest to a shareholder, double taxation of the business income is avoided because, although the interest is taxable to the shareholder, interest paid generally is deductible by the corporation. The IRS, however, carefully scrutinizes the characterization of debt from stockholders to be certain it is not disguised equity.

S Corporation

Shareholders of an S corporation generally have the same advantage of limited liability as shareholders in a regular or C corporation. However, like a partnership, an S corporation generally is not subject to federal taxes at the corporate level. An S corporation's items of income, gain, loss, deduction, and credit pass through to its shareholders and are reported by them on their individual income tax returns.

TaxPlanner

If you are forming a new business, you may want to consider setting up an LLC instead of an S corporation. Like an S corporation, LLC income is taxed at only the individual level. There are, however, other advantages to LLCs. Unlike an S corporation, there are generally no restrictions on an LLC's capital structure or on who may be a member. In addition, because an LLC with more than one member may be treated as a partnership for tax purposes, the special partnership allocation rules and basis adjustment rules that apply to partnerships, but not S corporations, may be available.

Although an LLC should be considered if you are forming a new business enterprise, an S corporation may be best if you are currently conducting business as a C corporation and would like to change your business tax status. Converting from C corporation to S corporation tax status is generally tax-free, while converting from a C corporation to a partnership or LLC generally is treated as a taxable liquidation with any gain taxed at both the corporate and shareholder levels. Another factor to consider is the treatment of flow-through income for self-employment tax purposes. An LLC member may be required to pay self-employment tax on his or her share of the LLC's flow-through income (even if such income is not paid out). In contrast, S corporation flow-through income is not considered earnings from self-employment.

A corporation must formally elect to be taxed as an S corporation by filing Form 2553 (Election by a Small Business Corporation) with the IRS, as well as meeting certain other requirements. The election to be taxed as an S corporation and eligibility requirements are discussed in detail in Chapter 16.

15

Determining Income, Deductions, and Taxes for Your Business

INTRODUCTION

Every type of business is required to compute its taxable income. The accounting period and accounting methods you choose to use for your business will determine when items of income and deduction are taken into account in computing taxable income. And the form in which you choose to do business will affect how such income is reported and taxed. This chapter tells you how to determine the taxable income of a business and how such income is taxed. In addition, the reporting requirements for all business entities, i.e., sole proprietorships, partnerships, S corporations, and regular corporations, are reviewed. This chapter also suggests strategies that could help you reduce your taxes.

ACCOUNTING PERIODS AND METHODS

Accounting Periods

Taxable income must be reported on the basis of a taxable year that, with few exceptions, will be an annual 12-month period. When a business is operated as a sole proprietorship, the taxable year of the business must be the same as that of the sole proprietor. Partnerships must have the same taxable year as that of the partners who own a majority interest in profits and capital. As a general rule, S corporations and personal service corporations (i.e., corporations whose principal activity is the performance of certain personal services, primarily by the employee-owners) must use a calendar year. However, partnerships, S corporations, and personal service corporations may use a different year if they can establish a business purpose for a fiscal year (e.g., the requested year is a natural business year). In addition, when first selecting a taxable year, these entities generally may elect to have a fiscal year that does not defer more than three months of income for their owners. A partnership or S corporation that makes such an election must make a deposit with the IRS that is intended to approximate the taxes that are being deferred for the partners or shareholders.

Generally, a C corporation may adopt a taxable year ending at the end of any month, assuming an annual accounting period is established. If an annual accounting period is not established, taxable income must be computed on a calendar-year basis.

Once an accounting period is chosen, permission from the IRS may be required to change to another year-end.

Accounting Methods

A business must compute taxable income in accordance with the method of accounting regularly employed in keeping its books. An "accounting method" includes not only the overall method of computing income, but also the accounting treatment of individual items. Federal tax law permits a variety of methods, including the cash method, the accrual method, the installment method (in limited situations), the special rules for long-term contracts, or any combination of methods that clearly reflect income.

For tax purposes, the choice of the cash method of accounting is restricted to individuals, sole proprietorships, certain farming businesses, certain personal service corporations, S corporations, certain partnerships, and small C corporations (i.e., C corporations with average gross receipts for the preceding three years of $5 million or less). C corporations (other than small C corporations), large partnerships with corporate partners, and businesses that are considered "tax shelters" must use the accrual method of accounting. (For a further discussion of the cash and accrual methods, see pages 262 and 281.)

Taxpayers with inventories must generally use the accrual method of accounting for purchases and sales of merchandise. However, the IRS recently announced that it will allow a business with annual gross receipts of $1 million or less to use the cash method of accounting, without regard to whether the business is required to maintain inventories. (See page 245 for more details.)

Unless otherwise required or permitted under the tax law, an accounting method may be changed only after securing permission from the IRS. The IRS may require a change in accounting method if the method used does not clearly reflect income.

Installment Sales.   An installment sale occurs when property is sold and the buyer is permitted to pay for it over a period of time that extends beyond the tax year in which the sale occurs. The installment method of reporting such sales income generally allows businesses to defer the payment of taxes until the year in which a payment is received rather than the year in which the sale occurs. (See page 128.)

Generally, the installment method is mandatory for eligible sales. A taxpayer may elect not to use the installment method, however, by reporting the entire gain for the tax year in which the sale is made on a timely filed return.

Effective for sales after December 17, 1999, the installment method is no longer available for a taxpayer using the accrual method of accounting.

TaxSaver

In certain cases, you may wish to "elect out" of the installment method and, instead, recognize the entire gain in the year of sale. This may be beneficial if you have capital losses or expiring net operating losses that may offset the recognized gain. Furthermore, if your tax rate is expected to increase in the year the cash is received, you may be better off recognizing the entire gain in the year of sale.

What to Include and What to Deduct from Income

A business generally must report any income it receives unless such income is specifically excluded by a provision in the tax code. Reportable income may be cash, property, or services received and includes payments for goods or services, interest, dividends, rents, royalties, gains from dealings in property, and income from the discharge of indebtedness. As indicated above, the method of accounting used by a business determines when income is to be reported. For example, a business using the accrual method generally must report income when it is earned rather than when it is received. Correspondingly, expenses are generally deducted when incurred. Under the cash method, items of income are reported in the year in which they are actually or constructively received and expenses are generally deducted when paid.

TaxSaver

The following may result in a deferral of income:
- *Delaying shipment on sales*
- *Making sales on consignment or approval*
- *For a cash basis taxpayer, selling qualifying assets on an installment basis*

Cost of Goods Sold

If you are in a business in which the production, purchase, or sale of merchandise produces income, you must identify the particular goods in inventory so that the proper costs can be calculated. The cost of merchandise sold during the year is determined by taking into account your inventory at the beginning of the year, adding to that the cost of goods purchased or produced during the year, and by subtracting the inventory remaining on hand at the end of the year.

When goods are so intermingled that they cannot be identified with particular purchases, the goods sold or used in manufacture are deemed to be the goods purchased first and the goods that remain in the inventory are deemed to be the goods purchased last—the first-in, first-out (FIFO) method. You may elect to compute the goods remaining on hand at the end of the year as being those purchased first—the last-in, first-out (LIFO) method. Under this method, the cost of goods sold during the year is deemed to be those purchased or used in manufacture last.

TaxSaver

In periods of rising costs, a LIFO inventory method generally will reduce taxable income. In certain cases a company using LIFO can affect taxable income by timing the purchase of goods.

In times of decreasing prices, the FIFO method of accounting generally will provide a larger tax benefit than the LIFO method.

Taxpayers with inventories generally must use the accrual method of accounting for purchases and sales. In other words, you may not deduct the purchase price of inventory when paid, but must wait until the inventory is sold. The inventory method used must conform to the best accounting practices in that particular trade or business and must clearly reflect income. Manufacturers are required to include both direct costs (such as material and labor) and indirect costs (such as those listed below) in inventory.

Uniform Inventory Capitalization Rules. Under the uniform inventory capitalization rules, certain indirect "period costs" must be capitalized into inventory. These indirect costs are generally associated with the expense of running a business over a specific time period, rather than the expense associated with the production and sale of a product. To the extent the inventory remains unsold these indirect costs may not be deducted. Among these costs are:

- Costs related to purchasing and storing inventory;
- Interest on debt either incurred or continued to finance the production of real property or certain tangible personal property;
- Taxes (other than income taxes);
- Successful bidding expenses;
- Depreciation;
- Utilities related to equipment or facilities;
- Engineering and design costs (other than research and experimentation);
- Compensation paid to officers attributable to production;

- Insurance costs related to equipment or facilities;
- Deductible contributions to pension, profit-sharing, stock bonus, or annuity plans for current service costs; and
- Past service pension costs incurred after December 31, 1987.

These rules generally relate to either real or tangible personal property you produce, or property acquired for resale. There are some exceptions, including: (1) property you produce for use other than in a trade or business; (2) self-constructed assets if substantial construction began before March 1, 1986; (3) property produced under a long-term contract; (4) certain development and other costs of oil and gas wells or other mineral property; (5) certain farming activities; and (6) property acquired by a small business (less than $10 million in gross receipts) and held for resale to customers. The uniform inventory capitalization rules generally apply to all types of taxpayers (i.e., individuals, corporations, and partnerships), although special capitalization rules apply to farmers.

While taxpayers with inventory generally must use the accrual method of accounting for purchases and sales, the IRS recently announced that it will allow businesses with annual gross receipts of $1 million or less to use the cash method of accounting, without regard to whether the businesses are required to maintain inventories. Under the new guidance, a taxpayer qualifies for the cash method if, for each tax year ending on or after December 17, 1998, the taxpayer's average annual gross receipts for the three-year period ending with the applicable prior tax year do not exceed $1 million. If a taxpayer has been in existence for less than a three-year period, the taxpayer must determine its average annual gross receipts for the number of years (including short tax years) that the taxpayer has been in existence. In the case of a short tax year, the taxpayer's gross receipts must be annualized by multiplying the gross receipts of the short tax year by twelve and then dividing the product by the number of months in the short tax year.

In addition to the gross receipts requirements, two additional requirements must be met in order for a taxpayer to be eligible to use the cash method. First, a taxpayer must satisfy a conformity requirement. A taxpayer must use the cash method to determine the income, profit, or loss of the trade or business for purposes of its books, records, and reports (including financial statements) to shareholders, partners, other proprietors, or beneficiaries and for credit purposes for the current and prior three tax years (excluding tax years ending before December 17, 2000). A taxpayer that uses the cash method of accounting for purposes of its books and records and reports, but on an isolated basis prepares financial reports using an accrual method (for example, to obtain a bank loan), will be considered to satisfy the conformity requirement.

Second, a taxpayer that does not want to account for its inventories is required to treat its merchandise inventory as a nonincidental supply. This means a taxpayer is permitted to deduct the cost of materials and supplies (other than incidental supplies) only in the amount actually consumed and used in operations during the tax year. Accordingly, no deduction is permitted for materials and supplies purchased but not consumed during the tax year (i.e., supplies on hand at year-end). However, the uniform inventory capitalization rules do not apply to such merchandise inventory.

For taxpayers currently using the accrual method of accounting that now qualify to use the cash method, certain procedures must be followed to change to the cash method. You should consult with your tax advisor to ensure that these procedures are complied with.

Business Capital Gains and Losses

Gains and losses from the sale or exchange of property must be taken into account in computing the taxable income of a business. Special rules apply to gains and losses arising from the sale or exchange of capital assets.

A sale is a transfer of property for money or for a mortgage, note, or other promise to pay money. An exchange is a transfer of property for other property or for services. The rules for figuring a taxable gain or a deductible loss apply to both sales and exchanges.

Capital assets are all assets other than the following: (1) inventory, (2) depreciable property, (3) real estate used in a business, (4) notes and accounts receivable acquired in the ordinary course of a business for services rendered or from the sale of inventory, or (5) in certain cases, copyrights or literary, musical, or other artistic compositions. Letters and memorandums prepared by or for you are also not classified as capital assets.

In the case of a C corporation, net capital gains on sales or exchanges of business assets are taxed at a corporation's ordinary income tax rate. Net capital losses, on the other hand, may not be deducted from ordinary income. They may, however, generally be carried back three years and any excess losses may be carried forward and applied against net capital gains recognized during the following five years. The loss carryovers are treated as short-term capital losses and are offset against any net capital gains in the carryback and carryforward years. Special limitations on the carryover of net capital losses apply following certain corporate acquisitions and changes in ownership. (See page 269.) In the case of a sole proprietorship, partnership, or S corporation, net capital gains on the sales or exchanges of business assets are combined with other capital gains and losses of the owner and, in the case of an individual, may be taxed at the lower individual capital gains tax rate. For individuals, see page 122 for capital gains tax rules.

TaxSaver

Corporations should review their tax positions before year-end and consider additional sales of capital assets to coordinate the timing of gains and losses and prevent the expiration of unused losses.

Depreciation Recapture. Any gain realized on sales and certain other dispositions of depreciable personal or other tangible business property (except buildings and their structural components that are "real property") is treated as ordinary income to the extent of depreciation deductions taken prior to the sale. Expensing certain assets in the year the property was placed in service is treated as depreciation for purposes of these rules. (See page 251.)

Gains realized on the disposal of depreciable real property, such as a building, must be recaptured under rules that are both more complicated and more beneficial than the rules for depreciable personal property. The rules also differ depending on when the property was acquired and how much depreciation has been claimed. In general, any gain equal to the excess depreciation over straight-line depreciation is ordinary income and any remaining gain on the disposition is a capital gain. (In the case of a corporation, an additional amount may be treated as ordinary income.) One important exception to this rule is nonresidential real property acquired from 1981 through 1986 under the Accelerated Cost Recovery System (ACRS). Depreciation on this ACRS property is recaptured up to the lesser of either the gain or the total depreciation taken on the property. However, there is no recapture on this type of property if the straight-line ACRS method was elected.

Deductions

Businesses are entitled to deduct ordinary and necessary business expenses paid or incurred during the taxable year, subject to various limitations. Deductible expenses may include:

- Salaries and wages;
- Repairs and maintenance;
- Bad debts;
- Rents;
- Taxes and licenses;
- Interest—both actual payments and imputed interest;
- Charitable contributions;
- Depreciation and amortization (including certain organizational costs);
- Depletion;
- Advertising;
- Contributions to pension and profit-sharing plans;
- Employee benefit programs;
- Insurance;
- Legal and professional services;
- Research and experimental expenses;
- Utilities and telephones;
- Travel, meals, and entertainment; and
- Net operating losses.

A deduction for certain dividends received may also be available.

Special rules regarding some of these deductions are discussed in the following paragraphs.

Salaries and Wages. You can deduct salaries, wages, and other compensation—including amounts paid to your relatives—as long as the amounts are reasonable in relation to the services provided. However, a sole proprietor cannot deduct any amounts paid to himself or herself. Also, partners in a partnership are not considered employees of the partnership, even if they provide services to the partnership. Thus, a wage deduction cannot be claimed for amounts paid by a partnership to its partners. Such amounts may be deductible as "guaranteed payments" however.

Bad Debts. You are allowed a deduction for specific debts that become wholly or partially worthless during the tax year. Ordinary deductions generally are allowed for debts created or acquired in connection with a taxpayer's trade or business (e.g., trade receivables). Capital losses are allowed with respect to nonbusiness debts (although C corporations are generally entitled to an ordinary deduction for nonbusiness bad debts). Certain businesses involved in the performance of services that use the accrual method of accounting may accelerate bad debt deductions by using a special accounting method that bases the bad debt deduction on the service provider's collection experience.

You cannot deduct losses from bad debts for receivables that you have not yet reported as income if you are a cash-method taxpayer. Accrual-method taxpayers include items in income when they have done everything required of them. Therefore, if a customer subsequently refuses to pay an accrual-basis taxpayer, a bad debt deduction eventually can be claimed, in effect reversing the original inclusion in income.

Rents. Rent expenses are deductible as incurred. Consequently, the IRS reviews leasing transactions carefully to ensure that they are not sales-financing arrangements set up to produce a rent expense deduction. Typically, a leasing transaction does not transfer the benefits and burdens of ownership to the lessee. This is different than a financing arrangement in which the parties contemplate a transfer as an indication of ownership. Court decisions on leasing expenditures generally have focused on the intentions of the parties; the substance, rather than the form, of the transaction; and whether and under what terms there is an option to purchase at the end of the lease term. The courts have looked unfavorably at arrangements that permit the lessee to purchase the leased asset at the end of the lease term for a nominal or "bargain" amount.

Note that prepaid rent is only immediately deductible to the extent that it relates to the year in which it is paid. The balance is deductible over the period to which the payment relates.

Taxes and Licenses. Federal income taxes can never be deducted, but certain other taxes—including real property, payroll, and contribution as an employer to FICA (Social Security)—are deductible.

Interest Expense. Interest on business loans is deductible; however, if you prepay interest, it only may be deducted in the tax year to which it relates. Special rules apply if you borrow to construct or manufacture assets. You should consult with your tax advisor.

Imputed Interest. When a debt instrument is issued for non–publicly traded property and the interest rate is not stated or is insufficient, a portion of each payment will be characterized as interest rather than principal. The recharacterized amount is recognized as interest income to the seller and as an interest expense to the borrower. The imputed interest rules apply to payments due more than six months after a sale or exchange of property where some or all of the payments are due more than one year after the date of sale, and where such payments exceed $3,000, but are no greater than $250,000. (Payments in excess of $250,000 are subject to the original issue discount rules, discussed below.)

As a general rule, unstated interest is computed by taking the sum of the installment payments and discounting them using the applicable federal rate (AFR). The AFR, which is published monthly by the U.S. Treasury Department, is based on the average yield on marketable U.S. obligations during the preceding month. The AFR is limited to 9%, compounded semi-annually, for certain debt instruments that have a principal amount under $3,960,100, and this amount is adjusted annually for inflation based upon the consumer price index. Special rules apply for sales of land between family members, sales of farms by individuals and small businesses, and sales of principal residences.

Accrual-method taxpayers must report interest income (expense) as it accrues, while cash-method taxpayers must recognize interest income (expense) as payments are made. (The accrual and cash methods of accounting are explained on page 242.)

Original Issue Discount (OID). In general, a debt instrument has original issue discount (OID) if the stated redemption price at maturity (all payments due under a debt instrument except interest that is unconditionally payable at a fixed rate at least once a year during the entire term) exceeds the issue price of the debt. The issue price depends on whether the debt is issued for money or property. The OID rules apply to long-term (more than one year) debt instruments, such as bonds or notes, that (1) are issued at a true discount, i.e., for less than the face amount of the debt; (2) require accelerated or deferred interest payments, e.g., the debt instrument has a stepped interest rate, payable at 6% for the first three years and 10% for the last five years, or the interest is not paid currently; (3) are issued with another property right, e.g., warrants, in exchange for cash or property traded on an established market; and/or (4) do not provide for "adequate stated interest," and are exchanged for non–publicly traded property (see discussion of imputed interest, above). The OID is generally recognized as an interest expense by the issuing party and as interest income by the debt holder as it accrues, without regard to their individual methods of accounting (cash or accrual).

Special rules, enacted in response to the explosive growth of junk bonds, apply to debt instruments issued after July 10, 1989, that have a term of more than five years, significant OID, and a yield that is more than five points over the AFR. A regular corporation that issues such an instrument may not deduct any portion of the OID on the instrument until interest is actually paid in property other than stock or obligations of the issuing corporation. Further, to the extent that the debt instrument's yield is more than six points over the AFR, no deduction is allowed for that portion of the OID, even when paid in cash.

In addition, interest expense deductions may be disallowed in their entirety for indebtedness of a corporation that is payable in equity of the issuer or a related party, if such indebtedness is issued after June 8, 1997. This provision in no way affects the amount of interest income that the holder of such debt instrument must recognize.

Charitable Contributions. A C corporation may deduct charitable contributions if such contributions do not exceed 10% of its taxable income computed before deducting such contributions, the dividend-received deduction (explained later), net operating loss carrybacks (also explained later), and capital loss carrybacks. Charitable deductions in excess of this 10% limitation can be carried over to the next five taxable years, subject to the same 10% limitation.

Deductions for property contributions are subject to the 10% limitation discussed above. However, no deduction is permitted for that portion of a contribution that would constitute ordinary income if the property contributed were sold at its fair market value (e.g., inventory). In effect, the deduction for contributions of inventory will be limited to the inventory's tax basis.

Corporations (other than S corporations, personal holding companies, and service organizations) are entitled to claim a deduction for contributions of inventory and certain types of property to a charitable organization. When such property is transferred specifically for the care of the needy, the ill, infants, or certain educational organizations, the amount of the deduction for such contributions may exceed the corporation's tax basis in the contributed property, but is limited to the basis of the property plus one-half of the unrealized appreciation. Furthermore, the amount of the deduction may not exceed 200% of the basis of the contributed property.

Example: During 2000, Fashion, Inc., a C corporation that manufactures women's coats, makes a contribution of women's coats to a shelter for the needy. The fair market value of the coats is $1,000 and the basis is $200. The corporation would be permitted to take a $400 deduction for the coats determined as follows: the deduction is limited to the corporation's basis in the property, $200, plus one-half of the unrealized appreciation, $400. Therefore, the deduction is limited to $600 ($200 + $400). However, because the amount exceeds 200% of basis, or $400, the second limitation is imposed, and the charitable contribution is limited to $400. The charitable deduction is also limited to 10% of the corporation's taxable income, as adjusted.

Corporations (other than S corporations, personal holding companies, and service organizations) are also entitled to claim a charitable deduction for contributions of research property. To be eligible for the deduction, the equipment must be constructed by the taxpayer and contributed to a qualifying educational institution such as a college, university, or a qualifying tax-exempt scientific research organization. The recipient must be the first to use the property. In addition, the contribution must be made within two years of substantial completion of construction and must be substantially used by the receiving institution for research purposes. The deduction for scientific contributions is limited to the donated property's basis plus one-half of the unrealized appreciation. However, the deduction may not exceed 200% of the property's basis.

An accrual-basis C corporation for which the board of directors authorizes a charitable contribution during the taxable year and then makes the contribution within two-and-a-half months after year-end may elect to treat the deduction as if it were made in the year authorized.

No charitable deduction is allowed in computing a partnership's taxable income, although each partner may claim a deduction for his or her share of the partnership's charitable contribution. An S corporation must separately state its charitable contributions. The S corporation's shareholders may deduct their share of the S corporation's contributions, subject to the limitations on contributions that apply at the shareholder level. Contributions made by a sole proprietorship are subject to the individual charitable contribution limitations.

See Chapter 6 for a detailed discussion of the documentation requirements for charitable contributions.

Depreciation. Depreciation is the annual deduction allowed for recovering the cost of fixed assets. Generally, depreciation deductions can be claimed on property purchased for business use. These deductions are calculated using the "cost recovery" systems that are explained in this section. The amount of the tax deduction will depend on which "cost recovery" system is used.

The depreciation allowance in the case of tangible property applies only to that part of the property that is subject to wear and tear, to decay or decline from natural causes, to exhaustion, or to obsolescence. The allowance does not apply to inventories or stock in trade, or to land apart from most improvements added to it. The allowance does not apply to natural resources that are subject to an allowance for depletion. No deduction for depreciation is allowed on personal assets, such as automobiles or other vehicles used solely for pleasure, a building used by the taxpayer solely as his or her residence, or furniture or furnishings therein.

Accelerated Cost Recovery System (ACRS). The cost of tangible assets placed in service after December 31, 1980, and before January 1, 1987, generally must be recovered according to the accelerated cost recovery system (ACRS). To qualify for deductions under ACRS, capital expenditures must be for "recovery property," which is any depreciable, tangible property that is used in a business or held for the production of income.

Under ACRS, capital expenditures generally are recovered over periods of 3, 5, 10, 15, 18, or 19 years. The applicable recovery period depends on the type of property and the date it was placed in service.

Modified Accelerated Cost Recovery System (MACRS). The modified accelerated cost recovery system (MACRS) generally applies to tangible property placed in service after December 31, 1986. Each item of property depreciated under MACRS is assigned to a property class. The property class establishes the period of time over which the cost basis of an item in the class is recovered. The class to which property is assigned is determined by its asset depreciation range (ADR) class life (a classification system established by the IRS). The ADR class life determines the property's recovery period and the method of depreciation that is used.

Under MACRS, tangible property falls into one of the following classes:
1. *3-year property.* This class includes property such as tractor units for over-the-road use and certain horses.
2. *5-year property.* This class includes property such as automobiles, trucks, property used in connection with research and experimentation, computers and peripheral equipment, and office machinery (typewriters, calculators, copiers, etc.). It does not include office furniture and fixtures.
3. *7-year property.* This class includes property such as office furniture and fixtures (desks, files, etc.) and, as designated, any single-purpose agricultural or horticultural structure. This class also includes any property that does not have a class life and that has not been designated by law as being in any other class. Because 7-year property is the default classification for property that does not have a class life and is not designated as being in any other class, most machinery and equipment is 7-year property.
4. *10-year property.* This class includes single-purpose agricultural or horticultural structures, any tree or vine bearing fruit or nuts, vessels, barges, tugs, and similar water transportation equipment.
5. *15-year property.* This class includes roads, shrubbery, municipal wastewater treatment plants, and certain telephone distribution plants.
6. *20-year property.* This class includes property such as farm buildings and, as designated, any municipal sewers.
7. *Residential rental property.* This class includes any real property that is a rental building or structure (including mobile homes) for which 80% or more of the gross rental income for the tax year is rental income from dwelling units. If you live in any part of the building or structure, the gross rental income includes the fair rental value of the part you

live in. A dwelling unit is a house or apartment used to provide living accommodations in a building or structure, but does not include hotels, motels, and inns in which more than half of the units are used on a transient basis. Residential rental property is depreciated over 27.5 years.

8. *Nonresidential real property.* This class includes any real property that is not residential rental property (defined above) and any real property that is Section 1250 property with a class life of 27.5 years or more. Section 1250 property includes all real property that is subject to an allowance for depreciation and that is not or has never been Section 1245 property (i.e., property subject to an allowance for depreciation that includes personal property and other tangible property used as an integral part of manufacturing, production, extraction, or the furnishing of transportation, communications, electrical energy, gas, water, or sewage disposal services). It also includes leased property (such as a building) to which the lessee has made improvements that are subject to an allowance for depreciation and the cost of acquiring a lease. This property is depreciated over 39 years.

The rate of recovery under MACRS is dependent upon three factors:

1. Depreciation method;
2. Recovery period; and
3. The applicable convention.

As indicated above, the class life determines a property's depreciation method and recovery period. The class life and when property is placed in service determine the applicable convention.

Three Conventions. There are three conventions: half-year, mid-quarter, and mid-month. These designations refer to when the property is deemed to have been placed in service during the year. All property within an individual class placed in service in a given taxable year must be depreciated using the same recovery method, period, and convention. Real estate is an exception to this rule. The recovery method and period are determined on a property-by-property basis.

Alternative Depreciation System. The alternative depreciation system (ADS), which utilizes the straight-line depreciation method and longer recovery periods, must be used for property used predominantly outside the United States, tax-exempt use property, tax-exempt bond-financed property, imported property restricted by presidential executive order, and listed property (defined below) used 50% or less for business purposes. In addition, you may elect to apply ADS in lieu of post-1986 MACRS deductions to any other class of property. ADS is also used for the purpose of computing the depreciation adjustment for post-1986 assets in connection with the alternative minimum tax rules (discussed below).

If you lease property, your depreciation deductions for any leasehold improvements you make are determined under MACRS without regard to the term of your lease. Thus, the costs of the improvements are depreciated over the applicable recovery period.

Short Taxable Year. If property is placed in service during a short taxable year (i.e., a tax year of less than 12 months) or used in a new trade or business, the first-year deduction must be allocated by calculating the depreciation deduction using the applicable method for the number of months the property was used.

For a discussion of recapture of depreciation on the sale of an asset, see page 246.

Sales or transfers of used property among related taxpayers for the purpose of receiving increased depreciation deductions are subject to certain restrictions, known as antichurning rules. The rules generally disqualify the property from being depreciated under a more rapid recovery method.

"Listed" Property. Any "listed" property placed in service after June 18, 1984, that is not used more than half the time in a qualified business use during any tax year does not qualify for MACRS depreciation, or for the asset expensing election (explained below). Instead, the property must be depreciated using the alternative depreciation system described above.

Listed property includes: (1) any passenger automobile; (2) any other property used as a means of transportation; (3) any property of a type generally used for entertainment, recreation, or amusement; (4) any computer and related peripheral equipment other than that used exclusively at a regular business establishment that is owned or leased by the person operating the establishment; (5) any cellular telephone or other similar telecommunications equipment; and (6) any other property specified by IRS regulations.

If you claim accelerated depreciation in excess of straight-line depreciation on certain pre-1987 leased real or personal property, the deduction will be considered a tax preference item for purposes of computing the alternative minimum tax. (See page 271.)

Section 179 Expensing. Instead of claiming a depreciation deduction, you may elect to expense (i.e., deduct currently) up to $20,000 per year of the cost of tangible personal property and other tangible property placed in service and used primarily in a trade or business. A depreciation deduction provides a recovery over a period of years, while expensing provides for a more immediate recovery. An immediate expense is not available for real property or property held for investment.

TaxAlert

The Small Business Job Protection Act of 1996 incrementally increased the allowable deduction for the equipment expensing election to $25,000 over a seven-year period. The allowable deductions for the remainder of the phase-in period are: $20,000 for tax year 2000; $24,000 for tax years 2001–2002; and $25,000 for tax year 2003.

The amount of the Section 179 expense cannot be greater than the income derived from the active conduct of any trade or business (computed without regard to the property to be expensed). Costs disallowed under this income limitation are carried forward to the succeeding taxable year and added to the allowable amount of such year.

In addition, the maximum allowable amount of the expense is reduced (but not below zero) by $1 for each $1 of property placed in service in a tax year exceeding $200,000. For example, the $20,000 expense allowed for 2000 is not available for taxpayers who place more than $220,000 of qualifying property in service during 2000.

TaxSaver

If you have incurred an operating loss in the current year, the expense will not be allowed in the current year, but can be carried over. If you expect to have taxable income in the following year, it may be more advantageous to take the expense in the current year and obtain the full benefit of that expense in the following year, as opposed to depreciating the asset over five or seven years.

TaxSaver

You should carefully consider the timing of your purchases of Section 179 property to maximize the tax deductions available.

In the case of a partnership or S corporation, the limitation applies to the partnership or corporation as well as to each partner or shareholder.

The dollar limitation on expensing must be apportioned among the component members of a controlled group. (See page 268.)

TaxSaver

An individual who is both a partner in a partnership and a sole proprietor should be careful to avoid a permanent disallowance that may result if the total election amount exceeds the limitations discussed above.

Amortization of Intangibles. Most acquired intangible assets—including goodwill and going concern value—may be amortized on a straight-line basis over a uniform 15-year period. This includes the cost of franchises, trademarks or trade names, and other non-self-created intangibles. Generally, a business is not entitled to an amortization deduction for self-created intangible assets—i.e., assets created by the taxpayer as opposed to assets that have been obtained through a business acquisition.

The following is a list of some of the intangible assets that can be amortized over a 15-year period using the straight-line method if the assets were purchased after August 10, 1993.

- Goodwill;
- Going concern value;
- Workforce in place;
- Information base, including business books and records;

- Know-how and similar items, including secret formulas, processes, designs, and patterns;
- Franchises, trademarks, and trade names; and
- Covenants not to compete and similar agreements entered into in connection with the direct or indirect acquisition of an interest in a trade or business (under prior law, these costs generally were amortized over the life of the covenant, typically three to five years).

Organizational and Start-Up Expenditures. Organizational and start-up expenditures incurred by a corporation generally are not deductible. An exception to this rule applies to companies that attach the appropriate election to their tax return for the year in which they begin business. These companies can amortize their organizational and start-up expenditures over a period of not less than 60 months.

Organizational expenditures are costs incident to the creation of the corporation that are capital in nature and that would be amortizable if incurred incident to the creation of a corporation having a limited life. Start-up expenditures are defined as amounts paid (or incurred) that: (1) would have been deductible if incurred in connection with the operation of an existing business; and (2) were in connection with (a) investigating the creation or acquisition of an active trade or business, (b) creating an active trade or business, or (c) engaging in a profit-making or income-producing activity that is converted into an active trade or business. In this last case, (c), the expenses incurred prior to the day on which the active trade or business begins would be deductible. The term "start-up expenditure" does not include any amounts paid or incurred for interest, taxes, or research and experimental expenditures.

TAX*SAVER*

You can amortize certain expenses incurred in creating a business or, in the case of partnerships, in anticipation of an activity becoming a business. A partnership can only deduct its organizational expenses if, like a corporation, it makes an election (described above) to do so over a period of not less than 60 months. Start-up expenses that don't qualify as organizational expenditures can be amortized by an electing partnership in computing its income. Expenses involved in investigating the acquisition of a partnership interest may be deducted by the partner on his or her personal return.

Advertising. Businesses generally are allowed to deduct the cost of advertising. It is not necessary to prove that the advertising immediately led to increased sales in order to claim a deduction.

Pension and Profit-Sharing Plans. Payments made by an employer to qualified employee retirement plans are deductible as long as the plans satisfy the qualification requirements established by the tax laws and IRS regulations. Investment earnings and gains attributable to contributions made under a qualified plan are not taxable to the employer or to the trust that holds the investment. In addition, accumulated amounts are not taxable to the employee until such amounts are distributed. For more information about deductions for pension and profit-sharing, Keogh, and SEP plans, see Chapter 2.

Employee Benefit Programs. Generally, a C corporation can fully deduct the cost of employee benefit programs, such as health insurance.

Sole proprietorships, partnerships, and S corporations generally can also deduct the cost of employee benefits programs for nonowner employees. However, the deduction for employee-owners (or partners) may be limited. In most instances a sole proprietor cannot deduct the amount paid for his or her own benefits. If, however, his or her spouse or children work in the business, the cost of their benefits is deductible. A sole proprietor, partner, or more-than-2% S corporation shareholder is allowed a deduction for health insurance premiums for personal and family coverage, but the deduction cannot exceed net earnings from the business. The percentages allowed as a deduction are as follows: 50% for 2000 and 2001, 60% for 2002, 80% for 2003 through 2005, 90% for 2006, and 100% for 2007 and thereafter.

TaxAlert

Medical Savings Accounts. *Beginning in 1997 and continuing for four years, the Health Insurance Portability and Accountability Act of 1996 authorizes self-employed individuals covered under a high-deductible health plan and employees of "small employers" (on average no more than 50 employees during either of the two preceding calendar years) covered under an employer-sponsored high-deductible plan to deduct contributions to Medical Savings Accounts (MSAs), exclude employer contributions to MSAs from income, earn income tax-free in their MSAs, and receive tax-free distributions from their MSAs to pay medical expenses. The number of eligible individuals who can set up MSAs is capped at a national level of 750,000. Deductions generally are limited to 65% of the inflation-adjusted annual deductible for individual coverage (for 2000 the deductible amount must be at least $1,550 and no more than $2,350) and 75% of the annual deductible for family coverage (for 2000 the deductible amount must be at least $3,100 and no more than $4,650). The maximum out-of-pocket expense for covered expenses cannot exceed $3,100 for individual coverage and $5,700 for family coverage.*

In general, an eligible individual cannot be covered under any health plan other than a high-deductible plan. However, insurance coverage, in addition to a high-deductible health plan, is permissible if the additional coverage is certain "permitted insurance" or is coverage for accidents, disability, dental care, vision care, or long-term care.

Insurance. Generally, business-related insurance premiums—for fire, theft, malpractice, and liability insurance, etc.—are deductible. Insurance premiums prepaid for a year are deductible when paid by a cash-basis taxpayer, even though the coverage carries over to the succeeding year. Premiums paid for more than a 12-month period must be deducted *pro rata*.

Legal and Professional Services.   You can deduct most fees for professional services (legal, accounting, etc.) incurred in your trade or business. If you use a paid tax professional to prepare your individual tax return, the portion of the tax preparer's fees attributable to completing Schedule C (and related schedules) may be allowed as a deduction on your Schedule C. Partners and S corporation shareholders may deduct a portion of their tax return preparation fees on Schedule E, to the extent they relate to reporting partnership or S corporation income. Fees paid in connection with the acquisition of a capital asset (title insurance, for example) should be added to the cost of that asset. Fees for advice on personal matters generally are not deductible.

Research and Experimental Expenses.   If you incur research and experimental expenditures in connection with a trade or business, you may elect to treat these expenditures as either: (1) deductions in the year the expenses are paid or incurred, or (2) deferred expenses that will be amortized over a period of not less than 60 months, beginning with the month you first realize benefits from the expenditures. The election will apply to all research and experimental expenditures you pay or incur or, if so limited by the election, to all expenditures for a particular project.

> **TAXSAVER**
>
> *Once made, the election applies to all such expenditures you incur unless a different method is authorized by the IRS. If you fail to make an election, your research and experimental expenditures must be capitalized. Expenditures for acquiring or improving land or depreciable or depletable property for use in connection with research and experimentation are not considered qualifying research and experimental expenditures. Depreciation (cost recovery) and depletion expenses attributable to such property, however, do qualify as research expenditures.*

Qualified research expenditures may also be eligible for a tax credit. (See pages 267–268 for additional information.)

Utilities and Telephones.   Utility and telephone bills generally are deductible. You cannot claim a deduction for the basic monthly charge you pay for local telephone service for the first telephone line in your home, even if it is used partly (or solely) for business. Charges for extra services—such as call forwarding, three-way calling, and call waiting—are deductible to the extent they relate to business use. A cellular phone for business purposes may be depreciated under the MACRS method of depreciation to the extent that business use of the telephone exceeds 50%. If your business use is less, you must use the straight-line method of depreciation over five years. If your business use of the phone does not exceed 50% for any one year, you must add back to your income part of the depreciation you've claimed in prior years.

Travel, Meals, and Entertainment. Business-related expenses of this nature generally can be deducted; however, the deduction for meals and entertainment is subject to a 50% ceiling. You cannot deduct expenses for the personal use of a car or truck but can deduct those expenses incurred during the course of business. Note that most dues paid for memberships in clubs are not deductible as business expenses. See Chapter 3 for more information about meals and entertainment expenses and the limited deduction for club dues.

Other Expenses. There are a variety of business expenses not specifically addressed above that can be claimed. Some of the more common expenses include: (1) dues for professional associations; (2) subscriptions to business-related publications; (3) bank service charges on business accounts; (4) security; and (5) trash removal fees.

Lobbying. No deduction is allowed for amounts paid or incurred for participation or intervention in a political campaign on behalf of a candidate for public office (campaign expenses) or for attempts to influence the general public, or segments thereof, with respect to legislative matters, elections, or referenda (grassroots lobbying expenses). In addition, no deduction is allowed for lobbying of foreign governments.

Furthermore, no deduction is allowed for the costs of any attempt to influence state or federal legislation and any communications with a *covered executive branch official* in an attempt to influence official actions or positions of that official. However, special rules apply to taxpayers in the business of lobbying.

TAX*SAVER*

A number of contacts with the government should not be considered lobbying contacts, including (but not limited to) those compelled by subpoena, statute, regulation, etc., those made in response to public notices soliciting communications from the public, and those made to a federal official with regard to judicial proceedings, criminal or civil law enforcement inquiries, investigations, or proceedings. Congress has expressed an intent that such contacts should not be considered lobbying. Thus, expenses incurred in dealing with the IRS and Treasury Department on matters involving private letter rulings, technical advice memoranda, and regulation commentary would remain deductible.

Net Operating Loss Deduction. If the corporation's deductions for the year exceed its income for the year, the resulting amount is a net operating loss. Net operating losses arising in taxable years beginning before August 6, 1997, generally may be carried back 3 years and forward 15 years and may be used to reduce taxable income incurred in those years. Net operating losses arising in taxable years beginning after August 5, 1997, generally may be carried back only 2 years but may be carried forward 20 years. You may elect to forgo the carryback period and carry forward the entire loss.

> ### *TaxSaver*
>
> *The election to forgo a net operating loss (NOL) carryback is irrevocable. Therefore, when deciding whether to forgo a net operating loss carryback, consider:*
> 1. *The marginal tax brackets in the carryback years versus the tax brackets in the carryforward years.*
> 2. *The time value of money (what will you be able to earn with the refund money).*
> 3. *The effect on tax credits.*

In general, a 10-year carryback period is available for the portion of the loss that is attributable to the costs of investigating, defending, or settling product liability claims and certain other statutory or tort liabilities ("specified liability losses"). In lieu of the 10-year carryback, the corporation may either elect a 2-year carryback or forgo the carryback period altogether, as mentioned above. Special limitations apply to the carryover of a net operating loss of a corporation that is a party to an acquisition or that experiences a change in ownership. (See page 270.)

A corporation generally may not carry back the portion of a net operating loss created by interest deductions arising from a major stock acquisition or a significant distribution or redemption (referred to as a corporate equity reduction transaction, or CERT).

Dividends-Received Deduction. In order to reduce the multiple taxation of corporate dividends, the law allows, with certain exceptions, a C corporation receiving a dividend from a domestic corporation to deduct 70% of the dividend. In the case of any dividend from a domestic corporation owned 20% or more by a recipient corporation, 80% may be deducted. This deduction is limited to 70% (80% if a 20%-or-more owned corporation is involved) of taxable income computed without regard to certain adjustments, including the dividends-received deduction itself.

An affiliated group—generally one or more corporations connected through stock ownership with a common parent corporation—may elect a 100% dividends-received deduction on intragroup dividends that are paid out of earnings. This applies as long as the distributing corporation and the recipient corporation were members of the group on each day of the taxable year.

How to Report Business Income

Sole Proprietorship Income

You must report your business income for the year from a sole proprietorship on Form 1040, Schedule C (or Schedule C-EZ for certain proprietorships). In addition to owing income tax, you as the sole proprietor may also be liable for self-employment tax. You may also be required to estimate your tax liability in advance and make payments during the year, instead of waiting until April 15 of the following year (see page 165). A net loss from the business generally can be deducted in computing your adjusted gross income. (Also, see the discussion of sole proprietorships in Chapter 14.)

Who Has to File Schedule C? You have to file Schedule C if you are the sole owner of an unincorporated business or are a self-employed professional. If you are the only member of a limited liability corporation (LLC), a schedule C may also be required (see page 235 for a discussion of treating a single member LLC as a sole proprietorship). These businesses include a wide variety of activities, such as owning a store; being a self-employed lawyer, doctor, accountant, or other professional; working as a freelance writer or independent consultant; or owning a manufacturing operation. Schedule C must be filed whether you pursue this activity full- or part-time and whether you also have another job; however, farmers use a special schedule, Schedule F. Schedule C cannot be filed if your business, trade, or professional practice is in the form of a corporation, partnership, or joint venture.

If you operate your own business while you are also employed by another one, you have to separate your deductions relating to each business.

Example: A freelance writer who is also employed as a reporter needs to separate deductible expenses relating to the freelance writing activity from the reimbursable expenses relating to being a reporter.

If you operate more than one sole proprietorship, you must file a separate Schedule C for each trade or business.

Example: During the day, Dave operates a store that sells party favors. At night, he operates a security service. The businesses are separate and distinct, and a separate Schedule C should be filed for each one.

Who Doesn't Have to File Schedule C? Not every income-producing activity is considered a trade or business. For example, investing in stocks and other securities for your own account (rather than for clients) is not considered a trade or business. It doesn't matter if you pursue this activity full-time or whether you generate substantial profits. Your income from these activities will be considered dividends, interest, or capital gains, as appropriate. Your deductions, if any, will be treated as miscellaneous itemized deductions and only will be deductible to the extent that they exceed 2% of your adjusted gross income.

An activity that you pursue as a hobby—even if you make money at it—will not be classified as a business by the IRS, and you do not need to file Schedule C; of course, your hobby income is reported as "other income" on your return. Expenses of a hobby, however, may be deductible to the extent of income that the activity produces. To determine whether an activity is a trade or business, as opposed to a hobby, the IRS is likely to consider several factors. If, for example, you do not keep careful records of your income and expenses, do not maintain a separate bank account, and spend little time on the activity, the IRS may not consider the activity to be a trade or business. All the facts in regards to the activity are taken into account. No one factor alone is decisive. Here are a few:

- Whether your losses from the activity are due to circumstances beyond your control (or are normal in the start-up phase of your type of business);
- Whether you change your methods of operation in an attempt to improve the profitability of the activity;
- Whether the activity makes a profit in some years, and how much profit it makes; and
- Whether you can expect to make a future profit from the appreciation of the assets used in the activity.

Example: John is a successful doctor. He is also an avid polo player. He raises horses that he uses in polo matches but he also sells them to his friends. Over the years, the expenses of raising and selling the horses have exceeded his income from this source. The IRS probably will view the horse-raising operation as a hobby.

How to Complete Schedule C. Schedule C contains four basic sections. A line-by-line discussion of how to fill out the form is beyond the scope of this book but is provided in *The Ernst & Young Tax Guide*, published annually. What follows are some suggestions to consider when completing the form:

Business Address. You should use your home address if you use part of your home as your principal place of business. If you don't, you may have a difficult time claiming a home office deduction (see page 53). If you plan to claim a deduction for home office expenses, you must also complete Form 8829, *Expenses for Business Use of Your Home*. Although filing a Form 8829 will not automatically result in an audit, the return may be more closely scrutinized.

Accounting Method. Most small businesses use the cash method of accounting, i.e., reporting income when it is actually received and expenses when they are actually paid. Remember that you are also required under the cash method to report income when it is "constructively" received. For example, if interest is credited to your business money market account on December 31, 2000, it must be reported as income in 2000, even though you don't get your bank statement until 2001. Or, if you receive checks from customers in 2000, you generally must report this income, even though you don't deposit the checks in your business account until 2001. If your business involves inventory, then you ordinarily must use the accrual method of accounting for purchases and sales of merchandise, unless your gross receipts are $1 million or less (see page 242). In some cases, you may use a combination of the cash and accrual methods. You should consult with your tax advisor.

Income. If your business provides only services, you will have no cost of goods sold. Your gross receipts will equal your gross profit.

What Can Be Deducted. For an expense to be deducted it must (1) be paid (or incurred, if you use the accrual method) by you within the taxable year in carrying on your trade or business; (2) not be a capital investment; and (3) be ordinary and necessary. Extravagant expenses run the risk of being disallowed. Although certain costs in manufacturing or producing property must be capitalized, this provision does not apply to writers, artists, and photographers. The IRS is on the alert for taxpayers who try to claim deductions on Schedule C that otherwise would be subject to the 2% floor on miscellaneous itemized deductions. For more information on the expenses commonly incurred by a business, see the discussion above.

Partnership Income

Even though a partnership is not a tax-paying entity (see discussion in Chapter 14), it must compute its income each year and file a partnership return (Form 1065). Form 1065 is due on the 15th day of the 4th month following the close of the partnership's taxable year (April 15 for calendar-year partnerships; if the due date for filing a return falls on a Saturday, Sunday, or legal holiday, the return will be due on the next business day). Extensions of time are available. The partnership also may have to file state and local returns in each jurisdiction in which it does business and where its partners reside. Failure to do so may subject the partnership (and each partner) to penalties.

Schedule K-1. A Schedule K-1 shows each partner's distributive share of the partnership's income or loss, deductions, and credits. A Schedule K-1 for each partner should accompany the partnership return sent to the IRS, and each partner should receive a copy of his or her own Schedule K-1. Each partner's distributive share generally is determined by the partnership agreement. Each partner needs to enter the information provided on Schedule K-1 in the appropriate place on his or her personal tax return.

A general partner is considered to be self-employed, rather than an employee of the partnership. Therefore, if you are a general partner, your share of partnership income will be subject to self-employment tax. In addition, you cannot exclude from your income the value of certain fringe benefits—health insurance, for example—that the partnership provides for you and your family.

Limitation on Deduction of Partnership Loss. A partner may not deduct losses in excess of his or her adjusted basis for his or her partnership interest. Generally, your basis in a partnership is the original capital contribution. This basis is adjusted over time to take into consideration any additional capital contributions, an allocable share of partnership liabilities, and previously reported items of partnership income, gain, loss, deduction, and distributions.

Special Allocation of Losses and Other Items. Under certain circumstances, the partnership agreement can provide for tax benefits to flow disproportionately to one or more of the partners. This special allocation of partnership items must be equalized at some point in the future and should be reviewed by your tax advisor to ensure that you are in complete compliance with these complex rules.

S Corporation Income

Corporations electing S corporation status generally are not subject to corporate income taxes. (S corporations are discussed in Chapter 14 and in greater detail in Chapter 16.) However, an S corporation must file an annual tax return on Form 1120S for its taxable year. Form 1120S generally is due on the 15th day of the 3rd month following the close of the taxable year (March 15 for calendar-year S corporations; if the due date for filing a return falls on a Saturday, Sunday, or legal holiday, the return will be due on the next business day). Extensions of time are available. Attached to the return is a Schedule K-1 for each shareholder, which reports his or her share of the S corporation's income, loss, deductions, and credits. The S corporation also must send each shareholder a copy of his or her Schedule K-1.

If a qualified subchapter S subsidiary (QSub) election is made for a subsidiary that is wholly owned by an S corporation, the subsidiary is treated as a division of the parent and all of its income, deductions, credits, etc., are included directly in the return of the parent S corporation (the QSub rules are discussed in more detail on page 273). This is also the case if an S corporation is the sole member of an LLC that is not treated as a corporation for federal tax purposes.

Regular or C Corporations

A corporation's federal income tax return (Form 1120) is due on or before the 15th day of the 3rd month following the end of its taxable year (e.g., March 15, 2001, for the calendar year 2000; if the due date for filing a return falls on a Saturday, Sunday, or legal holiday, the return will be due on the next business day). An automatic extension of time to file of up to six months may be granted if an extension request (Form 7004) is properly filed. An extension of time to file, however, does not extend the time to pay the tax due. A corporation must pay the balance of tax due as shown on its tax return on or before the original due date of the return. Penalties are imposed for failure to pay corporate income taxes when due under circumstances similar to individuals. (See page 168.)

Tax Rates. Current corporate tax rates are in the Appendices at the back of this book.

Estimated Tax Requirements. A C corporation is required to make estimated tax payments if it expects to have a year-end tax bill of $500 or more. Form 1120-W is available from the IRS to assist you in estimating your company's tax and in determining the deposits to be made. Payments are due on the 15th day of the 4th, 6th, 9th, and 12th months of the corporation's taxable year. If the due date for filing a return falls on a Saturday, Sunday, or legal holiday, the return will be due on the next business day.

Corporations may be penalized for not paying enough tax for an installment period. In general, the required quarterly installment is the lesser of:

1. One-fourth of the tax shown on the return for the current year; or
2. One-fourth of the tax shown on the return for the preceding year.

In order to calculate the required quarterly installment based on the prior year's tax, the following conditions must be met:

1. The prior year's return must have covered a 12-month period;
2. A tax liability of $1 or more must have been shown on the prior year's return; and
3. The corporation cannot be a "large" corporation, although a large corporation may use this method for the first installment for the year. A "large" corporation is a corporation with taxable income of at least $1 million in at least one of the three preceding tax years.

The required quarterly installment may also be based on either annualized or seasonal income for the current year. If it is based on the company's annualized income, the required quarterly installment is equal to 100% of the tax, allocated evenly and cumulatively to each of the quarterly periods. To calculate its annualized income, the company must place its taxable income for the corresponding portion of the tax year on an annualized basis (i.e., multiply taxable income for the corresponding portion of the tax year by 12 and divide by the number of months in the period), compute the tax, and, after deducting prior installments for the year, pay the tax according to cumulative percentages.

Only certain corporations with a seasonal pattern in income can base their required quarterly installments on seasonal income. If it is based on seasonal income, the required quarterly installment is computed by annualizing income, assuming that income earned in the current year is earned in the same seasonal pattern as in the three preceding tax years. One hundred percent of the tax, allocated evenly and cumulatively to each quarterly period, and computed by using annualized seasonal income, must be paid under this method.

If estimated payment installments are determined by using either the annualized method or the seasonal income method, and some other method is used for a subsequent installment (i.e., 100% of the current-year liability or 100% of the prior-year liability), you may need to adjust subsequent payments. IRS rules require that 100% of the reduction in estimated taxes resulting from using the annualized or seasonal income methods for previous installments must be paid with the subsequent installment to avoid an underpayment penalty. The tax computed under each exception includes all taxes, such as the alternative minimum tax (AMT), minus any allowable credits.

Underpayment Penalties. Corporations will be penalized for paying less than the required quarterly installment. The penalty is equal to the amount of the underpayment multiplied by the applicable federal rate (AFR). (See page 249 for more about the AFR.) The penalty is assessed from the installment due date to the earlier of the date on which a subsequent installment is paid or the original due date of the return.

A payment of estimated tax is applied against underpayments of required installments in the order in which the installments are required to be paid, regardless of the installment to which the payment relates. Thus, if an underpayment exists for a corporation's first quarter, any second quarter payment first will be applied to the underpayment for the first quarter. An overpayment of a required installment may be applied to subsequent underpayments, unless the overpayment is already allocated to an earlier underpayment. No penalty is imposed for an underpayment of estimated tax if the tax shown on the return is less than $500.

Large corporations may not use the prior year's tax exception, except to determine the amount of the first installment for the tax year.

Quick Refund of Overpaid Estimated Tax. If a corporation overpays its total tax liability by making estimated tax payments that are higher than necessary, it may apply for a quick refund on Form 4466. The refund request must be made within two-and-a-half months after the close of the corporation's taxable year and before the date on which the corporation files its tax return. In addition, the overpayment must be equal to at least 10% of the corporation's expected tax liability and, in any case, must not be less than $500.

Tax Credits. Certain nonrefundable credits are available to businesses. They are presented below in the order in which they are applied against the tax. Any corporation claiming a credit should consult with its tax advisor.

Foreign Tax Credit. The U.S. income tax system generally taxes the worldwide income of taxpayers. Most foreign jurisdictions also tax the same income in their jurisdiction, thereby creating a double tax on such income. To minimize this impact, at the option of the corporation, foreign income taxes imposed on foreign source income may either be deducted in computing taxable income or taken as a credit against U.S. taxes. In addition, foreign income taxes paid by certain foreign corporations from which dividends are received or deemed to be received will be considered "paid" by the corporate shareholder and may be included in computing its foreign tax credit.

TAXSAVER

In general, it will be preferable for a corporation to elect the credit against U.S. taxes rather than to claim a deduction for foreign taxes paid. A credit offsets tax liability on a dollar-for-dollar basis. A deduction will bring a benefit of only 35 cents on the dollar at the top marginal tax rate.

A foreign tax may be allowed as a credit against a corporation's U.S. tax only if it is treated as an *income* tax under U.S. tax law. The same is true if it is a tax substitute for an income tax imposed on the general population of a foreign country. Under U.S. tax law, a "creditable" tax is any foreign tax that attempts to tax net realized gains. Examples of creditable taxes include: income-withholding taxes, flat or progressive taxes on gross income less reasonable deductions, and gross-receipt taxes that are "in lieu" of an income tax. Noncreditable foreign taxes are capital, stamps, sales, VAT, and other consumption taxes. Foreign taxes that are not creditable taxes are still allowed as a deduction from income.

Nonconventional Fuel Credit. Subject to certain limitations, taxpayers producing fuel from nonconventional sources (shale oil, tar sands, etc.) generally are allowed a credit of $3 per barrel for the fuel produced that is equivalent to a barrel of oil.

General Business Credit. Each of the five credits discussed below (investment, work opportunity, alcohol fuel, increased research, and disabled access) is calculated separately and then combined for purposes of applying an overall limitation. Beginning with credits arising in taxable years after December 31, 1997, unused general business credits may be carried back 1 year and forward 20 years. Unused general business credits arising in taxable years beginning before January 1, 1998, may be carried back 3 years and forward 15 years. Transition rules are provided for pre-1984 credit carryforwards under prior law. General business credits are deemed to be used in the order listed below:

Investment Credit. The investment credit is made up of the following three components: (1) the rehabilitation credit, (2) the energy credit, and (3) the reforestation credit. (See page 161.)

Work Opportunity Credit. A "work opportunity credit" is available to employers hiring individuals from one or more of eight targeted groups. The credit generally is equal to 40% of qualified first-year wages. The credit applies to wages paid or incurred to a qualified individual who begins work after September 30, 1996, and before January 1, 2002. Consult your tax advisor for further details.

Alcohol Fuel Credit. A credit is allowed for certain sales and uses of alcohol as a fuel.

Credit for Increased Research. A nonrefundable credit equal to 20% of a taxpayer's excess of the qualified research expenses for the taxable year over a base amount is allowed. The costs eligible for the credit must be paid or incurred prior to July 1, 2004. The base amount generally is calculated using historical research and development expenses and gross receipts. The base amount cannot be less than 50% of the costs for the current year. You may elect an alternative research credit (with lower fixed-base percentages and credits). Once this election is made, it must remain in effect unless revoked with Treasury Department approval.

The term "qualified research" refers to research and development undertaken to develop new or improved products, processes, techniques, inventions, computer software, etc., whether used in the taxpayer's trade or business, or held for sale, lease, or license. Any deduction allowed for research and development expenditures must be reduced by the research credit claimed. However, you may elect not to claim the full amount of the credit to avoid the reduction of the deduction.

In addition, certain corporations are allowed an additional 20% credit for basic research payments. In general, basic research payments are payments in cash to certain qualified organizations for basic research.

Generally, basic research payments are payments to tax-exempt organizations for the conduct of research with no immediate commercial objective. This aspect of the credit also involves computing a base amount related to qualified organization expenses and donations.

Disabled Access Credit. Certain small businesses are allowed a 50% credit against their income tax for "eligible access expenditures" that are at least $250 but no more than $10,250. Eligible expenditures are those paid to enable small businesses to comply with the Americans with Disabilities Act of 1990. Allowable expenditures include amounts paid to remove architectural barriers that affect a disabled person's access to a business or costs for special services and equipment for the disabled. Businesses with gross receipts under $1 million or 30 or fewer full-time employees during the preceding tax year are eligible for the credit.

Companies that spend more than $15,000 to eliminate architectural barriers or are too large to qualify for the credit may deduct expenditures up to $15,000 each year.

Special Rules and Taxes for C Corporations

This section is intended to familiarize a business executive with some of the special rules and taxes that can apply to C corporations. In all cases, the rules and taxes only apply in a limited number of situations. In addition, you should consult with a professional tax advisor if any of the items discussed are applicable to your company or personal situation. Whenever possible, we have tried to point out tax strategies that you and your tax advisor may want to discuss. Taxpayers who are involved with closely held corporations should pay particular attention to the special rules discussed below.

Controlled Groups of Corporations. Controlled groups are corporations that are related by common ownership. To prevent abuses that could result from the establishment of multiple corporations, restrictions are placed on certain tax benefits available to controlled groups of corporations.

A controlled group can only benefit from lower tax rate brackets to the extent that it would if it were taxed as a single corporation. In addition, the benefit of the graduated tax rate structure must be divided equally among the group of controlled corporations, unless the corporations consent to a different allocation. The income of a controlled group must be aggregated for purposes of computing the 5% surtax on income between $100,000 and $335,000, and the 3% surtax on income between $15 million and $18,333,333.

Members of a controlled group are also limited to one $40,000 exemption for purposes of calculating the alternative minimum tax. (See page 271.) Controlled corporations also are subject to the following additional limitations:

1. One $250,000 accumulated earnings credit;
2. One $20,000 limitation for the expensing of fixed asset additions (page 254); and
3. One $1 million base amount for the large corporation test related to the calculation of estimated taxes (page 265).

S corporations generally are excluded from a controlled group for purposes of the above restrictions.

Consolidated Returns. Corporations that make up an "affiliated group" (which uses a different qualification test than a controlled group) may elect to report their income and deductions on a consolidated income tax return. The primary benefits of filing a consolidated return are: the ability to offset income of profitable group members with losses of unprofitable group members, the ability to postpone reporting gains on intercompany sales, and the ability to offset capital gains with capital losses between members. In general terms, an affiliated group is one or more chains of corporations connected through stock ownership with a common parent corporation. To be considered connected through stock ownership, the parent corporation must directly own 80% of at least one other corporation. Direct stock ownership of at least 80% in the aggregate is also required for all other members of the group. The ownership is computed in terms of voting power and value of stock. For this purpose, certain preferred stock is not counted in calculating the 80% threshold. An election to file a consolidated return generally is binding on the affiliated group for all future years.

The Treasury Department has established extensive regulations governing the filing of consolidated tax returns. These regulations set forth rules for using net operating loss carryovers, computing intercompany profits and losses where the group has sales among its members, establishing accounting periods and methods, determining earnings and profits of group members, and numerous other matters.

TAXPLANNER

If multiple corporations are desired (e.g., for liability protection), one option to consider is single member limited liability corporations (LLCs) instead of a consolidated group. When a single member LLC is owned by a corporation, the LLC is treated as a division of the owning corporation unless the LLC is required, or elects, to be treated as a corporation. The use of single member LLCs may eliminate much of the complexity associated with the consolidated return rules. You should consult with a professional tax advisor before making a decision.

Tax-Free Changes in Corporate Ownership. Corporations can in certain cases reorganize, liquidate, or acquire other corporations without the corporation or its shareholders recognizing gain or loss. The recognition of the gain or loss is deferred because the corporation's or the shareholder's original basis is carried over to the new entity. Income taxes are not payable until some future date when a taxable sale, exchange, or termination occurs.

A successor corporation in a tax-free reorganization, liquidation, or acquisition generally can carry over unused net operating losses, general business credits, job credits, foreign tax credits, and capital losses from the predecessor corporation. This transfer of tax attributes is limited if there has been a substantial change in stock ownership or, in some cases, if there has been a change in the corporation's business. In addition, if the principal purpose of an acquisition is to obtain tax benefits that would not otherwise be available, those benefits may be disallowed by the IRS.

TAXSAVER

If you are seeking to acquire a corporation with net operating losses or other carryforward items, you should plan carefully to avoid the limitations that apply when a substantial percentage of the corporation's stock changes hands.

Likewise, corporations seeking outside equity investors need to exercise care in planning transactions. If the change in corporate ownership exceeds certain limits, the ability to use the loss and credit carryovers may be limited or denied.

Accumulated Earnings and Personal Holding Company Taxes. Certain corporations that do not distribute their earnings for a taxable year may be subject to either a tax on an excess accumulation of earnings or a tax on undistributed personal holding company income. In computing these taxes, the amount of earnings is determined in accordance with specific provisions of the Internal Revenue Code. Consideration is given to dividends paid and certain other adjustments. Documentation of a corporation's reasonable business needs is often critical in defending against assessment of the accumulated earnings tax. Such reasonable needs may include business expansion or acquisition, or potential liabilities that are contingent upon the outcome of litigation.

TaxSaver

Throughout the year, corporations should monitor their accumulation of earnings and the types of income they receive in order to detect potential exposure to these taxes. If a corporation determines that one of these taxes may apply, there are methods available to reduce or eliminate any resulting tax liability.

For example, if a corporation is vulnerable to the accumulated earnings tax, the use of "consent" dividends may be appropriate. "Consent" dividends are hypothetical (in that they are not actually paid) distributions to a shareholder who consents to treat some or all of the corporation's income as a dividend, even though no cash is received. Because special rules apply to consent dividends, you should consult a professional tax advisor.

Note: *Corporations with significant accumulated earnings tax exposure should also review whether electing S status makes sense because the tax does not apply to S corporations.*

Corporate Alternative Minimum Tax. The alternative minimum tax (AMT) is based on a corporation's regular taxable income increased by tax preference items and increased or decreased by adjustments to arrive at an amount upon which the corporate AMT rate of 20% is applied. In general, it is a "separate" tax system that attempts to prevent a corporation from realizing too much benefit from certain favorable tax provisions. The AMT is available as a credit to offset a future year's regular tax liability for years in which the regular tax exceeds its AMT liability.

It is beyond the scope of this book to explain in detail how the AMT is calculated. In any case, you will need to seek professional tax advice.

TaxAlert

For taxable years beginning after December 31, 1997, the AMT does not apply to eligible small business corporations. The determination of whether a corporation is an eligible small business corporation is made based on its average gross receipts.

TaxSaver

A company should be aware that planning techniques used to reduce its regular tax might not provide a current tax benefit if the company is subject to the alternative minimum tax. Moreover, in certain cases, regular tax planning techniques can even subject the company to the AMT. For example, the use of modified accelerated cost recovery system depreciation could result in an AMT liability.

Although traditional regular tax planning techniques (e.g., accelerating deductions and deferring income) can result in an AMT liability, the company nevertheless may want to make sure that such techniques are employed because the minimum tax credit can be used to offset a future year's regular tax liability.

TaxOrganizer

Because the AMT is, in effect, an independent income tax system apart from the regular income tax, a company needs to keep separate records for items such as depreciation on assets acquired after 1986, AMT net operating loss carryovers, and AMT foreign tax credit carryovers. For example, because different amounts of depreciation are allowed under the two tax systems, separate basis amounts must be tracked for purposes of computing gain or loss upon a sale of such assets.

Although many companies have recognized the need to maintain a separate set of records for AMT purposes (because the AMT system has been with us since 1986), it may not be as widely known that a third set of records is required for adjusted current earnings (ACE) purposes.

TaxAlert

The 1997 Tax Act conforms the recovery periods used for purposes of the AMT depreciation adjustment to the recovery periods used for purposes of the regular tax under present law. This change applies to property (including pollution control facilities) placed in service after December 31, 1998.

16

S Corporations

Introduction

Income earned by C corporations is taxed at the corporate level when earned and taxed again at the shareholder level when distributed as dividends. An S corporation election permits a corporation to avoid this "double taxation." S corporation income generally is only taxed at the shareholder level. This in itself can be a tremendous tax-saving opportunity.

Yet, for legal purposes, an S corporation is indistinguishable from any other corporation. S corporation shareholders have limited liability and other rights and protections identical to shareholders of regular corporations. If your corporation meets the requirements to qualify for S corporation status, you should seriously consider making an S election.

This chapter discusses how to elect S corporation status, the advantages of being an S corporation, and other considerations associated with operating as an S corporation.

Electing S Corporation Status

A corporation must meet certain requirements to be an S corporation. Specifically, a corporation can elect S corporation status only if the following conditions are met:

- The corporation is a domestic corporation.
- The corporation has only one class of stock (but the voting rights within the class can differ).
- The corporation has no more than 75 shareholders.
- The corporation's shareholders are limited to individuals, estates, and certain qualifying trusts, and certain tax-exempt organizations.
- No shareholder of the corporation is a nonresident alien.
- The corporation is not a Domestic International Sales Corporation (DISC) or former DISC, an insurance company, a bank using the reserve method of accounting for bad debts, or a corporation with a possessions tax credit election in effect.

TAX ALERT

While an S corporation cannot have a corporate shareholder, a corporation that is wholly owned by an S corporation may effectively achieve S corporation status by electing to be treated as a qualified subchapter S subsidiary (QSub).

To elect S corporation status, the corporation must meet all of the above requirements on the day the S election is filed and on every day of each year for which the election is to be effective.

To be effective for the current year, an S election must be made during the preceding year or within the first two-and-a-half months of the current tax year. All persons who are shareholders on the day the election is made must consent to the election. In addition, if the election is filed within the first two-and-a-half months of the year in which it is to be effective, all persons who held stock prior to the filing of the election must consent, even if they don't own stock on the day the S election is filed. An S election is made on a Form 2553, *Election by a Small Business Corporation.*

TAX ALERT

For taxable years beginning after December 31, 1997, an Employee Stock Ownership Plan (ESOP) is an eligible S corporation shareholder. Amendments made by the 1997 Tax Act to the ESOP rules as they apply to an S corporation significantly enhance the potential benefits of establishing an ESOP for S corporation employees. Specifically, the rule requiring the ESOP to pay tax on S corporation income allocated to the shares of S corporation stock it owns was repealed. In addition, an ESOP established and maintained by an S corporation can distribute benefits in cash instead of employer securities. The change is very helpful in avoiding unintended terminations of the corporation's S election and can also be used to prevent direct ownership of the S corporation's stock by former employees.

ADVANTAGES OF BEING AN S CORPORATION

Income earned by a regular corporation is taxed at the corporate level when earned and is generally taxed again at the shareholder level when distributed as dividends. Thus, the income of a regular corporation is subject to "double taxation." An S corporation's income or loss is reported directly on the shareholders' returns, generally escaping tax at the corporate level. The income is taxable to the shareholders even if it is not distributed, but generally it is not taxed again when distributed. The income increases the shareholder's stock basis, potentially reducing gain or increasing loss when the stock is sold. Additionally, the shareholders may be able to shelter the income with losses from other sources. If a corporation is profitable, electing S status can be especially advantageous because the double taxation of its income may be eliminated.

Example: Assume Corporation A earns $500,000 during its 2000 tax year and distributes its after-tax earnings to its shareholders. If Corporation A operates as a regular corporation, the total amount of tax the corporation and its shareholders will pay is $300,680 ($170,000 + $130,680), and only $199,320 of the earnings are available to the shareholders, computed as follows:

Corporation A taxable income	$500,000
Corporate-level tax at 34%	170,000
Income distributed and taxed to shareholders	$330,000
Shareholder-level tax at 39.6%	130,680
Remaining income available	$199,320

On the other hand, if Corporation A operates as an S corporation, the total amount of tax incurred by the corporation and its shareholders is only $198,000, leaving $302,000 available for the shareholders—a savings of $102,680. This is computed as follows:

Corporation A taxable income	$500,000
Corporate-level tax at 34%	N/A
Income distributed and taxed to shareholders	$500,000
Shareholder-level tax at 39.6%	198,000
Remaining income available	$302,000

To the extent the income is not distributed to an S corporation shareholder, the income will increase the shareholder's basis in the corporation stock. Upon disposition of the stock, therefore, the shareholder's gain is reduced.

Note that the highest individual tax rate (39.6%) currently exceeds the highest corporate tax rate (35%). If the corporation anticipates retaining all of its earnings for a significant period of time, this rate differential may make C corporation status more favorable.

If the corporation is incurring losses, an S election may also be advantageous. Like S corporation income, S corporation losses are reported directly on the shareholders' individual returns. The losses may offset income from other sources. However, a shareholder's currently deductible share of the corporation's losses is limited to his or her basis in the corporation's stock and debt of the corporation owed to the shareholder. The losses may be subject to other limitations as well. See the discussion of the at-risk and passive activity loss rules in Chapter 1.

TAXSAVER

Shareholders of S corporations that incur losses often find themselves unable to claim deductions if the losses exceed the shareholder's basis in the cor-

poration's stock. An S corporation shareholder generally can obtain basis in S corporation debt only by actually loaning money to the corporation. If an S corporation borrows money from a bank, the loan does not provide the shareholders with basis against which a loss could be claimed, even if the shareholders guarantee such loans. Consult your tax advisor about restructuring these loans so that the shareholders can utilize the losses being passed through by the company.

OPERATING AS AN S CORPORATION

Pass-Through of Income and Losses. S corporation income is taxable directly to the corporation's shareholders based on their respective ownership percentages. A loss for the corporation's taxable year is deductible on a *pro rata* basis but may be limited to the shareholder's basis, amount at risk, or passive activity income. In cases where a shareholder either joins or leaves the S corporation during the year, income or loss for that shareholder is usually allocated in proportion to the number of days that the shareholder held the stock during the taxable year. In certain cases, however, the corporation may elect or be required to "close the books" and treat its tax year as two separate years for purposes of allocating income or loss.

An S corporation is required to separately identify items that would be subject to special treatment on the shareholders' individual returns. These items include interest, dividend, and royalty income; capital gains and losses; certain gains and losses on business property; investment interest expense; and charitable contributions. Items not subject to any special limitations are passed through in aggregate. Tax credits also generally pass through directly to the shareholders.

Health insurance premiums paid by an S corporation for the benefit of shareholder-employees owning more than 2% of its stock are deductible by the S corporation and includible in the shareholder's income as additional compensation. The shareholders can generally claim a deduction based on the amount of health insurance premium included in their income. The percentages allowed as a deduction are as follows: 50% for 2000 and 2001, 60% for 2002, 80% for 2003 through 2005, 90% for 2006, and 100% for 2007 and thereafter.

Taxable and nontaxable income that flows from the S corporation to the individual shareholder increases the shareholder's basis in his or her stock. Likewise, deductible and nondeductible expenses decrease a shareholder's basis in his or her stock. Distributions from an S corporation are generally tax-free to the extent of a shareholder's basis (however, such distributions reduce basis). If the S corporation was a regular corporation prior to electing S status, a distribution in excess of the earnings accumulated since electing S corporation status may be taxed as a dividend to the shareholder.

Corporate-Level Taxes. S corporations generally are not subject to corporate tax, but if an S election is made for a corporation that operated as a regular corporation for a period of time, certain taxes may apply. A brief discussion of these taxes follows.

LIFO Recapture Tax. If a regular corporation using the LIFO (last-in, first-out) method of accounting for inventory elects S corporation status, the corporation must include its LIFO reserve in income for its last taxable year as a regular corporation. The LIFO reserve amount that must be included in income is the excess of the inventory value computed under the FIFO (first-in, first-out) inventory method over the value computed under the LIFO method. The increase in tax attributable to including the reserve in income is payable over four tax years, with the first payment due on the due date (without extensions) of the last regular corporate return.

Built-in Gains Tax. S corporations that were formerly regular corporations, and that elected S corporation status after December 31, 1986, may be subject to a special "built-in gains" tax. The tax is paid at the corporate level. It generally applies to gain accrued in the corporation's assets *before* it elected S status, to the extent that the gain is recognized during the corporation's first 10 years as an S corporation. (Certain income may also be subject to the built-in gains tax.)

The tax does not apply to the appreciation of assets occurring after the date the corporation makes its S election.

The tax, if applicable, will be imposed using the highest regular corporate rate, currently 35%.

The corporate-level tax reduces the amount of the gain from the disposition of an asset that passes through to S corporation shareholders.

There is a "taxable income limitation" to the amount of the built-in gains subject to this tax. The taxable built-in gains are limited to the current year's taxable income, generally determined as if the corporation was a regular corporation. If the S corporation election was made on or after March 31, 1988, any recognized built-in gain not subject to tax because of this taxable income limitation must be carried over to the subsequent tax year and is subject to that year's taxable income limitation. If the taxable income limitation prevents the recognition of built-in gain income beyond the 10-year period, these gains will escape tax at the corporate level.

Unexpired net operating losses, capital losses, business credit carryforwards, and alternative minimum tax credit carryforwards may be used to offset the built-in gains tax.

Passive Investment Income Tax. An S corporation with regular corporation earnings and profits and passive investment income (for example, interest, dividends, and certain rents) exceeding 25% of its gross receipts may have to pay a special tax. If these conditions exist for three consecutive tax years, the corporation's S election terminates.

Any new corporation that can qualify for S corporation status can reap a huge tax benefit on the subsequent sale of corporate assets. A regular corporation would have to pay tax at the corporate level on any gain from the sale of assets; an S corporation would not. That can amount to an enormous tax benefit for an S corporation. But, as explained above, an existing corporation that has been a regular corporation and did not elect to become an S corporation by December 31, 1986, cannot simply elect S status and hope to avoid the corporate tax on gains from the sale of assets it held at that time unless the corporation waits at least 10 years before selling the assets. Note, however, that any appreciation occurring after becoming an S corporation will escape double taxation.

Taxable Year. Generally, an S corporation is required to report on a calendar-year basis unless it can demonstrate to the satisfaction of the IRS a valid business purpose for a fiscal year-end. However, a newly formed S corporation can elect a year-end (ending not earlier than September 30) by making a "required payment" to the IRS, which is intended to eliminate the tax benefit from the deferral. A C corporation electing S status may also make this election, but it can only elect a year ending not earlier than the later of its current year-end or September 30.

In most cases, an S corporation or partnership would have to demonstrate to the IRS that the different fiscal year is its "natural business year."

The use of a year other than a calendar year can result in a deferral of taxes, and with a natural business year the corporation does not have to make a "required payment" to offset the benefit of the deferral.

Terminating S Corporation Status. Once an S election is made, it is generally effective for all subsequent tax years. However, a corporation's S election will terminate if the corporation violates any of the eligibility requirements explained earlier in this chapter. In addition, an S election will terminate if the corporation has regular corporation earnings and profits and more than 25% of its gross receipts is from passive investment income for three consecutive years. Shareholders of an S corporation who hold more than one-half of the number of issued and outstanding shares may also revoke the corporation's S election.

A company should take steps to safeguard against unwanted transfers of stock that would terminate its S election. For example, a minority shareholder not otherwise able to individually revoke the company's S election could nevertheless do so by transferring stock to a shareholder not qualified to hold S corporation stock. One way of protecting against unwanted transfers is to execute agreements limiting a shareholder's ability to transfer stock.

When to Consider Terminating S Corporation Status. The following factors should be taken into account when evaluating whether you should terminate an S election:

- *The top corporate tax rate (35%) is lower than the top individual tax rate (39.6%). In addition, the alternative minimum tax rate for C corporations can be lower than the applicable individual rate for S corporation shareholders. However, keep in mind that C corporation income is generally subject to double tax. In addition, as discussed below, after a corporation's S election terminates, a waiting period applies for purposes of reelecting S status. And, upon reelection, the corporate-level taxes that apply to S corporations that were once C corporations, discussed earlier, may apply.*
- *Because a C corporation is not subject to the rules limiting the number and kind of shareholders discussed earlier, it has much more flexibility and more financing alternatives and opportunities.*
- *Preferred stock is prohibited in an S corporation and not in a C corporation. S corporations cannot have more than one class of stock. Unlike C corporations, all outstanding shares of an S corporation generally must have the same rights to distributions and liquidation proceeds.*
- *A dividend-received deduction, usually 70%, is available to C corporations but not S corporations.*
- *A C corporation has more favorable exclusions for certain employee benefits (e.g., exclusion of health insurance benefits).*

Once a corporation's S election has terminated, the corporation generally cannot elect S status again for five years. A provision in the Small Business Job Protection Act of 1996 waives the requirement that IRS permission be obtained to reelect S status for terminations occuring in taxable years beginning before January 1, 1997. Also, under certain limited conditions, the IRS may permit the corporation to reelect S status before five years have passed. In addition, if the event that caused the S election to terminate was inadvertent, the IRS may grant a waiver of the inadvertent termination and allow the corporation to continue to be treated as an S corporation.

STATE TAX CONSIDERATIONS

While S corporation income generally is exempt from corporate tax at the federal level, not all states exempt S corporations from state taxes at the corporate level. This can result in double state taxation on corporate earnings or dividend distributions.

Most states recognize S corporation status. However, a few states tax S corporations in the same way they tax C corporations.

Some states require a separate S election at the state level while others base their acceptance on the federal election. In addition, a number of states require an S corporation to withhold state income tax on income that is distributable to its shareholders as a means of ensuring that nonresident shareholders comply with state tax laws. Penalties are frequently assessed on taxpayers who do not comply. Lastly, many states allow an S corporation to file one composite tax return on behalf of its nonresident shareholders to reduce the administrative burden on multistate S corporations with several shareholders. Because corporations engaged in multistate commerce are subject to the tax rules of many states, state corporate tax can be *very* complicated. Please consult your tax advisor.

17

Year-End Tax Planning for Businesses

Introduction

There will probably not be an increase in business taxes in the next few years because the government is operating at a significant "surplus"; also, 2000 is a presidential election year.

Timing of Income and Deductions

A business's overall accounting method can substantially affect tax planning. Most individuals and many owners of service businesses use the cash method of accounting for tax purposes. However, most other businesses must use the accrual method of accounting.

Under the cash method, items of income are reported when actually or "constructively" received (that is, when unrestricted use of the funds is available). Items of expense are reported when actually paid. Under the accrual method, the right to receive an income item and the liability to pay an expense item generally determine when those items are reported. For tax purposes, however, an accrual method taxpayer usually may not deduct a liability until goods or services are provided.

The typical business will want to defer income and accelerate expenses (although this strategy would need to be reevaluated if it appeared likely that tax rates were going to rise substantially). Consider the following potential suggestions for accomplishing this goal:

- Delay deliveries on sales (but consider the potential property tax).
- Make sales on consignment or approval (delaying billing and payment).
- Make the maximum deductible charitable contributions.
- Contribute the maximum deductible amount to tax-qualified retirement plans.

- In certain cases, corporations on the LIFO (last-in, first-out) inventory method can affect taxable income by timing the purchase of inventory.

TaxALERT

Remember to consider the impact of the alternative minimum tax (AMT). With the relatively small differences between the AMT rate and the regular corporate tax rate, more corporations are subject to AMT than ever before. However, because the corporate AMT tax can be fully credited against future corporate income tax, its effect may not be severe.

TaxSAVER

As discussed in Chapter 15, the IRS recently announced that it will allow a business with annual gross receipts of $1 million or less to use the cash method of accounting without regard to whether the business is required to maintain inventories. If your business has annual gross receipts of $1 million or less and currently uses the accrual method of accounting, you should discuss with your tax advisor whether a change to the cash method of accounting would be beneficial.

DEPRECIATION

The date new property is placed in service can significantly affect the amount of your 2000 depreciation deduction. In general, personal property is treated as if it was placed in service at the midpoint of a tax year (July 1 for calendar-year taxpayers) no matter when it was actually purchased and placed in service. However, it's not always that simple. If more than 40% of the personal property purchased during the tax year is placed in service during the last three months of the year, different procedures apply. Under these circumstances, all personal property purchased and placed in service throughout the year will be treated as being placed in service in the middle of the quarter in which it was placed in service. This will usually result in a lower first-year depreciation deduction than if the property were treated as having been placed in service at the midpoint of the tax year.

In certain situations, however, having depreciable property subject to the more-than-40% rule is advantageous. Thus, you should review your fourth-quarter acquisition plans to determine whether you want the more-than-40% rule to be activated.

In general, real property is treated as placed in service in the middle of the month in which it is actually placed in service.

For tax purposes, depreciation is calculated using the modified accelerated cost recovery system (MACRS). An alternative depreciation system must be used when determining if the AMT applies. The difference between depreciation calculated under MACRS and the alternative depreciation system is an adjustment item used in computing the AMT. If you wish to avoid the AMT, you should consider leasing instead of purchasing depreciable assets.

Taxpayers may expense up to a certain amount of capital purchases for tangible personal property in the year acquired, provided such expenses do not exceed the taxable income derived from the business. The amount allowed as an expense is $20,000 for tax year 2000; $24,000 for tax years 2001–2002; and $25,000 for tax year 2003. To limit this write-off for larger businesses, the maximum amount is reduced dollar-for-dollar by the cost of eligible property in excess of $200,000.

Other Business Expenses. If you employ your children in your unincorporated business, their earned income will be taxed at their tax rates, and you will get a deduction for their salaries. Also, for children under age 18, neither you (as employer) nor they will be subject to FICA tax on wages you pay to them.

Capital Asset Transactions

Corporations generally compute capital gains and losses in the same manner as individuals. For capital losses, however, corporations may only offset such losses against capital gains and not against any portion of ordinary income. Excess capital losses can generally be carried back three years and forward five years to offset capital gains. Unused capital losses expire and are lost forever. Corporations should review their tax positions before year-end. Additional sales or exchanges of capital assets should be considered to coordinate the timing of gains and losses and prevent expiration of unused losses.

Charitable Giving

A "regular" (or "C") corporation may be able to reap special benefits from its charitable contributions. As a means of accelerating the maximum deduction (generally 10% of taxable income) into the current tax year, a regular corporation that uses the accrual method of accounting may deduct contributions made within two-and-a-half months after the close of the tax year, provided the contributions have been authorized by the board of directors by year-end. The IRS requires that a statement regarding the board's action be attached to the return. For a regular corporation using a calendar year, contributions must be made by March 15, 2001. In addition, gifts of *current* inventory may not be subject to the 10% limitation (see Chapter 15).

Executive Compensation

In general you may claim a business deduction for reasonable salaries or other compensation for personal services rendered. However, a publicly held corporation is precluded, subject to some exceptions, from taking a deduction for compensation in excess of $1 million paid to either its chief executive officer or any of the four other most highly compensated officers. These five employees are known as "covered" employees. This rule does not apply to (1) payments to a tax-qualified plan, (2) fringe benefits that are excludable from gross income, and (3) qualified performance-based compensation, including stock options or other stock appreciation rights, provided it meets certain independent director and shareholder approval requirements.

TaxSaver

There are a number of strategies that companies and top executives can consider to minimize the effect of the $1 million annual cap on compensation deductions.

One strategy is to use nonqualified deferred compensation arrangements to minimize or completely avoid the $1 million limitation with respect to base salary. These arrangements may be elective, nonelective, or a combination of both. The goal would be to defer base salary to a point in time when it is deductible.

There are two basic structures that can be used. First, base salary could be deferred under an agreement that provides that it will be paid when the employee is no longer a covered employee. Alternatively, the deferral agreement could provide that the deferred base salary will be paid when it is first deductible. This approach could create problems in administration, however, because deductibility will depend on the other components of the employee's compensation package, e.g., bonuses and stock option exercises.

Highly paid employees and employers should also consider converting their bonus plans to arrangements that meet the requirements for performance-based compensation.

Companies should also consider granting stock options and stock appreciation rights (SARs) at fair market value. If the options or rights are granted at fair market value and the other requirements for performance-based compensation are met, the income from the exercise of the stock options or SARs will not be counted as part of the $1 million limitation.

TaxAlert

Compensation that is tied to preestablished performance goals is exempted from the $1 million deductibility limitation. However, for year 2001 incentive plans to receive an exemption, performance goals must be established and approved by the compensation committee no later than March 31, 2001.

Dividends-Received Deduction

The law permits a corporation to deduct 70% (or, in some cases, 80% or 100%) of qualifying dividend income that it receives from taxable domestic corporations. A special provision limits this to 70% of the recipient corporation's taxable income, computed without regard to certain adjustments, including the dividends-received deduction itself.

Dividends-received deductions that are limited as a result of the net income limitation are lost forever. However, this rule does not apply if the recipient corporation would have a net operating loss (NOL) after taking into account the dividends-received deduction. In such a case, the dividends-received deduction is allowable and increases the NOL carryover.

A corporation with qualifying dividend income should plan carefully to ensure that this deduction is not lost because of these rules.

Estimated Tax Filing Requirements

Businesses should conserve cash by making payments only when taxes are owed and only in the required amounts. Overpayments are essentially interest-free loans to the government, while underpayments may result in a nondeductible penalty.

A lower estimated installment amount may be paid if it is shown that use of an annualized income method or, for corporations with seasonal incomes, an adjusted seasonal method would result in a lower required installment. (See Chapter 15.)

State Tax Considerations

In your year-end business tax planning, you should consider the substantial role state taxes play in a business's overall tax liability.

Taking Advantage of Net Operating Losses. A company may be able to utilize losses generated by an affiliated company in states in which the companies are required to file separate returns. To do so, income-generating assets may have to be transferred to the company with the loss, certain other intercompany transactions may have to occur, or the companies may have to merge. You will need to consult your tax advisor to plan how to maximize your tax benefits.

Distributions and Transactions between Different Companies. Intercompany transactions that do not give rise to current taxable income under the federal consolidated return rules may be subject to direct or indirect state taxes. For example, some states tax a portion of dividends paid by one company to another. On the other hand, some sales of tangible property between companies and some management fees that one company pays another may be exempt from state taxes. You should consult your tax advisor to determine whether state taxes could be reduced or eliminated by restructuring certain distributions and other transactions between companies.

Appendices

2000 Income Tax Rates

The tables for 2000 reflect the rate brackets indexed for inflation.

Married Individuals Filing Joint Returns and Certain Widows and Widowers[a]

| If 2000 taxable income is: | | The tax is: | |
Over—	But not over—		Of excess over—
$ 0	$ 43,850	$ 0 + 15%	$ 0
43,850	105,950	6,557.50 + 28%	43,850
105,950	161,450	23,965.50 + 31%	105,950
161,450	288,350	41,170.50 + 36%	161,450
288,350	—	86,854.50 + 39.6%	288,350

Standard Deduction: $7,350
Personal Exemption: 2,800

Phaseout of Personal Exemption:
Threshold Phaseout Amount: $193,400
Phaseout Amount Completed after: $315,900

Single Individuals[a]

| If 2000 taxable income is: | | The tax is: | |
Over—	But not over—		Of excess over—
$ 0	$ 26,250	$ 0 + 15%	$ 0
26,250	63,550	3,937.50 + 28%	26,250
63,550	132,600	14,381.50 + 31%	63,550
132,600	288,350	35,787.00 + 36%	132,600
288,350	—	91,857.00 + 39.6%	288,350

Standard Deduction: $4,400
Personal Exemption: 2,800

Phaseout of Personal Exemption:
Threshold Phaseout Amount: $128,950
Phaseout Amount Completed after: $251,450

Unmarried (or Legally Separated) Individuals Who Qualify as Heads of Households[a]

| If 2000 taxable income is: | | The tax is: | |
Over—	But not over—		Of excess over—
$ 0	$ 35,150	$ 0 + 15%	$ 0
35,150	90,800	5,272.50 + 28%	35,150
90,800	147,050	20,854.50 + 31%	90,800
147,050	288,350	38,292.00 + 36%	147,050
288,350	—	89,160.00 + 39.6%	288,350

Standard Deduction: $6,450
Personal Exemption: 2,800

Phaseout of Personal Exemption:
Threshold Phaseout Amount: $161,150
Phaseout Amount Completed after: $283,650

[a]Does not take into account the alternative minimum tax; net long-term capital gain taxed at maximum rate of 20%.

286

2000 Income Tax Rates

Married Individuals Filing Separate Returns[a]

If 2000 taxable income is:		The tax is:	
Over—	But not over—		Of excess over—
$ 0	$ 21,925	$ 0 + 15%	$ 0
21,925	52,975	3,288.75 + 28%	21,925
52,975	80,725	11,982.75 + 31%	52,975
80,725	144,175	20,585.25 + 36%	80,725
144,175	—	43,427.25 + 39.6%	144,175

Standard Deduction: $3,675
Personal Exemption: 2,800

Phaseout of Personal Exemption:
Threshold Phaseout Amount: $96,700
Phaseout Amount Completed after: $157,950

Estates and Nongrantor Trusts[a]

If 2000 taxable income is:		The tax is:	
Over—	But not over—		Of excess over—
$ 0	$ 1,750	$ 0 + 15%	$ 0
1,750	4,150	262.50 + 28%	1,750
4,150	6,300	934.50 + 31%	4,150
6,300	8,650	1,601.00 + 36%	6,300
8,650	—	2,447.00 + 39.6%	8,650

[a]Does not take into account the alternative minimum tax; net long-term capital gain taxed at maximum rate of 20%.

Corporate Income Tax Rates[b]

If 2000 taxable income is:		The tax is:	
Over—	But not over—		Of excess over—
$ 0	$ 50,000	$ 0 + 15%	$ 0
50,000	75,000	7,500 + 25%	50,000
75,000	100,000	13,750 + 34%	75,000
100,000	335,000	22,250 + 39%	100,000
335,000	10,000,000	113,900 + 34%	335,000
10,000,000	15,000,000	3,400,000 + 35%	10,000,000
15,000,000	18,333,333	5,150,000 + 38%	15,000,000
18,333,333	—	6,416,667 + 35%	18,333,333

[b]Does not take into account the alternative minimum tax.

2000 Dollar Limits for 401(k) and Other Retirement Plans

§401(k) participant pre-tax contribution limit	$ 10,500
Defined benefit plan limit	135,000
Defined contribution limit	30,000
Annual compensation cap for benefits/allocations	170,000

Social Security and Medicare Taxes

Old-Age Benefit Tax on Employers and Employees

Social Security rate on the first $76,200[a] in wages	6.20%
Medicare rate on wages	1.45%
Maximum Social Security Tax for the Calendar Year 2000	$4,724.40

Self-Employment Tax[b]

Social Security rate on the first $76,200 of self-employment income	12.4%
Medicare rate on self-employment income	2.9%
Maximum Social Security Tax for the Calendar Year 2000	$9,448.80

[a]The wage base can increase based on a statutory formula. Any change is published in the Federal Register not later than November 1 each year. The wage base has been eliminated for Medicare taxes. The Medicare tax applies to all wages and self-employment income.
[b]A self-employed individual may deduct one-half of his or her self-employment tax for the year as a business expense in arriving at adjusted gross income.

Unified Estate and Gift Tax Rates

Taxable transfers over (1)	But not over (2)	Tentative tax on amount in col. (1) (3)	Rate of tax on excess over amount in col. (1) (4)
$ 0	$ 10,000	$ 0	18%
10,000	20,000	1,800	20%
20,000	40,000	3,800	22%
40,000	60,000	8,200	24%
60,000	80,000	13,000	26%
80,000	100,000	18,200	28%
100,000	150,000	23,800	30%
150,000	250,000	38,800	32%
250,000	500,000	70,800	34%
500,000	750,000	155,800	37%
750,000	1,000,000	248,300	39%
1,000,000	1,250,000	345,800	41%
1,250,000	1,500,000	448,300	43%
1,500,000	2,000,000	555,800	45%
2,000,000	2,500,000	780,800	49%
2,500,000	3,000,000	1,025,800	53%
3,000,000	—	1,290,800*	55%

Plus 5% of the cumulative transfers in excess of $10,000,000 but not exceeding $17,184,000.

Unified Estate and Gift Tax Credit

The unified estate and gift tax credit for 2000 is $220,550. This has the effect of exempting estates of $675,000 or less from estate taxes.

Computation of Maximum Federal Estate Tax Credit for State Death Taxes

Adjusted taxable estate[a] more than— (1)	But not more than (2)	Maximum credit amount in col. (1) (3)	Rate of credit on excess over amount in col. (1) (4)
$ 0	$ 40,000	$ 0	None
40,000	90,000	0	.8%
90,000	140,000	400	1.6%
140,000	240,000	1,200	2.4%
240,000	440,000	3,600	3.2%
440,000	640,000	10,000	4.0%
640,000	840,000	18,000	4.8%
840,000	1,040,000	27,600	5.6%
1,040,000	1,540,000	38,800	6.4%
1,540,000	2,040,000	70,800	7.2%
2,040,000	2,540,000	106,800	8.0%
2,540,000	3,040,000	146,800	8.8%
3,040,000	3,540,000	190,800	9.6%
3,540,000	4,040,000	238,800	10.4%
4,040,000	5,040,000	290,800	11.2%
5,040,000	6,040,000	402,800	12.0%
6,040,000	7,040,000	522,800	12.8%
7,040,000	8,040,000	650,800	13.6%
8,040,000	9,040,000	786,800	14.4%
9,040,000	10,040,000	930,800	15.2%
10,040,000	—	1,082,800	16.0%

[a]The taxable estate less $60,000.

Tax Calendar

Your 2000 individual income tax return is due on April 16, 2001, if you are a calendar-year taxpayer. You shouldn't wait until then to get your tax affairs in order, however. The calendar that follows, although not intended to be comprehensive, is designed to highlight important forms you need to file and when. It includes tax dates not only for individuals but for corporations as well. Key dates for employers are also highlighted. Taxpayers whose years end on dates other than December 31 must adjust these dates to their situation. Due dates that fall on a Saturday, Sunday, or legal holiday are automatically extended to the next business day.

Individuals

January 15, 2001
- Form 1040-ES (declaration of estimated tax) for fourth quarter of prior year

April 16, 2001
- Form 1040 (individual income tax return, including the employment taxes for household employees) for prior year or Form 4868 (request for automatic four-month extension)
- Form 709 or 709A (gift tax return) for prior year or extension request (Form 4868 or letter)
- Form 1040-ES for first quarter of current year

June 15, 2001
- Form 1040-ES for second quarter

August 15, 2001
- Form 1040 for prior year, if previously extended by Form 4868 (if additional time is needed, a further two-month extension may be obtained by filing Form 2688 or by letter)
- Form 709 or 709A, if previously extended by Form 4868 or letter (alternatively, request additional time to file by filing Form 2688 or by letter)

September 17, 2001
- Form 1040-ES for third quarter

October 15, 2001
- Form 1040 for prior year, if request for automatic four-month extension and additional two-month extension were previously filed

Corporations

March 15, 2001
- Form 1120 (corporate income tax return) (Form 1120S for an S corporation) for prior year or Form 7004 (request for automatic six-month extension)

April 16, 2001
- Deposit estimated tax for first quarter of current year

May 15, 2001
- Form 8752 (Required Payment or Refund under Section 7519) for an S corporation using a year other than a calendar year

June 15, 2001
- Deposit estimated tax for second quarter of current year

September 17, 2001
- Form 1120 (Form 1120S for an S corporation) if previously extended by Form 7004
- Deposit estimated tax for third quarter of current year

December 17, 2001
- Deposit estimated tax for fourth quarter of current year

Employers

Includes businesses and individuals. (Consult your tax advisor for the various dates that employment taxes must be deposited.)

January 31, 2001
- Form 941 (employer's quarterly federal tax return) for fourth quarter of prior year
- Form 940 (employer's federal unemployment tax return) for prior year
- Distribute withholding statements and information returns, including Forms W-2 (Wage and Tax Statement), W-2P (Statement for Recipients of Annuities, Pensions, Retired Pay, or IRA Payments), and 1099-R (Total Distributions from Profit-Sharing Retirement Plans, Individual Retirement Arrangements, Insurance Contracts, etc.) to employees

February 28, 2001
- File Form W-3 (Transmittal of Income and Tax Statements) with Forms W-2 and/or W-2P and for prior year with IRS and Social Security Administration
- File Form 1096 (Annual Summary and Transmittal of U.S. Information Returns) with Form 1099-R for prior year with IRS

April 30, 2001
- Form 941 for first quarter of current year

July 31, 2001
- Form 941 for second quarter

October 31, 2001
- Form 941 for third quarter

Index